Building Your Mutual Fund Portfolio

A Passport to Low-Risk, High-Return Investing

Albert J. Fredman
Russ Wiles

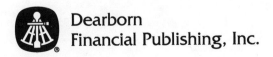

Dearborn
Financial Publishing, Inc.

Dedication

For my lovely wife Kathy and aspiring sons Doug, Glenn and Eric.

A.J.F.

To my wife Linda, a fellow writer, for her love, patience, encouragement and valuable suggestions.

R.W.

Managing Editor: Jack Kiburz
Senior Associate Editor: Karen A. Christensen
Associate Project Editor: Stephanie C. Schmidt
Editorial Assistant: Jill Strubbe
Interior Design: Lucy Jenkins
Cover Design: DePinto Studios

©1996 by Albert J. Fredman and Russ Wiles

Published by Dearborn Financial Publishing, Inc.

96 97 98   10 9 8 7 6 5 4 3 2 1

Library of Congress Cataloging-in-Publication Data
Fredman, Albert J.
   Building your mutual fund portfolio : a passport to low-risk, high-
return investing / Albert J. Fredman and Russ Wiles.
      p. cm.
   Includes index.
   ISBN 0-7931-1234-6
   1. Mutual funds. 2. Portfolio management. I. Wiles, Russ.
II. Title.
HG4530.F728 1995
332.63'27--dc20   95-11311
                                                        CIP

CONTENTS

FOREWORD

Building your mutual fund portfolio is, for me, a continuous activity that hopefully is a lifelong pursuit. A portfolio at any time is the result of resources, needs, perceptions and, unfortunately, unplanned inertia. Each of these factors change, or should change, over time.

Thus, investing is not a single act, but a series of acts or—as I prefer to think of investing—a long journey. The trek has only one certainty and that is when it begins. As with any trip, conditions of travel make the trip enjoyable, arduous or most likely both. Most conditions on one's investment trip are unpredictable; for example, changes in markets, economies, taxes and personal needs.

Investing must first be distinguished from spending or saving. Most important, investing is using assets today to generate benefits for tomorrow. The level and value of the future benefits are uncertain with potential losses of purchasing power, if not actual dollars. Any loss could be harmful to one's lifestyle or psyche. Thus, many of us approach the investing trip with trepidation. For most people, setting off on a perilous trip is not fun. Few of us would have volunteered to sail with Columbus or fly with astronaut Alan Shepard. Similarly, most of us are uneasy, nervous or just plain scared about investing.

We know little for certain about investing. History provides a useful guide of past human experiences and shows human nature does not change. The constant motivations of fear (the fear of loss and the fear of failing to meet our needs) and of greed (the greed of wanting more assurances we will have the desired resources) are the "yin and yang" of investing. In each investor's actions one can trace combinations of fear and greed. Though markets are the aggregation of individual and institutional actions, markets rarely are in a perfect state of equilibrium between these two polar motivations, and thus fluctuate. These fluctuations often seem to be erratic.

If we look to investment commentators to guide us, we see that most focus on enthusiasm or despair as they assess the current primary trend. Their gaze may be useful for trading but not for investing, as they rarely examine our entire investment needs and personality.

Historically, investing was an activity for the wealthy; until recently it was restricted to a small portion of the population, perhaps less than 1 percent. Today, in the United States, mutual funds are the investment of choice for a large and growing part of our population. In this country, marketing skills have commingled with investment skills to build the mutual fund business. The complexities and uncertainties of individual investing have created a market for mutual funds, but how do we select a mutual fund? Approximately three funds exist for every company listed on the New York Stock Exchange. With this large number, competition is intense. Many funds make seemingly contradictory claims and compound our dilemma by producing documents understood only by lawyers.

Mutual fund investors need a guidebook. Like a traveler, they need to recognize useful sign posts (trends) and tools (passports, maps, skis and umbrellas) that can be helpful along the way. My old friends Russ Wiles and Al Fredman have written such a guidebook. Together they have formed a brilliant pairing of the most thorough and readable mutual fund columnist with a college professor who explains mutual funds in easy-to-understand language. After reading *Building Your Mutual Fund Portfolio,* you will enjoy your investment journey and profit from the experience.

A. Michael Lipper
President
Lipper Analytical Services

PREFACE

Financial horror stories have been in vogue. In 1994 the worst bear market in bonds since the 1930s shocked many investors. It produced a painful lesson in what interest-rate risk is all about. Adding insult to injury, a few managers of supposedly staid bond funds used risky derivative strategies that backfired, magnifying losses for investors. That same year a peso crisis sent Mexican stocks spiraling downward, souring skittish investors on the world's emerging markets, which had shined so brilliantly in 1993. Meanwhile, a money market mutual fund "broke a buck" or fell below $1 a share in price for the first time ever. As for the stock market, it always seems to be vulnerable to taking a spill.

What does all this mean to you as an investor? One thing is certain: Events and factors such as these add to the confusion and fear in the minds of countless investors. To help clear up the misconceptions and set you on a profitable path, we have written *Building Your Mutual Fund Portfolio: A Passport to Low-Risk, High-Return Investing*. We cover the landscape of basics, from balancing risk and return to reducing your costs to finding the best mix of funds for your portfolio. The better you understand the different forms of risk, the better you will be able to manage and live with your investments.

Our primary focus is asset allocation or slicing your investment pie into percentages of stocks, bonds and cash. Asset allocation involves mixing and matching different types of stock and bond funds, while maintaining a modest stake in money market funds, to maximize your returns for a given level of risk. By spreading your wealth among the right assortment of funds, you will enjoy a calmer, more profitable investment journey.

Financial travelers face many hazards and potholes along the highways and byways to wealth. These include inflation, taxes, high investment costs, misleading advice, complex products, gimmicks, fear and greed, impatience and a high-roller outlook. Your first step toward successful investing is simply knowing how to avoid the key mistakes. So it's vital to have the right roadmap to help you create the best possible mix of funds, then to fine-tune that mix as you journey on your road to wealth.

At last count, about $2.5 trillion was invested in almost 6,000 stock, bond and money market funds, according to the Investment Company Institute, the mutual fund industry's Washington-based trade association. There's certainly no dearth of choices for even the most discriminating shoppers. We help you narrow the alternatives to build the best all-weather investment package for your needs. Too many people haphazardly jump in and out of investments, giving little or no consideration to the broader portfolio concept.

Because at least some capital appreciation is crucial to most investors, *Building Your Mutual Fund Portfolio* pays attention to the ways in which you can achieve growth. Possible avenues include small-stock funds, mid-cap funds, large-stock funds and international funds. We'll show how index funds, which beat most actively managed portfolios, make excellent core holdings. We also provide comprehensive coverage of closed-end funds, those quirky mutual fund relatives that can help you get extra mileage from your investment dollars.

These days many people worry about an impending bear market. We can't prevent a broad decline, but we can encourage you to hang tough through one. Think of it this way: the stock market rises in about seven out of every ten years, so you can welcome bear markets as a time to do some bargain hunting. Above all, don't panic and sell out at rock-bottom prices. This won't be necessary if you've put together an all-weather portfolio that you can live with through thick and thin. We expose the pitfalls of market timing, or making extreme changes in your asset allocation in anticipation of a bear market.

Building Your Mutual Fund Portfolio is intended for all types of investors, whether you want to invest a few hundred dollars or millions. Highlighted material spread throughout the book will enrich your journey with cautionary notes about investment dangers, gems of wisdom from portfolio managers and interesting sidetrips. An epilogue containing 101 tips provides a comprehensive checklist to make your journey more cost-effective and profitable.

Most of you will probably want to put together and manage your own portfolios. But if you'd rather leave the details to an adviser, this book tells how to evaluate the wisdom of your counselor's recommendations. It's dangerous to turn your wealth over to someone else if you lack even the most rudimentary investment knowledge.

Writing a book is a journey in itself. Caroline Carney and Karen Christensen of Dearborn Financial Publishing have helped make *Building Your Mutual Fund Portfolio* a reality. We appreciate their efforts. Lipper Analytical Services and Morningstar generously provided data for this book.

Bon voyage!

Albert J. Fredman and Russ Wiles

CHAPTER 1

Coping with Dangers En Route

Traveling and investing are more similar than you might think. Both involve realizing dreams, hopeful expectations and opportunities for fun and excitement, tempered at times by uncertainty, fear, potential dangers, inconvenience, wrong turns and rip-offs. Like travelers, investors hope for smooth sailing and an enriching experience, while avoiding perils lurking in the byways of unfamiliar places.

Travelers and investors also share a financial connection: Both a major trip and an investment strategy involve large sums of money. Before you can set out on any extended voyage, you need to budget your income, carefully plan your route and make provisions for emergencies. You also need "street smarts," which in the investment world means an ability to distinguish between legitimate financial opportunities and deals that are simply too good to be true. As your tour guides, we will help you avoid the major financial potholes found along the ever-dangerous road to wealth.

Viewing the Mutual Fund Landscape

First, let's make sure we're all headed in the same direction.

A *mutual fund* is a professionally managed portfolio of stocks or bonds. Each fund holds dozens if not hundreds of individual investments or securities. Also, each fund tends to pursue a particular

1

focus—such as big stocks, small stocks, foreign shares or tax-free bonds. This makes it easy for investors to own several funds with differing objectives. Figure 1.1 gives you an overview of the more popular fund categories.

Just as you can take many different routes on a trip, some investment trails provide a more enriching trip, some may get you there safely but without memorable stories, and some may not get you there at all. Our primary focus in *Building Your Mutual Fund Portfolio* is on *asset allocation*. Mutual funds offer a simple, low-cost way to build a tailor-made portfolio. By spreading your nest egg among the right assortment of funds, you will smooth out your overall fluctuations. Asset allocation would be impossible for many people if they relied solely on individual stocks and bonds because of the complexities of analyzing different securities and the difficulty and expense of purchasing them in small quantities.

The Seven Biggest Dangers

Anyone trying to build a mutual fund portfolio faces no shortage of obstacles. In this chapter, we'll confront seven common investment perils—keep in mind that the key to investing isn't avoiding risk, but rather reducing it to a tolerable level. People who keep all of their cash locked up in banks aren't investors—they're savers—and they're destined to wind up as losers over the long haul. That's because risk is tied to reward. To increase the value of your wealth over time, you must accept some uncertainty. Savers are like people so afraid of flying that they miss out on visiting many of the world's great attractions.

1. Inflation Risk

The biggest peril is not taking much, if any, risk at all. Here's why: *Inflation* or *purchasing power risk* is a subtle danger that can slowly erode your portfolio over the years, bit by bit. Over the long term, inflation has averaged a little above 3 percent annually. Seemingly innocuous savings vehicles such as Treasury bills ("T-bills") and certificates of deposit (CDs) are most vulnerable to this danger because they have achieved the lowest long-run returns of the major asset classes. It's true that these ultra safe products pose no risk of default

FIGURE 1.1   Fund-Category Map

Category	Primary Focus
Domestic Equity	
Aggressive growth	Maximum capital appreciation from volatile stocks
Small company	Appreciation from smaller firms
Growth	Appreciation from larger companies
Growth and income	Appreciation and income from larger stocks
Equity income	Income with modest appreciation from larger firms
Foreign Equity	
International	Appreciation from foreign stocks
Global	Appreciation from both foreign and domestic stocks
Emerging market	Appreciation from companies based in developing nations
Other Equity and Hybrid	
Index	Appreciation from replicating an index such as the S&P 500
Sector	Appreciation from an industry such as health care or precious metals
Asset allocation	Appreciation and income from a changing mix of stocks, bonds and cash
Balanced	Appreciation and income from a fairly stable mix of stocks and bonds
Fixed Income	
General bond	Income from corporate or U.S. government bonds
High-yield bond	Income and appreciation from bonds rated below "investment grade"
International bond	Income from foreign government and corporate bonds
Ginnie Mae	Income from mortgage-backed bonds
Tax-exempt bond	Tax-free income from municipal bonds
Money market	Income from Treasury bills and other short-term debt securities

and their principal is highly stable, so you're not going to be taken on a financial roller coaster. The problem is that they simply don't produce enough income to protect your capital against the highly corrosive effects of inflation.

Even higher-yielding bonds can get clobbered. This presents problems for people who allocate too much of their money to the fixed-income area. Take a fifty-something couple who plan on collecting $10,000 of annual interest from their $175,000 portfolio of insured municipal bonds over the next 25 years. The buying power of these $10,000 payments will shrink dramatically, as we see in Figure 1.2, which shows their purchasing power at five-year intervals, given several rates of inflation. For example, in 15 years the $10,000 in payments would buy only what $5,553 can buy today, assuming moderate 4-percent inflation in the meantime. When the bonds mature in 25 years, the couple would get back their $175,000, but inflation would reduce that as well—to a real value of only $65,645. So taking too little risk can be riskier than you might think.

The rationale for holding stock mutual funds is that they have a proven history of performing much better than bond funds and savings instruments. Just take a look at some data provided by fund researcher Lipper Analytical Services: Over the 35 years from 1960 through 1994, general equity funds returned 11.8 percent a year in contrast with the 7.6 percent generated by taxable bond funds—an average difference of 4.2 percentage points annually. For this superior performance, you must accept wider fluctuations.

The risk of being out of the stock market can be even greater than being in it. Inflation erosion is the price you pay when you stay on the sidelines. Too many people play it too safe for their own good. Of the roughly $2.5 trillion socked away in mutual funds, almost 30 percent is in money market portfolios. Avoiding volatility can be extremely hazardous, especially if you're working with a long time horizon. It's like shunning commercial aircraft and doing all of your traveling in a more dangerous vehicle—the automobile.

2. Market Risk

Stocks offer the best returns to offset inflation, but their fluctuations can be severe. *Market risk* refers to the danger that a substantial decline in stock prices generally will reduce the value of your portfolio. In the 1973–1974 *bear* or down market, the Standard & Poor's 500 index lost nearly 50 percent of its value over a gut-wrenching 21 months. This was the market's worst tumble since the horrendous bear phase of the early 1930s, which came on the heels of the October 1929 crash. During the October 1987 panic, the S&P 500 plunged roughly 34 percent, but this downdraft lasted only a few months.

How badly can stock mutual funds get hit if the market careens into a deep ditch? Figure 1.3 shows the worst 12-month periods since 1969 for each of Lipper Analytical Service's general stock-fund categories. Even though stock funds advanced 10.2 percent annually on average over this 25-year span, they still took some spills.

FIGURE 1.2   Purchasing Power of $10,000

Years Hence	Inflation Rate			
	3%	4%	5%	6%
5	$8,626	$8,219	$7,835	$7,473
10	7,441	6,756	6,139	5,584
15	6,419	5,553	4,810	4,173
20	5,537	4,564	3,769	3,118
25	4,776	3,751	2,953	2,330

FIGURE 1.3   Worst Rolling 12-Month Performances
by Fund Categories Since 1969

Category	Total Return
Capital appreciation	−45.4%
Growth	−44.0
Mid cap	−45.4
Small-company growth	−46.7
Growth & income	−35.4
Equity income	−30.1
General equity	**−40.5%**

Source: Reprinted by permission of Lipper Analytical Services, Inc.

In a worst-case scenario, stock investments could plunge some-where between 30 and 47 percent. It could take perhaps five years just to get back to breakeven and ten years to approach long-term average results. That's precisely why you need to hold stock funds as long-term investments!

You can't avoid market risk, but you can learn how to steer through it carefully and reduce potential pothole damage by following an approach known as *asset allocation*. This involves selecting the right mix of stocks, bonds and cash so you build a portfolio of mutual funds that delivers perhaps 80 percent of the long-run returns of stocks with only half the downside exposure.

TRAVELER'S ADVISORY:
Don't Sell the Market Short

These facts about the stock market are worth remembering:

- Bull or rising markets, on average, last more than twice as long as bear markets.

- Stocks gain far more in bull markets than they lose in bear markets.

- On average, about seven of every ten years see rising stock prices.

- The only thing you can say for sure about the stock market is that it will fluctuate.

---

3. Sector Risk

This reflects the danger associated with having too much exposure in one area of the market. It's a problem for those who don't have adequate diversification across different industries. For instance, if you concentrate in volatile health-care, financial, technology or gold funds, your holdings could gyrate wildly. Certain problems are industry-specific and can strike even more stable sectors like utilities, which were hit hard in 1994 by the sharp upward spikes in long-term interest rates coupled with competitive pressures. Typical, broadly based stock funds protect you against sector risk because their managers normally diversify among at least six or eight industries.

Lists of the best and worst mutual funds over shorter periods of a month, quarter or year include a disproportionately large number of sector funds. Those funds often rank near the top and bottom because they tend to be pretty risky. Investors who buy them sacrifice diversification for the chance of making a fast buck. We suggest that you limit sector funds to just a small portion of your portfolio.

**FIGURE 1.4   Price Impact of a One Percentage Point Increase
in Interest Rates***

Years to Maturity	Decrease in Bond Price		
	7% Coupon	4% Coupon	Zero Coupon
2	1.8%	1.9%	1.9%
5	4.1	4.3	4.6
10	6.9	7.6	9.0
20	10.4	11.6	17.1
30	12.2	13.5	24.5

*All bonds initially priced to yield 6 percent to maturity.

4. Interest-Rate Risk

This peril rates near the top of the list of dangers confronting bond-fund investors. Rising rates inevitably lead to falling bond prices. In 1994, for example, investors experienced a big jolt when the Federal Reserve began raising short-term rates for the first time in five years to keep inflation under control and squeeze speculative excesses out of the market. Since 1982 bondholders had earned exceptionally high returns as interest rates gradually worked their way to lower ground. This pleasant ride was temporarily interrupted in 1987, when rates surged for about nine months.

The longer a bond's term to maturity, the greater its potential volatility. But this is not the only variable that determines interest-rate risk—the size of the bond's interest or coupon payment also plays a role. Lower-yielding bonds tend to fluctuate more, with *zero-coupon bonds* (those that make no periodic interest payments) most volatile of all. Mutual funds that hold zeros are called *target-maturity* funds and, naturally, expose you to plenty of interest-rate risk.

Figure 1.4 compares the price impacts of a one percentage point increase in rates on bonds with different coupons and maturities. In all cases, prices fall further with longer maturities, but the 4-percent and zero-coupon issues decline more. Most vulnerable is the 30-year zero bond, which plunges 24.5 percent with a one percentage point uptick in general interest rates.

The point is to be mindful of the potential volatility of longer-term bond funds. Many people were stunned in 1994 when the values of their U.S. government or high quality municipal-bond funds sank as interest rates ratcheted higher and higher. If your time horizon is relatively short and you want to minimize your exposure to interest-rate risk, stick mainly with money market and short-term bond funds. If your horizon is lengthy and you can tolerate some volatility, allocate more of your assets to longer-term bond funds to earn potentially higher returns.

Interest-rate risk affects stocks as well as bonds in part because stocks and bonds compete for investor dollars. When bonds start to offer more attractive yields, individuals sell their stocks and shuttle over to the bond market. A pronounced upward trend in rates definitely spells bad news for equity investors.

You can effectively ignore interest-rate gyrations by holding bond funds for the long haul. But if you can invest for many years, it's wiser to allocate the lion's share of your assets to stocks, which offer much higher growth potential.

5. Credit Risk

If you lent money to a friend, your biggest worry would be getting your cash back. In the bond world, this describes *credit* or *default risk*—the danger that the bond issuer won't have enough money to make interest payments and repay the principal borrowed. For all practical purposes, government securities don't carry this risk, but corporate and municipal bonds do. Various credit-rating firms give letter grades to reflect a bond's credit risk. The two best known credit-rating agencies are Moody's and Standard & Poor's.

Within the so-called *investment-grade* category, bonds with triple-A ratings are of the highest quality, carrying minimal credit risk. Double-A-rated bonds have only a bit more risk; single-A issues have still more; and triple-B securities carry the most credit risk within the investment-grade category. Issues rated below triple-B are known as *high-yield* or *junk* bonds. Investors who own shares in junk-bond funds are exposed to the most credit peril—and they earn higher yields to compensate for this.

But even junk-fund investors do not need to stay awake at night worrying about default woes. Mutual funds greatly reduce bankruptcy dangers by diversifying across 50 to 100 or more bonds, and fund managers frequently monitor the credit risks of their holdings so they can quickly dump bad apples before they start to rot.

Keep in mind that high-yield bond funds can get hit particularly hard in a recession, when worsening economic conditions push some teetering bond issuers into deeper trouble, including defaults. This happened in the 1989–1990 junk-bond debacle. But you can expect high-yield portfolios to bounce back when the storm clears.

6. Currency Risk

This consideration is more important these days because the investment process has become global. More than two-thirds of the total value of the world's stock markets exists outside the United States. Thanks to mutual funds, even small investors have easy access to various international stock and bond markets.

Whenever you purchase a foreign stock or bond, you are investing in both a security and a currency. If you buy a Japanese stock, you also have a position in the yen. Suppose the stock gained 15 percent during a period when the yen appreciated 10 percent against the dollar. Your total return would be about 25 percent. On the other hand, if the dollar strengthened (the yen weakened), your results would suffer. If the yen lost 10 percent when the stock rose 15 percent, your return would be about 5 percent. Currency risk is a wind that can blow at your back or in your face.

But currency risk is not a great problem for long-term investors in foreign-stock funds. Over many years, currency fluctuations tend to be more or less a wash. The main factors driving your returns as an international investor will be the performances of the companies and stock markets themselves, not fluctuations in currencies. Over time, these performances have been impressive.

7. Asset-Class Risk

Stocks, bonds and cash (or money market instruments such as T-bills) are the three major asset classes. If you have a disproportionate amount in any one of them, you may be taking on excessive risk. Too much in a money market fund for long exposes you to inflation risk. Bond funds return more than money funds, but can be particularly hard hit when interest rates surge. Stock funds appreciate most of all, but they can decline furthest in a bad market.

To reduce your risk to a tolerable level, you might need to diversify across all three main asset classes, even if you emphasize one group,

FIGURE 1.5   Sample Wealth Indexes for Hypothetical Investments

Fund	Annual Return	Value of $1 at End of				
		10 yrs.	20 yrs.	30 yrs.	40 yrs.	45 yrs.
Small stock	11%	$2.84	$8.06	$22.89	$65.00	$109.53
Big stock	10	2.59	6.73	17.45	45.26	72.89
Long-term bond	7	1.97	3.87	7.61	14.97	21.00
Money market	5	1.63	2.65	4.32	7.04	8.99

such as stocks. Trim your risk even further by diversifying into various subcategories of funds such as foreign stocks, foreign bonds and gold.

Asset Wealth Indexes—The Magic of Compounding

Although the past is not necessarily a useful predictor of the future, it can serve as a rough guidepost to gauge how you might fare. It's impossible to pinpoint future returns of different asset classes or portfolios, yet the performances of stocks, bonds and cash should maintain their same relative standings in the future because of the direct link between volatility and reward.

Suppose you put $1 into four different portfolios—small stocks, big stocks, long-term corporate bonds and money market instruments. If the four funds generate annual returns of 11 percent, 10 percent, 7 percent and 5 percent, respectively, you would see the compound amounts, known as *wealth indexes,* at the end of the various periods displayed in Figure 1.5. Wealth indexes show how your capital can grow, but do not confuse them with stock price indexes such as the S&P 500.

The differences become more pronounced as the time horizon lengthens, illustrating the "magic of compounding," which refers to the exponential growth of accumulated earnings on an investment. After 45 years, the investment in the big-cap stock fund swells to 3.5 times the bond fund and 8.1 times the money fund. These eye-popping differences become even more pronounced with the small-stock fund. Thus, more aggressive investments have the potential to sparkle over longer periods, provided you don't get saddled with sub-par performers. Compounding is one of the great wonders of the world, right up there with the pyramids in Egypt and the Coliseum in Rome.

AT THE HELM: PETER LYNCH

It's hard to name someone more committed to the notion of long-term investing than Peter Lynch. In fact, it's hard to name a more famous investment professional, period.

From 1977 to 1990, Lynch ran Fidelity Magellan, compiling a sizzling track record that transformed this fund into the largest and most famous one around. A person who sank $10,000 into Magellan in 1981, when it first offered shares to the public, could have cashed in those chips for more than $70,000 by the end of the decade. Lynch outperformed the benchmark Standard & Poor's 500 index by 20 percentage points or more each year from 1978 through 1982. And even after Magellan hit $1 billion in assets in 1983—quite a distinction back then—Lynch continued to beat the market.

Lynch stepped down from the helm of Magellan in 1990, but he has remained active as a Fidelity trustee and as a mentor to the company's legion of portfolio managers and analysts. For years he has urged individual investors to search for promising young companies in their own back yards—and to build their portfolios around stocks for superior long-term results. Notably, Lynch kept Magellan fully invested in equities at all times, believing that it was futile to predict short-term market fluctuations. Coming from this famous stockpicker, that's a lesson worth heeding.

Be aware that Figure 1.5 illustrates what four imaginary funds *might* do. Still, you skew the odds in your favor if you place stock investments at the long-term core of your portfolio. A heavy stock fund exposure works best because corporations can offset inflation by raising prices as costs ratchet upward. They can even restructure, if necessary. And they can innovate to sell new products and capture more markets. For solid companies, the long-term rate of profit increases should outpace inflation.

Street Smarts

- Reaping the rewards of traveling and investing requires thoughtful planning, knowledge of the dangers and an understanding of the modes of transportation.
- Allocating too much of your assets to bank accounts and money market funds makes you vulnerable to inflation risk.
- Stock funds expose you to short-term volatility, but the payoff is amazing long-term growth through the magic of compounding. The longer your time horizon, the more you can safely allocate to stocks.
- High quality bond funds are not risk free. They make you vulnerable to interest-rate perils, as many unsuspecting individuals learned in 1994, on the heels of a decade of double-digit returns. Simply put, bond prices come down when interest rates ratchet upward. If you can't tolerate this danger, stick with shorter-term bond investments.

CHAPTER 2

Establishing Goals for Your Journey

Setting your goals or objectives is an important part of the planning stage. To prepare for a trip, you start by pulling out maps, reading tourbooks, pouring over brochures, sending away for visas and perhaps later getting your shots. But planning your investments is actually much easier than setting up a vacation itinerary. You have to contend with less legwork, fewer red-tape hassles and, best of all, no needles.

At the most basic level, each investor's objective is to make money. How you achieve that is the tricky part. Your strategy depends on factors such as your age and health, the level and stability of your income and net worth, your emotional ability to handle risk, tax bracket, and investment knowledge.

Your objectives will reflect some combination of the following three factors: (1) a desire for capital appreciation, (2) a need for current income or (3) a preference for capital preservation (or stability). The more aggressive you are, the more you should gear your investments toward appreciation.

If you want growth, you will have to accept some money-losing quarters or years. That's the trade-off between risk and return. High profits and stability don't normally go hand in hand. And if you're looking for big capital gains, you can't expect to earn much in the way of current income: Small, fast-growing stocks (and funds) are most likely to score big gains, but they pay little or no dividends.

The All-Equity Path

Suppose you invested exclusively in stock funds. Figure 2.1 traces annual returns for Lipper's general-equity fund category over the past 35 years. You can see the ups and downs one could expect in a portfolio made up exclusively of different types of domestic stock funds, ranging from the volatile capital-appreciation category to the conservative equity-income group. The worst yearly returns occurred in 1973 and 1974. Also note the performance contrasts between longer periods. For instance, stock funds produced a robust 16.3 percent compound annual return during the 10 years ended December 1988, versus a paltry 2.5 percent a year over the decade ended December 1978. For the full 35-year period, general-equity funds returned a handsome 11.8 percent annually.

Mapping Your Route

You might think of the risk-reward trade-off as choosing between alternative vacation itineraries. The farther you go, the more enriching your trip, but also the more complicated it can get. Similarly, the higher your long-run growth potential, the greater the short-term volatility with which you must live. The basic "itineraries" would look like the following.

Itinerary 1: Capital Preservation

This portfolio resembles a vacation at Aunt Myrtle's house in the suburbs. You're not going to get pickpocketed or catch any strange foreign viruses, but you might get bored after the second day. The ultra-stable core of this type of portfolio consists of money market mutual funds, CDs, short-term bond funds and the like. Very little, if anything, would be held in stock funds or even longer-term bond portfolios, which can lose ground when interest rates rise fast.

A key problem with a capital-preservation portfolio is reduced purchasing power: Defensive investments rarely pay enough to stay ahead of inflation for long. Itinerary 1 really makes sense only for investors with short time horizons who can't take any risks, such as older retirees or people planning to use the money to purchase a house within a year or two.

FIGURE 2.1   Annual Total Returns of General Equity Funds

Year	Return	Year	Return	Year	Return
1994	−1.7%	1982	26.0%	1970	−7.2%
1993	12.7	1981	−0.8	1969	−12.7
1992	9.3	1980	34.5	1968	17.4
1991	36.3	1979	29.6	1967	37.3
1990	−5.7	1978	11.9	1966	−4.8
1989	25.2	1977	2.4	1965	23.2
1988	15.8	1976	26.6	1964	14.2
1987	1.1	1975	34.5	1963	19.2
1986	14.7	1974	−24.3	1962	−13.8
1985	28.5	1973	−21.9	1961	26.1
1984	−0.9	1972	13.3	1960	3.4
1983	21.9	1971	21.1		

Source: Reprinted by permission of Lipper Analytical Services, Inc.

Itinerary 2: Income

Here, what you're taking is a trip to San Diego—good weather, lots to see, but nothing terribly exotic. Itinerary 2 includes more volatile investments, such as mutual funds oriented around intermediate-term bonds. You might earmark a portion of your assets to "hybrid" funds that maintain a mix of stocks and bonds, such as those in the balanced or asset-allocation camps. You might even include a stake in a conservative stock fund, such as a utility or equity-income product. You could round out the portfolio with some exposure to a long-term bond fund or two.

Itinerary 3: Growth and Income

This is the vacation-in-Honolulu portfolio. You face some danger of being lashed by a hurricane or getting sunburned beyond recognition, but you can probably anticipate having a pretty good time. You would hold a blend of mainstream stock and bond funds. The stock portion provides growth, while the bonds add stability and income. The relative tilt toward growth or income depends on your objectives, risk tolerance and other personal factors.

Itinerary 4: Conservative Growth

Itinerary 4 resembles a sidetrip to the Big Island of Hawaii. You're willing to accept a new danger—the possibility of being melted in a volcanic eruption—in return for the promise of more spectacular results. You can build this type of portfolio around a mix of stock funds—especially those holding large, blue chip companies such as General Electric, General Motors or Microsoft. Some small-company and international funds might round out the portfolio. Though risky in themselves, these latter two categories add new layers of diversification to the overall portfolio and boost its money-making potential.

Itinerary 5: Aggressive Growth

This is the cliff-diving-in-Acapulco itinerary. You're willing to take big risks in return for a thrilling payoff. You put heavy emphasis on the small-stock and foreign areas—including some of the more volatile funds that have large stakes in the emerging economies of East Asia, Latin America and other developing regions. For extra thrills, you might also include industry-sector funds, such as those specializing in technology or medical stocks.

Life-Cycle Investing

Your portfolio's composition depends largely on how old you are. Your age often is closely related to your time horizon and risk tolerance—two other critical variables in the asset-allocation equation. At the minimum, your stock-fund holdings should include a sampling of the small, large and international-stock categories, as illustrated in Figure 2.2. These ballpark asset-allocation ranges will help you get started. For instance, a couple in their mid-20s might allocate between 10 and 30 percent of their total investment portfolio to small-stock funds, and so on.

The financial profiles of different people in any age bracket can vary widely, so it's impossible to offer hard and fast benchmarks. Nevertheless, the wide age-specific asset ranges in Figure 2.2 provide general guidelines. Your age probably ranks as the most important factor determining your investment horizon, but you need to consider other variables as well.

FIGURE 2.2   Broad Age-Specific Portfolio Allocations

Portfolio Categories	Decade of Life						
	20s	30s	40s	50s	60s	70s	80s
Small stocks	10–30%	10–30%	10–25%	10–20%	0–10%	0–5%	—
Large stocks	10–30	20–30	25–40	25–50	25–50	20–35	10–30%
Foreign stocks	10–30	10–30	10–30	10–25	5–20	0–15	0–10
Bonds	0–20	5–25	5–30	10–50	20–60	30–70	40–80
Money market	5–20	5–20	5–20	10–25	10–25	15–40	20–80

When you invest for the long haul, you have less to worry about in the short term. Daily, weekly, quarterly and even yearly ups and downs won't matter so much because you have time to recoup losses. Market declines can be frustrating, but prices generally bounce back eventually, just as inclement weather clears up sooner or later. Over time, the stock market has had a definite upward bias. Still, you should stash some cash in a money market fund or similar investment as a short-term reserve for possible emergencies.

Here are some examples of time horizons for different types of investors, which illustrate how your objectives change as you age:

- *Young single executives.* These people might well seek the aggressive growth typical of an Itinerary 5 portfolio. They won't retire for many years, even if they hope to call it quits by age 55. They do not need to live on income from their investments, and they understand—and can tolerate—an occasionally large stock-market decline. These factors tilt them toward the more volatile and powerful stock-fund categories.

- *A couple in their 50s.* As this husband and wife move within sight of retirement, they will likely shift their portfolio toward more conservative and higher-yielding investments, perhaps making a transition from Itinerary 4 to Itinerary 3, or from 3 to 2.

- *A well-heeled retired couple.* These people want to hang on to what they've got. They don't need to build more wealth, though they might want to spend some of the income their investments throw off. They are Itinerary 1 folks all the way, perhaps favoring a mix of short municipal-bond funds for stability and tax-free yields.

TRAVELER'S ADVISORY:
Invest All You Can

The surest way to build more wealth is to invest more. It's safe to say that most people do not stash away enough for retirement. Social Security isn't designed to provide recipients with a comfortable lifestyle. Besides, people are living longer, so they've got to accumulate more assets for a lengthier retirement. And increasingly, people are viewing retirement as a liberating time of fun and leisure, so you don't want to scrimp if you don't have to. Think of all the vacations you could take with a sufficiently large nest egg!

The greater your income, the more you will tend to sock away. Most people should be able to invest at least 10 percent of their income, so think of this number as a minimum. Individuals in their early twenties are an exception, because they typically are strapped for cash as they finish college and face basic big-ticket purchases such as cars, appliances and housing. One benefit of growing older is that you may find yourself able to invest more.

Investor Questionnaire

If you seek guidance from a financial planner or other investment counselor, you normally will be asked to answer a series of questions to determine your objectives, time horizon and risk tolerance. We have developed a similar questionnaire. Your responses will help determine what sort of investor you are and what mix of mutual funds you should maintain.

For each question, circle the number on the left that corresponds to your chosen response. Then add up your responses to arrive at your total score. No answers are right or wrong—just respond in the way that best describes your personal situation or preferences.

A. In which age group do you fall?
1. 65 or over
2. 55–64
3. 45–54
4. 30–44
5. Under 30

B. What is your investment time horizon—when do you think you will need or want to tap into your portfolio?
1. Within 2 years
2. 3–4 years
3. 5–9 years
4. 10–19 years
5. 20 years or longer

C. What are your investment objectives?
1. Capital preservation and a satisfactory current income are my goals. I'm not striving for growth.
2. Income is my top priority. Growth is secondary.
3. I want a balance of income and growth.
4. I'm basically growth oriented, but I want to play it somewhat safe.
5. I want maximum growth. Income is not critical.

D. How would you describe your financial needs?
1. I depend totally on my investments for monthly income, occasional big-ticket expenditures and emergency needs.
2. I depend on my portfolio for income and emergency needs.
3. I depend somewhat on my portfolio for income and emergency needs.
4. I do not depend on my portfolio for income, but it could serve me in an emergency.
5. My portfolio is devoted to long-term savings. I don't need any income from it and probably wouldn't have to turn to it to meet a financial calamity.

E. What is your attitude toward fluctuations in the value of your portfolio?
1. I'm willing to accept the lower long-run returns associated with maximum stability.
2. I'll accept a little volatility for somewhat higher returns.
3. I can take an average amount of volatility for average returns.
4. Growth is my goal, and I'm prepared for the higher volatility.
5. Maximum appreciation is my goal. I can live with substantial volatility.

F. How do you feel about investing in fixed-income investments?

1. I want the highest quality, most stable investments, even though they don't offer the best returns. U.S. Treasury bills and the like are my top choice.
2. Stability is important, but I'm willing to assume a little risk to garner higher returns than T-bills offer.
3. I'm willing to assume a fair amount of volatility because I want above-average income from the fixed-income component of my portfolio.
4. Volatility is no problem. Higher-yielding munis, junk corporates and the bonds of emerging foreign nations are my cup of tea. I want the highest total returns I can achieve with my fixed-income investments.
5. I'm totally committed to stocks; fixed-income securities don't even have a place in my portfolio, with the exception of modest cash reserves.

G. How do you feel about investing in stocks?

1. I won't even consider them.
2. I'll invest just a modest amount of my portfolio in blue chip stock funds.
3. I'd be willing to put about half of my portfolio into stock funds, most of which should focus on S&P 500-type stocks.
4. I want to invest mainly in stock funds for their higher long-run returns, including those that target small domestic companies and others that hold foreign shares.
5. I'm willing to hold the most volatile stock funds to maximize long-run appreciation, such as those emphasizing small stocks, volatile industry sectors or emerging stock markets.

H. Suppose you had a $600,000 portfolio that plunged 25 percent to $450,000 in a global bear market. The outlook for recovery anytime soon is bleak. How might you feel?

1. Terrible. I could never tolerate this.
2. Badly. I'd certainly face sleepless nights.
3. Not good, but I probably wouldn't lose too much sleep.
4. I wouldn't be thrilled, but I'd have to accept potentially extreme volatility as the price to be paid for long-term growth.
5. No problem. This would be a great buying opportunity. The long-term direction of the stock market is up, and down markets are just part of the game.

I. How do you feel about the global economic outlook?
1. I'm fairly pessimistic about the United States and the rest of the world.
2. I have mixed feelings.
3. I'm moderately optimistic.
4. I'm optimistic.
5. Highly optimistic. I feel that smaller businesses worldwide and emerging economies have tremendous potential long term.

J. Which of the following statements best describes your attitudes toward travel and adventure?
1. I prefer not to travel—there are too many hassles, dangers and uncertainties. I like staying at home and having the comfort and security of familiar surroundings. Day trips meet my travel needs just fine.
2. An occasional weekend trip is all I need. I try to limit my brief excursions to familiar places within about a 120-mile radius of my home. I've been to Las Vegas or Atlantic City a few times, but gambling is not for me.
3. I try to get away for at least one or two weeks a year, but I don't stray off the beaten path. Most of my trips are domestic—to places like San Francisco or Washington, D.C. I'm somewhat skittish about venturing abroad.
4. I like traveling domestically to out of the way places as well as to familiar stomping grounds. I look forward to occasional trips abroad to places like England, Mexico or the Caribbean.
5. I like to travel abroad as much as I can afford to. Far away, exotic spots in Eastern Europe, Southeast Asia and Latin America excite me. It's a thrill to explore new places on my own or with a companion. I'd even consider a jungle safari or a mountain trek.

Now, add up your scores for all questions except J, which we included merely for fun. The higher your tally, the greater your capacity to be aggressive and the more capital-gains oriented you are.

Here's the strategy that matches up with your score:

0–14 points: Capital preservation
15–23 points: Conservative income
24–32 points: Growth and income
33–41 points: Conservative growth
42–45 points: Aggressive growth

Of course, your score provides just a rough idea of what sort of portfolio you should build. For example, you can achieve a growth objective in different ways. Some investors may want large holdings in foreign-stock funds, whereas others stick exclusively to domestic products. If you have a fairly big portfolio, you may want to buy some individual stocks to complement your mutual fund positions.

Implementing Your Plan

After determining your basic objectives, it's time to build your portfolio. This involves selecting individual funds and fund families. In addition, you need to set up a schedule for putting money away. A low-pain way to accomplish this involves making regular monthly transfers through an automatic investment plan. Most fund companies offer these plans—you merely need to establish a link between your bank account and fund. Suppose you choose to invest $100 monthly. Your bank can automatically transfer the money to your fund on approximately the same day each month. These fixed-dollar purchases buy more shares when prices are low, which benefits you during down markets. Chapter 6 covers this important strategy, called *dollar cost averaging*.

If you're saving for retirement, start with an individual retirement account (IRA) or other tax-sheltered plan, such as a 401(k) or a SEP-IRA (if you're self-employed). All of these accounts provide tax-deferred compounding, which enables you to build more wealth. The main point is to develop some type of systematic, disciplined plan.

Street Smarts

- Spend a few moments to determine your objectives, time horizon and risk tolerance, then select a broad investment itinerary with some exposure to stocks, bonds and cash. Sticking with a suitable mix will help you avoid those unpleasant potholes as you journey through the years.
- Your time horizon is the most important determinant of your asset mix, but you should also favor the highest-returning investments with which you can rest comfortably at night.
- The surest way to build more wealth is to invest more. At the minimum, strive to sock away at least 10 percent of your gross income each year, preferably on a regular weekly, monthly, or quarterly basis.

CHAPTER 3

Putting Together a Balanced Itinerary

Think back to early 1992, when health and biotechnology mutual funds had just come off a year during which they gained 74 percent on average. It was their seventh straight advancing year, and with a rapidly aging U.S. population, the future looked bright indeed. But if you had sunk much money into a health/biotech fund at that time, your portfolio would have needed first aid. With the emergence of Bill Clinton and his health-reform crusade, these funds got their noses bloodied in 1992 and 1993. High-flying sector funds tempt investors with the promise of quick profits, but people who chase after them often do so with disastrous results, as this example showed.

Enter asset allocation. It will protect your portfolio against the risk of staking too much in a single type of investment by providing a balanced itinerary. The name of the game is to avoid betting the ranch on a possible winner by apportioning your money across different asset classes. By slicing and dicing, you improve your odds of success by not suffering any debilitating setbacks. Over time you should do very well, provided you have the proper allocation and stick with it.

Major asset classes include stocks, bonds, cash, real estate and precious metals. Decide on an appropriate mix after defining your investment situation, for which your age, investment objectives and risk tolerance figure prominently. Our main focus is on the split between stocks, bonds and cash. You can make real estate and precious metals allocations through mutual funds that specialize in these sectors, or

---

TRAVELER'S ADVISORY:
The Glitter of Gold

Should you allocate some of your assets to gold? Financial advisers often recommend keeping about 5 percent of your portfolio in gold-related investments, such as a gold mutual fund. These funds invest in mining companies, whose shares are thought to be a good hedge against economic and political chaos and runaway inflation, as gold prices often fare brilliantly when other investments tumble. But you probably wouldn't want to commit more than 5 percent or so to gold portfolios, which are volatile and unpredictable and could do much worse than your other stock funds over the long haul. That said, one of the better such funds to consider is Vanguard Specialized Portfolios—Gold and Precious Metals, largely because of its relatively low expenses.

---

you might choose the real thing—rental real estate or gold coins and bars. Though important, your own home doesn't count as part of your investment portfolio. Regard it first and foremost as shelter.

Anchor Your Short-Term Savings

Separate your short-term cash needs from your long-term investments. Asset allocation deals with building wealth over many years using money you won't need to withdraw anytime soon. Set aside cash in a money market mutual fund or similar conservative investment—perhaps even a short-term bond fund—to provide for the following needs:

1. *Unexpected emergencies.* Financial planners usually recommend that you have three to six months' living expenses available to meet a surprise contingency.
2. *Large anticipated expenditures.* You should also determine how much money you will need over the next five years to pay for college tuition, a down payment on a house or other major purchases.

You don't want to have to liquidate part of your long-term investment portfolio to meet needs such as these. That can force you to unload stock funds at an inopportune time, and it can easily throw your portfolio out of balance. The cash and short-term bond allocations we'll be discussing are part of your investment portfolio, separate from your savings.

Strategic Asset Allocation

In apportioning assets, you face a tradeoff between risk and return. The greater the exposure to stocks, the higher your long-run results, but the greater your volatility or risk. Conversely, if you keep too much in cash, you may not earn enough to offset inflation. This risk is particularly painful if you've got a long time horizon. And if you allocate too much to long-term bonds, you could get clobbered if interest rates rise substantially. With rates near 30-year lows in early 1994, this risk turned out to be a very big concern in retrospect. Bonds and bond funds also subject you to inflation risk, albeit to a lesser extent than with cash.

Assigning *weights* (or percentages) to the different investment classes is known as *strategic asset allocation*. Your allocation should mirror your investment strategy. For example, a healthy 65-year-old married man who recently retired might initially put 40 percent into stocks, 40 percent into bonds and 20 percent into cash. This person might need to spend some interest but still needs to build wealth, as he and his spouse might live for another 25 or 30 years. They also might want to leave something to their children.

The allocation weights reflect your long-term itinerary. It's often wise to specify the percentages as a target range so you can make appropriate tilts to take advantage of unique market opportunities or valuation extremes. For instance, the investor cited above might shoot for 35 to 45 percent in stocks, 35 to 45 percent in bonds, and 15 to 25 percent in cash. Avoid the temptation to set these ranges too wide, however, as you could derail your plans if you get too far off course. Monitor your portfolio and rebalance it, if necessary, following a major market move or after a year or two, to keep the allocations within their appropriate ranges. Some possible ranges for different investors appear below. Chapter 2 discusses these types of investors in terms of their risk-reward itineraries.

Investment Objective	Stocks	Bonds	Cash
Aggressive growth	80–90%	5–15%	0–5%
Conservative growth	65–80	15–25	5–10
Income	15–40	50–70	10–20

A Simple Formula

One rough-and-ready rule is to allocate a percentage equal to your age into bonds and money market securities. A 25-year-old person thus might assign a weight of 25 percent to bond funds and the remaining 75 percent to stock investments. The older you get, the more you would want in bonds and cash. But as long as you're younger than 100, you would have at least a little invested in stocks. One problem with this rule of thumb is that it can cause you to become too conservative. Always invest as much as you comfortably can in stocks regardless of what this formula tells you because they promise the best long-term reward.

When Should You Alter Your Weights?

Revise your allocation plan when your circumstances change. As you grow older, you would probably tilt more toward fixed-income investments, reflecting increasing conservatism and more emphasis on income and capital preservation. But a middle-aged investor who has paid off his or her mortgage or kids' tuition bills may decide to boost the stock percentage for long-term growth.

But if little has changed, don't alter your weights unless you set them incorrectly in the first place. If you deviate too much, you may be exposing yourself to excessive risk. Avoid the temptation.

Why Hold Cash?

Even aggressive investors might want to keep 5 to 10 percent of their assets in money market funds. Cash investments can help smooth out the ups and downs of your overall portfolio. Also, they represent reserve buying power, enabling you to take advantage of unusually good values in the stock or bond markets when such values are widespread. This is one reason that fund managers themselves hold a modest amount of cash.

You might want to move a portion of your cash allocation into short-term bond portfolios as a nice compromise. They return more

---

TRAVELER'S ADVISORY:
Money Market Returns Bounce Around

Money market funds, which invest in T-bills, short-term corporate IOUs known as "commercial paper" and the like, offer the utmost in stability of principal. In fact, their prices stay at $1 a share. But their returns (which tend to vary directly with changes in inflation) fluctuate dramatically over the years, as Lipper data show.

In 1980, 1981 and 1982, for example, money funds returned 12.9, 17.2 and 12.6 percent, respectively. Conversely, in 1992, 1993 and 1994 they achieved 3.3, 2.6 and 3.7 percent. Over the 23-year period from 1972 through 1994, money-fund returns averaged 7.6 percent a year—an abnormally good span. The lower results of recent years probably are more typical of what you can expect. Even so, moderate doses of these investments make sense in most portfolios because they often fare best when stocks and bonds are being hammered down by sharply increasing interest rates and inflationary worries.

---

than money market funds (provided the yield curve is upward sloping, as it usually is) and offer fairly good principal stability compared with longer-term bond funds. But even short-term funds expose you to some principal volatility if interest rates ratchet up sharply. Most such portfolios were flat to modestly lower in 1994, for example.

Category and Sector Allocation

After breaking your portfolio into the basic investment classes, the next step in setting up your asset allocation program is fine tuning, which is more complex. The following questions will guide you in this step:

1. *What kinds of stock funds should you hold?* You can choose among large and small cap, growth and value, domestic and foreign, utility or technology, passive or actively managed, and more. You may want small holdings in gold or real estate

portfolios, too. (A stock's "cap" or capitalization measures its size, as calculated by the per-share stock price multiplied by the number of shares outstanding.)

2. *What types of bond funds should you own?* Bond funds differ by average maturities, credit ratings, taxability and so on.

3. *What kinds of money market funds should you buy?* Some invest only in government debt, whereas others purchase corporate notes. And money funds differ depending on whether their yields are tax free or not.

4. *How many funds should you hold?* This depends on the size of your portfolio and the amount of time you devote to your investments. Small investors might have just two or three funds whereas someone with a $1-million portfolio could easily own 16 or more.

Checking the Map Periodically

With a strategic allocation, you specify long-term target weights for stocks, bonds and cash. Stick with these targets unless your circumstances change. But you also might want to do some *tactical asset allocation* or periodic rebalancing. The idea here is to fine-tune your portfolio in accordance with current market conditions.

For example, if your strategic allocation calls for you to maintain 65 to 80 percent in stocks and you presently have 85 percent following a strong rally, you might trim your holdings. Or you might boost your exposure a bit if stocks have been sliding and you view the market as undervalued.

Because of tax consequences, you may hesitate to sell an appreciated stock-fund position to restore the original mix. This can be avoided by adding new money to the underweighted categories if you have additional cash to invest. But if you're strapped for cash, you could move the weights gradually by making all subsequent additions into just one or two categories until these categories catch up to your target weights. Or you could funnel the dividends kicked off by, say, the overweighted stock category into money market and bond funds. Still another option is to make the adjustments in tax-deferred accounts such as your 401(k) or IRA to avoid the tax consequences of selling appreciated stock funds.

Asset allocation, which generally requires that you always maintain at least some investments in each asset class, has an advantage over aggressive market timing. With the latter, you may move completely out of stocks when you feel the market is due for a plunge or invest entirely in them if you're anticipating a surge. However, extreme moves do not always pay, because it's simply too easy to mess up. You face a very big risk by moving completely out of the market, and even greater dangers by switching 100 percent into it. Sharp moves can result in inferior long-term portfolio performance.

Tracking What You Own

Too many people have only a vague idea of what their portfolios look like. Yet it's important to keep track of what you own. If you own just a few funds, it's easy to list them and determine your allocations. If you have access to a personal computer, you can use a spreadsheet such as Microsoft Excel or Lotus to track your weightings. This is particularly useful for larger portfolios. All you have to do is spend an hour or so initially setting up the worksheet in a format you like. Then, you can quickly update your portfolio by plugging in any new prices and any revised number of shares owned. Delete funds that have been sold and add new acquisitions to the list. It's wise to keep a separate worksheet of funds sold for tax purposes.

Figure 3.1 shows an allocation worksheet for a husband and wife in their early 40s who are pursuing a growth strategy with 12 funds. As you can see, the worksheet readily summarizes key portfolio traits, from total dollar size to category weightings.

The different ways in which you set up your spreadsheet are limited only by your imagination. In addition to mutual funds, you might add individual stocks and bonds, closed-end funds and more. Holdings in tax-deferred retirement accounts such as IRAs, 401(k)s and variable annuities also should be represented.

Guideposts for Allocating Your Assets

Keep the following suggestions in mind when you implement your asset allocation program:

1. *Set weights for your exposure to stocks, bonds and cash.* Base these weights on your age, time horizon, risk tolerance and performance expectations.

FIGURE 3.1 Sample Portfolio Allocation Worksheet

Date:	Shares	NAV	Total Value	Investment Weight
Stock Funds:				
Gold	500	8	$4,000	1.4%
Real estate	500	11	5,500	2.0
Small-cap growth	1,500	11	16,500	5.9
Small-cap value	2,000	12	24,000	8.5
Emerging markets	1,000	14	14,000	5.0
Small-cap international	800	17	13,600	4.8
Large-cap international	2,500	15	37,500	13.3
Large-cap growth	4,000	12	48,000	17.0
Large-cap value	4,000	14	56,000	19.9
Subtotal			**$215,100**	**76.4%**
Bond Funds:				
High-yield	2,500	9	$22,500	8.0%
Short-term corporate	2,000	12	24,000	8.5
Subtotal			**$46,500**	**16.5%**
Cash:				
Money market fund	20,000	1	$20,000	7.1%
Subtotal			**$20,000**	**7.1%**
Total			**$281,600**	**100.0%**

2. *Remember that holding too much cash can be risky.* The long-run returns on money funds are likely to average around 3 percent a year. Hold cash to 10 percent or less of your portfolio, if possible.

3. *Invest as much as you can in stocks.* The more you allocate to equities, the higher your returns will be, provided you've got the time to be patient.

4. *Spread your stock investments among different categories, styles and sectors, including small companies and foreign corporations.* Holding different types of stock funds can help calm the short-term fluctuations a bit in your overall portfolio. If you've got a long time horizon, the small stock and foreign allocations could help boost your overall returns.

5. *Commit to stocks for the long haul.* Don't invest money that you're going to need in a couple of years to make a large down payment on a home. That money belongs in a short-term bond fund or cash account.

6. *Decide on your rules for rebalancing.* You may want to check your weights once a year or after a major market move. Base any such "tactical" allocations on a market forecast.

7. *But refrain from making large tactical shifts.* For example, if your strategic or long-term guideline calls for a stock weighting between 40 and 50 percent, don't drop to 30 percent. Tighter ranges make more sense.

8. *Don't make frequent small alterations.* This may complicate your recordkeeping and tax preparation.

9. *Remember that you don't need to sell something to change your mix.* You can often accomplish the same goal by investing new money into one or two main categories.

10. *Use mutual funds for allocation decisions.* Funds represent an easy, low-cost way to switch among investment categories. Of course, fund switching is still a taxable event unless you're moving within a tax-sheltered retirement account such as an IRA.

11. *Keep track of your holdings.* A computerized spreadsheet can help you keep your portfolio on course. The number of funds you should own depends on the amount of money you're working with, the investment route you're following and the time you have to monitor your holdings.

CHAPTER 4

Selecting the Best Vehicles for Transportation

We have a tendency to believe that history repeats itself. We assume that last year's Super Bowl champion will be a strong contender this year. We suppose a director's upcoming film will be a smash hit because his or her most recent one was.

So too with mutual funds. Many prospective shareholders buy, or are tempted to invest in, last quarter's top performers. Such funds often see a big influx of money following a sizzling three-month run. Should you hop aboard these fast-moving vehicles? Unfortunately, such short-term performance can turn on a dime. Worse yet, those funds that make quarterly top-ten lists often are among the most volatile.

So do not jump blindly into hot funds when shopping for the best vehicles for your investment journey. Instead, view mutual-fund selection as a two-step process:

1. Determine which investment categories you want, using the principles of asset allocation.
2. Find the best, or at least most appropriate, funds within each category.

How should you get started? Many investors learn about mutual funds by talking with friends, attending financial seminars, reading financial books and magazines or turning to the business section of their local newspaper. You can find out about popular funds in many ways. Celebrity managers who fare well get lots of press.

Hitching Up With a Fund Family

Begin your search by checking to see what some leading fund groups offer. The big players can afford the best managerial talent and research, top-notch investor services and the most complete product lineup. Some examples follow:

- *Fidelity Investments.* By far the biggest family, Fidelity has captured about 13 percent of the total mutual fund market. Although its media-relations people often are hard-pressed to give an exact fund count on request, Fidelity offers more than 200 investment portfolios, of nearly every conceivable type. The company's strength is growth-stock investing, underscored by the great long-term performance of the Fidelity Magellan Fund, the industry's largest.
- *Vanguard Group.* The second-largest family, Vanguard is a penny-pincher's paradise. Vanguard's low costs make the group highly competitive, especially in the bond and money market arenas, where expenses matter most. In addition, Vanguard has emerged as a dominant player in index funds—passively managed portfolios that track popular market benchmarks such as the Standard & Poor's 500. At last count, the company offered about 100 funds, but had fewer than a dozen in the foreign arena.
- *Scudder, Stevens & Clark* and *T. Rowe Price.* These two companies have a fairly extensive lineup of no-commission mutual funds, with strength in the international area. Like Fidelity, Scudder has assembled a network of walk-in investor centers in selected large cities. At these offices, fund investors can buy and sell shares, pick up literature and receive answers to their questions in person.
- *Niche families.* No-load fund groups with a particular slant include Lindner (value investing), Montgomery (growth investing and emerging markets), Mutual Series (value investing and special situations) and Royce (small company value investing).

This list can go on and on. We haven't even mentioned the many fine load-fund complexes, such as American Funds, Putnam or Franklin/Templeton. Appendix 1 contains the phone numbers of most fund families referred to in this book. For comprehensive information on fund groups, see *The Value Line Mutual Fund Survey,* which provides commentary on 100 leading families.

Sorting the Numbers

Mutual fund investing needn't be terribly complicated or time-consuming. Still, you should understand various terms, especially those relating to a fund's performance numbers and fees. Just as it helps to know a few foreign words when traveling abroad, knowing some key words and phrases helps you in mutual fund investing. Here are a few terms:

Total Net Assets. This term, which reflects total portfolio assets minus liabilities, tells you how big a fund is. Midsize funds have net assets between about $250 million and $500 million; small portfolios have less than $50 million or so. The really tiny ones are smaller than $10 million, whereas the biggest tabulate their assets in the billions. Fidelity Magellan, the largest mutual fund, had more than $40 billion at last count.

Funds that invest in small companies often have an easier time when they themselves are on the small side. They can buy meaningful stakes in these thinly traded stocks without bumping up their prices in the process. Big funds, with their voracious appetite for shares, could cause havoc in the market price of a little company. In general, small-company portfolios function best with assets less than $300 million or so. But funds that earmark large stocks or bonds can benefit from a greater size because of economies of scale, which lead to lower expense ratios. By examining assets over several years, you can see whether a portfolio has grown, stayed roughly the same or decreased in size. Popular, good-performing funds exhibit vigorous asset growth. But those that have fared poorly often lose shareholders.

Net Asset Value (NAV). This term, quoted in newspaper financial tables, refers to the fund's price per share. With the help of computers and independent pricing services, each fund company tabulates its NAV daily, typically within 90 minutes of the market's close. To calculate the NAV, each security held by the fund must be priced. Then the total values of all securities (including cash equivalents) are added up, and expenses and other liabilities deducted. The result is the fund's *total net assets*. Dividing this by the number of shares gives you the NAV. For example, if Fund A has total net assets of $800 million on a day when 50 million shares are outstanding, its NAV would be $16 ($800 million ÷ 50 million).

By watching daily or weekly fluctuations, you can get a feel for how volatile a fund might be. But the NAV by itself doesn't tell you much, because the NAV drops each time a fund pays a dividend or capital-gains distribution. Thus, it doesn't really matter whether a fund's price is $1, $10 or $100 a share. You should focus on the total return, another commonly published number, because it reflects both price changes and income.

Measuring Performance—Yield versus Total Return. "Total return" and "yields" are not synonymous, no more than "England" is "Great Britain." Bonds and stocks produce returns consisting of two sources: yield and price appreciation (or depreciation). The *yield* measures the income kicked off by an investment. Taken together, the two components add up to the *total return.*

For example, a high-grade bond trades at $800 at the beginning of the year and pays $60 interest for the year. Its yield is 7.5 percent ($60 ÷ $800). Suppose interest rates decline, and the bond rises to $850 at year end. The total return equals $110 ($60 interest + $50 price gain). As a percentage, the return is 13.75 percent ($110 ÷ $800 initial price). You calculate total return in the same way for stocks and mutual funds.

$$\frac{\$60 \text{ Income} + \$50 \text{ Price change}}{\$800 \text{ Initial price}} = 13.75\% \text{ Total return}$$

Total return serves as a complete measure of performance in both good and bad markets. Assume interest rates instead rise and the bond in our example falls to $700 at year end. The investment now produces a $40 net loss ($60 interest − $100 price decline). So even though the yield is still 7.5 percent, the total return equals −5 percent (−$40 ÷ $800).

$$\frac{\$60 \text{ Income} - \$100 \text{ Price change}}{\$800 \text{ Initial price}} = -5\% \text{ Total return}$$

This simple example should convince you that total return is the preferred measure of performance. Too often unsophisticated investors fall into the "yield trap," looking only at this yardstick and grabbing the highest-yielding bond or bond fund because it appears more enticing. But excessively high yields usually reflect severe credit or interest-rate risks and might not last for long.

The Income Ratio. The *ratio of net investment income to assets* measures what the portfolio earned in stock dividends or bond interest. Note that the numerator contains *net income* (gross income less fund expenses). Basically, the income ratio represents the fund's yield, so it is not a complete measure of performance like total return. As you might expect, bond funds have higher ratios than stock portfolios,

FIGURE 4.1   Hypothetical Fund Returns

| | Year | | | | | |
	1	2	3	4	5	5-yr. avg.
Fund A	10%	−35%	20%	5%	90%	11.4%
Fund B	14	−20	24	9	35	10.7

especially appreciation-oriented stock funds, whose numbers may be near zero. The average income ratio for equity funds recently approximated 1.1 percent, versus 5.7 percent for taxable bond funds, according to Morningstar, a research and ranking service. A ratio could even be a negative number if expenses exceed income. Don't worry about low income ratios on funds that are shooting for appreciation.

Sizing Up Total Return.   You should view a fund's total return relative to those of its peers and an appropriate market benchmark. For example, judge a growth and income fund against other growth and income funds and the S&P 500. *The Wall Street Journal* is a notable source of total-return figures over various periods, ranging up to five years. Lipper Analytical Services provides the data, and fund results for different periods appear on different days.

Look for consistent performance and be sure to study returns in individual years. The five- or ten-year numbers can mask a lot of volatility along the way. Figure 4.1 shows the investment results of two aggressive-growth portfolios. If you looked at the five-year average only, you would choose Fund A, because its 11.4 percent return exceeds B's 10.7 percent. But B actually did better than A in every year except the most recent. A's unusually high 90 percent return in year five may turn out to be a flash in the pan. Notice that B's returns are much less volatile and it lost considerably less in year 2, dropping 20 percent versus A's 35-percent plunge.

The bottom line: Be leery of volatile funds in which one or two exceptional years have fueled impressive average returns. Often these are smaller portfolios that assume substantial risk. Observe how a fund fared in tumultuous years such as 1987, 1990 and 1994. Could you hang on through a decline of that magnitude?

You also want to make sure that the fund is being run the same way it was in the past, especially if you are looking at averages over three or more years. A new manager may be at the helm, or the portfolio

---

TRAVELER'S ADVISORY:
Using the Right Benchmarks

Suppose your capital-appreciation fund's NAV tumbled 6 percent yesterday. Should you panic? That depends partly on whether rival portfolios also got clobbered.

Gauging a fund's day-to-day, week-to-week or year-to-year performance relative to its peers is usually better than using an index, such as the S&P 500. Lipper Analytical Services provides "equal-weighted" indices for a spectrum of categories. The equal-weighting feature ensures that each fund in a particular index has the same influence—no single fund dominates. Thus equal-weighted indices offer an ideal way to gauge a fund's recent performance. Several of these indices appear daily in Part C of *The Wall Street Journal*.

---

may have grown much larger. Either development could change the fund's character.

Performance is paramount, but low costs can tilt the odds in your favor. It's important to understand the potential impact of sales loads, expense ratios and portfolio turnover ratios on the bottom line, as each can exert a drag on the total return. A fund's costs are, in fact, more predictable than its performance.

Sales Loads. These represent the commissions you pay on funds sold through most brokers, banks and financial planners. You'll find these charges in the fee table of the fund's prospectus or disclosure statement. You should be familiar with several types of loads:

- *Front-end loads.* These charges are levied on your initial purchase and typically range between 3 and 6 percent. Commission discounts known as *breakpoints* may be offered to people who make very large investments—usually starting at $50,000 or $100,000. Deeper discounts apply at higher dollar levels. On some portfolios, the front-end load may vanish completely if you're investing, say, $1 million or more.

- *12b-1 fees.* More than half of all funds now impose these annual distribution charges, which cover marketing costs and—in the case of broker-sold products—shareholder servicing by the broker. In many cases, 12b-1 fees are just another, less-noticeable way to charge a commission. The 12b-1 fee, which can be as high as 1 percent a year, is included in the fund's expense ratio. High 12b-1 charges of 0.5 percent or more can be a serious drain on performance when compounded over the years.
- *Deferred sales loads.* Also known as back end or *contingent deferred sales charges,* these costs are imposed when you exit a fund. The penalty might be as high as 5 or 6 percent if you redeem during the first year. The charge declines thereafter and phases out completely after five or six years. The deferred sales charge generally applies to funds with high 12b-1 fees, but no front-end loads.

You can avoid all three types of charges by sticking with commission-free or no-load funds. Some of these portfolios do levy a modest 12b-1 fee, but it will be limited to 0.25 percent a year. Most no-loads impose no such costs. The subject of fees can get quite involved. Many broker-sold products now offer various fee options in the form of different share classes, namely A, B and C shares. Chapter 21 covers these share classifications and their accompanying charges.

The Expense Ratio.   This ratio is a standardized number that measures a fund's annual costs. It totals the management fee, administrative outlays, 12b-1 fees and other costs on a per-share basis. Contrary to what you might think, the expense ratio does not include brokerage commissions incurred by the fund when the manager buys and sells securities. The average expense ratio for stock funds was recently 1.45 percent, according to Morningstar. That represents a charge of $14.50 a year on each $1,000 invested. In contrast, municipal-bond funds came in a bit below at 0.84 percent, or $8.40 per $1,000. Index portfolios have some of the lowest expense ratios. Note that several of the weakest fund groups charge some of the highest costs.

When you look at total-return numbers, keep in mind that expenses have already been subtracted out. That is, published performance results are net of fees. Even so, the expense ratio still deserves serious consideration. Although some sizzling performers carry very high expense ratios, you can never be sure whether those stratospheric returns will continue. The high costs most likely will. Expenses weigh especially heavy for bond funds because they generate lower returns than stock products. Moderate costs leave more income for shareholders.

Portfolio Turnover Ratio. This ratio measures a fund's trading activity. High turnover results in steeper brokerage commissions and other transaction costs that eat into total returns. These expenses are magnified if a fund trades securities that characteristically have low liquidity and high trading costs, such as small stocks or junk bonds.

A turnover of 100 percent implies that each stock or bond is replaced once a year on average. A 50-percent reading means that every other security is replaced annually. The average stock fund recently had a 75-percent turnover rate, according to Morningstar. Sometimes you'll see funds with high turnover and consistently good total returns. If the management has been successful, it's hard to fault them for trading frequently. But a fund with high turnover and poor returns definitely makes a bad choice. Index funds have the lowest turnover ratios, which can be just 4 or 5 percent. Aggressive-growth funds typically have the highest readings—sometimes 300 to 400 percent or more.

Reading a Fund's Prospectus

Anyone who has traveled along unfamiliar turf knows how important a good map can be. Not all maps are very good, of course. The typical mutual fund prospectus is a poor map, full of complexities, jargon and legal mumbo jumbo. That's too bad because the prospectus is the most important disclosure document required of fund companies. The rise of independent research publications such as *Morningstar Mutual Funds* and *The Value Line Mutual Fund Survey* can be traced partly to the fact that investors aren't getting all the information they need from fund companies themselves.

On the bright side, prospectuses are getting better. A fairly new SEC rule, dating to 1994, now requires fund companies to provide limited total-return numbers in the document, including a comparison of the fund's performance against a relevant market benchmark. Fidelity Investments is among the groups that have succeeded in developing readable, helpful prospectuses. One of the earliest and best examples of a good prospectus comes from the Gateway Trust in Cincinnati. Gateway's document provides all sorts of revealing insights, including various ways to measure the fund's risk and returns, and detailed information on Peter Thayer, the portfolio manager.

AT THE HELM: PETER THAYER

Manager of the Gateway Index Plus Fund since 1977, Peter Thayer owns more than $350,000 worth of shares in the fund, enjoys birdwatching and collects Rookwood Pottery. That's more than you may care to know about him, but those facts are available and highlighted in the fund's prospectus.

Every mutual fund issues a prospectus or disclosure document. Like owner's manuals, these small booklets are filled with the key information you need to make decisions. That's the ideal anyway. In practice, most prospectuses are verbose, legalistic, intimidating—and largely unread by shareholders. The poor quality of the typical prospectus represents one of the major failings of the mutual fund industry.

But Gateway Index Plus' prospectus is different. When the revamped document came out, Thayer and other Gateway execs bragged about setting a new standard for mutual funds. We think they have. This prospectus contains all of the usual disclosures, along with risk and return numbers expressed in several ways, performance charts, definitions of key investment terms and, of course, a profile of the portfolio manager.

At a time when fund managers always seem to be coming and going, Thayer's tenure at Gateway Index Plus is comforting. As president and co-founder of the fund's management company, he's not likely to leave anytime soon. Gateway Index Plus has been a steady performer that follows a conservative path in the stock market. If you don't believe us, you can read about it in the prospectus.

The Financial Highlights Table

Even less-enlightened fund companies must provide reams of data in their prospectuses. The problem is that you can find these facts hard to locate and interpret. A good place to start is the financial-highlights table. The numbers in this chart go back for ten years or the life of the fund, whichever is less. The table includes information on the following:

- *Dividends*
- *Capital-gains distributions*
- *NAV*
- *Total returns*
- *Net assets*
- *Expense ratios*
- *Net income ratios*
- *Portfolio turnover rates*

As noted, a fund's total returns over various periods provide the most important measure of performance. Analyzing the financial-highlights table sheds light on how these critical numbers are derived. The top half of the table starts with the fund's NAV at the beginning of the year and traces the factors that caused it to change, including gains and losses on portfolio holdings, investment income, and dividend and capital-gains payouts.

Analyzing ABC Small Cap

To help you understand how the numbers tie together, Figure 4.2 contains excerpts from the financial-highlights table of a hypothetical small-company stock fund.

Lines 1 and 2 tell that the distributions consist entirely of capital gains, with nothing coming from dividend income—common with a fund of this type because small companies often don't pay dividends. Capital gains can vary widely from year to year. By themselves, the NAV numbers in Line 3 say little, because they will be reduced by the amount of distributions paid to shareholders. Total return (Line 4) is the important number, because it pulls together all these changes into a single figure. The total returns by themselves look interesting, but you need to check further to see how ABC Small Cap did relative to its peers and a benchmark like the Russell 2000. To find this detailed information, you might have to consult mutual fund guides such as those published by Morningstar and Value Line.

Net assets (line 5) tell how the fund has grown. Size increases for two reasons: new investor money and portfolio gains. ABC Small Cap has experienced considerable growth. Size is an important factor to monitor on small-company funds. When their assets swell beyond $300 million or so, these types of funds have a more difficult time confining themselves to the manager's choice picks because small stocks

FIGURE 4.2 Excerpts from ABC Small Cap's Financial-Highlights Table

Per-Share Data and Ratios	Year-end December 31		
	1995	1994	1993
1. Dividends from net income ($)	0.00	0.00	0.00
2. Capital gains distributions ($)	1.52	0.83	3.09
3. Net asset value ($)	10.80	10.75	9.50
4. Total return (%)	14.6	21.9	39.9
5. Net assets (000s $)	600,000	250,000	100,000
6. Expense ratio (%)	2.5	2.4	2.3
7. Net income ratio (%)	–0.5	–0.4	–0.1
8. Portfolio turnover (%)	250	275	300

are illiquid and funds generally don't want to invest too much in any one company. At $600 million, ABC has grown rather large, so size is a negative here.

The expense ratio (line 6) is rather high and appears to be trending upward—another red flag. ABC's slightly negative income ratio (line 7) mirrors its capital-appreciation objective and does not represent cause for alarm. Expenses commonly top income when the stocks in a portfolio generate little or no dividends.

Finally, portfolio turnover (line 8) is very high, another negative. This is a concern with a small-stock fund because it costs more to buy and sell small stocks than the big, actively traded blue chips. So, you don't want your portfolio manager trading too frequently.

What's in the Portfolio?

Now we move from the prospectus to the fund's annual and semiannual reports. These documents describe the investment holdings. You might also be able to get more timely information by calling the fund company directly.

What Percent of the Portfolio Is in Cash?   A "fully invested" fund virtually always keeps at least 90 to 95 percent of its assets in stocks or bonds with the remainder in cash (that is, Treasury bills and the like). However, some funds reserve the right to make substantial changes in their cash allocations. Their managers want the option of retreating to cash when they think stocks or bonds are overpriced and headed for a decline. But it's easy for anyone making big bets on the market's direction to mess up. Portfolios that switch heavily into cash often lag their peers over the long term because less risk leads to lower returns.

What Are the Top-Ten Holdings?   By looking at the fund's dominant stocks, you get a feel for the kinds of companies management likes. Do these stocks seem right for the fund's objectives, or do they appear out of place? The portfolio should include the kinds of securities you were expecting.

Which Sectors Does the Fund Invest In?   Funds that place heavy bets on volatile industries such as technology or health care are more risky than others with a more even distribution. *Sector weightings* (the percentages invested in different industries) tell you what groups the manager favors or avoids. A fund's performance during any year or quarter may depend heavily on its sector preferences.

What Are the Country Allocations?   Global and international portfolios may diversify across two dozen or more stock markets. It's important to look at these country allocations. You want to know where the manager of, say, T. Rowe Price International is investing assets, and how the breakdown differs from that of Scudder International. Of special interest is each fund's tilt toward or away from volatile emerging markets such as Mexico, China and India.

How Much of Your Domestic Fund Is Invested Abroad?   Increasingly, funds you think of as domestic dabble on foreign exchanges. A typical growth portfolio might have 10 or 15 percent of its assets outside the United States. That can have an important impact on performance and risk. For instance, if foreign stock markets outdistance the S&P 500 in a particular year, a growth fund with a 20-percent stake in these nations could significantly outperform its competitors.

Know Your Navigator's Style

The two major approaches or styles of equity investing are growth and value. These stock-selection strategies tend to do well at different times in the economic cycle, so it often pays to represent both among your fund holdings. For a good part of the 1980s, value investing sparkled, but then it lagged growth in 1989, 1990 and 1991. Value made a comeback in 1992 and continued as the better performing style in 1993. Growth managed to inch ahead of value in 1994 and 1995.

Value investors look for companies that are undervalued or "cheap" according to traditional yardsticks, including low price-earnings (PE) ratios, low price-book value ratios, low price-cash flow ratios and high dividend yields. (The PE is the stock's price divided by its earnings per share; the *price-book ratio* divides price by common stockholders' equity per share; and the *price–cash flow ratio* divides price by cash flow, where the latter equals earnings adjusted for noncash items such as depreciation.)

Cheap stocks can include former "blue chips" that have fallen on hard times. Companies in basic industries such as auto, chemical and steel manufacturing sometimes offer special values when these sectors hit their cyclical nadirs. Utility and financial stocks with high dividend yields often attract the value conscious. Some penny pinchers also look for "hidden assets" on the balance sheet and pay attention to a company's "break-up" value. Simply put, they're trying to buy a dollar's worth of assets for less. Value investors trace their roots back to the work of the legendary Benjamin Graham, the father of modern security analysis.

Conversely, *growth* managers seek out companies with sales and earnings that are expected to ratchet upward sharply in the future. Growth stocks pay little or no dividends because it's more profitable for these companies to plow this money back into their businesses to finance future expansion. Growth investors don't mind buying exciting stocks with high PEs and low yields, but at the first sign of trouble they're often quick to bail out. Growth managers frequently target such sectors as the communications, entertainment, health care and technology industries.

Growth and value investing are not necessarily mutually exclusive. At times, certain stocks seem to fall into both camps simultaneously. Also, some fund managers blend the two styles. They may be looking for companies with above-average earnings potential, but they buy only if the shares appear cheap. This is known as GARP or "growth at a reasonable price."

A fund's name often doesn't tell you which style management follows. Names can even be misleading. ABC Growth Fund may have value in its heart. But if you look at the right numbers, you can tell. Here are some signposts to help identify a portfolio's true stripes:

- Growth funds tend to have high turnover rates, but value managers often hold their stocks for years, waiting patiently for them to blossom.
- Growth funds normally have higher PE ratios.
- Funds in the "equity-income" category have a value orientation unless they are mislabeled, which sometimes happens.
- Growth funds tend to focus on midsize or small companies, which generally have more sales and earnings potential than the big caps. But there are many small-cap value funds, too.
- Because growth stocks generally pay little or no dividends, value funds tend to have higher income ratios or yields.

Of course, a fund's statement of objectives should give you a reasonable clue about the manager's style. But looking at the above data provides greater insight because the statement of objectives could be written vaguely on purpose.

When doing your homework, look at the fund's composite PE ratio. This statistic averages the PE multiples of each stock in the portfolio. You can find it in the Morningstar or Value Line guides listed in Appendix 2. Higher PEs indicate greater volatility because they have further to fall in a correction or bear market. Growth funds normally fluctuate more than their value relatives.

You can determine the size range of companies your portfolio invests in by examining the median market capitalization of its holdings. Funds that buy small stocks should have median market caps below $600 million or so—and preferably below $300 million. Check in Morningstar and Value Line and compare with the S&P 500, which had a median market cap of roughly $15 billion at this writing.

In addition, Morningstar and Value Line provide a useful box that categorizes a stock portfolio in terms of style (value, blend or growth) and the size of companies it targets (large, medium or small). As a rule, large-stock value funds are considered least risky, and small-company growth portfolios most volatile.

Risk Measures—Paying Attention to Potholes

In addition to examining a fund's return, you need to evaluate its risk. Figure 4.1 illustrates volatility by the year-to-year variations in the annual returns of the two aggressive-growth portfolios. The more extreme the ups and downs, the greater the volatility or risk. If you are

---

TRAVELER'S ADVISORY:
Fund Ratings Aren't Predictive

The comprehensive ratings provided by both Morningstar and Value Line capture risk and return in a tidy little numerical score. Researchers at these companies rate funds according to their "risk-adjusted performance" over various periods. The higher a fund's performance relative to its fluctuations, the better its score. Ratings are convenient summary measures that can help narrow your list of candidates, but don't pick portfolios solely on this basis. The ratings represent only a starting point for a more in-depth analysis. They don't predict future results; they merely describe what has happened so far.

---

a long-term investor and don't have to worry about selling shares to meet emergency needs, you need not be concerned about volatility, unless it just plain makes you uncomfortable.

Standard Deviation

You can measure volatility in several ways. The most insightful and dependable barometer is known as *standard deviation,* the degree to which a fund's returns fluctuate around their average. The higher the standard deviation, the greater the volatility. About two-thirds of the time, a fund's most current return will differ from its past average by no more than one standard deviation, plus or minus. So for a stock fund that has an average annual return of 12 percent and a standard deviation of 14 percent, you can expect to earn between 26 percent and −2 percent in about two of every three years. The best measure of risk, standard deviation allows you to compare all kinds of funds— stock, bond, international and sector.

The Beta Coefficient

Beta measures a fund's volatility relative to a market benchmark, commonly the S&P 500 index. A fund that seesaws in perfect sync with the market has a beta of exactly 1.0. More volatile portfolios such as aggressive-growth funds show betas higher than 1.0; more conservative investments have coefficients below 1.0. On gold, international and other funds that move independently of the S&P 500, beta readings are not meaningful. That is one reason this risk measure has lost some of its following over the years. In short, it's wise to check the standard deviation along with beta when you're examining volatility. You can find both of these and other risk yardsticks in the Morningstar and Value Line publications.

Street Smarts

- A good first step for new investors is to become familiar with the large, popular mutual fund families. As your portfolio grows, explore other, more specialized groups.
- Be a penny pincher. Compare expense ratios of similar types of portfolios, recognizing that costs vary noticeably among fund categories.
- Look for performance consistency—not just a few stellar quarters. And make sure the portfolio manager responsible for an outstanding record is still at the helm.
- The net income ratio is important if you're following a yield itinerary. But don't invest in a fund that delivers high income if its total returns have lagged.
- The financial-highlights table is the most important part of the prospectus. Excessive expenses, outrageously high turnover rates, a shrinking asset base and poor total returns stick out like potholes on your journey to wealth.

CHAPTER 5

Can Your Navigator Beat the Averages?

The typical mutual fund manager earns about $100,000 annually. Some top stock and bond pickers bring home multimillion-dollar paychecks in good years. Even young, inexperienced managers live well—certainly better than most people in their twenties and thirties. So is it too much to ask that your mutual fund at least match the performance of the broad market? Apparently it is.

Even though the market includes millions of amateur investors, mutual funds have a hard time beating it. Over the ten years through December 1994, for example, Lipper's general-equity fund category returned 12.8 percent annually. But the S&P 500 index did better, rising 14.4 percent a year. So too with international-stock funds. According to Lipper, they advanced at an annual clip of 15.7 percent over this period, trailing the 17.6-percent yearly surge in the MSCI-EAFE (the Morgan Stanley Capital International Europe, Australia, Far East index).

Want more evidence? Figure 5.1 shows the percentages of general-equity and small-stock funds outperformed by their benchmarks on an annual basis. Even the best individual funds don't beat the market year in and year out.

Why Do Professional Navigators Lag?

The following four reasons explain why underperformance is so common:

- Some managers simply make poor stock selection or timing decisions. They just aren't that good at their craft.
- Many funds lag the broad market averages in a given year because their investment style is out of favor.
- Cash holdings can hold a fund back in a bull market.
- Managers have to overcome the formidable hurdles of management fees and transaction costs because they must report returns minus ongoing expenses.

Poor investment selection and timing decisions obviously affect funds negatively. For example, an aggressive-growth manager may overweight industries that turn out to be disappointments while neglecting those that eventually sparkle. It's more instructive to look at the other, less obvious factors.

FIGURE 5.1   Actively Managed Funds Outperformed by Indices

Year	General-Equity Funds Outperformed by		Small-Cap Funds Outperformed by
	S&P 500	Wilshire 5000	Russell 2000
1984	78%	68%	54%
1985	74	78	58
1986	76	62	45
1987	76	57	43
1988	59	67	80
1989	82	73	22
1990	64	43	13
1991	45	57	38
1992	46	55	80
1993	40	46	64
1994	78	63	43

Source: Reprinted by permission of Lipper Analytical Services, Inc., and The Vanguard Group.

Style Differences

The media and most investors like to track the U.S. stock market via the Dow Jones Industrial Average, a grouping of 30 household-name corporations. But investment pros, including many fund managers, tend to peg their performance against the S&P 500 index, a broader and thus more indicative measure. One reason most funds don't match the market is that their holdings don't closely mirror the S&P 500. Managers emphasize or avoid certain stocks and industries, they mix in smaller companies and they might even dabble in foreign securities. And as noted, certain managers buy value stocks whereas others go for growth. Each fund has its own particular style.

During a year when growth stocks lag, you can expect growth-oriented fund managers to underperform the S&P 500. But when value lags, these helmsmen have an easier time beating the index, which is biased toward mature, less volatile, dividend-paying companies—that is, value stocks. So the style factor can work either way. It's important to be aware of style differences and the effect they can have on the bottom line. Although we have cited the S&P 500, this explanation applies to any market index.

Cash Holdings

Mutual funds typically keep 5 to 10 percent of their assets in cash, mainly Treasury bills, partly to handle unexpectedly large shareholder *redemptions* (or liquidations) and partly to have buying power available to jump on bargains when they arise. Many managers also accumulate cash if they anticipate a correction or bear market. A few equity portfolios move entirely into and then out of stocks at the manager's discretion.

When funds hold cash, they obviously can't enjoy gains on that money as stocks rise. As a result, they risk underperforming the S&P 500 or relevant benchmark if the market pulls a surprise and shoots higher. Too much cash can be the main factor explaining lagging returns during an upward phase, as T-bills almost always pay less when stocks as a whole are rising.

But how does cash affect funds in down markets? Because managers face redemptions, they can quickly lose their cash cushion if the decline is sudden and severe enough. In major meltdowns, such as in 1973–74 and 1987, stock portfolios suffered along with the S&P 500, as seen in Figure 5.2. These numbers do suggest, however, that cash cushions gave funds an edge during periods of modest declines, as in the 1980–82 period.

**FIGURE 5.2   Bear Market Performance of General
Equity Funds**

	S&P 500	Lipper General Equity Average	S&P 500 Advantage
January 1973–September 1974	−42.64%	−45.14%	+2.50%
December 1980–July 1982	−16.51	−9.67	−6.84
September 1987–November 1987	−29.58	−27.95	−1.63

Source: Reprinted by permission of Lipper Analytical Services, Inc.

Expenses and Transaction Costs

Good mutual funds represent highly cost-efficient investments, but they aren't free. The drag exerted by costs is probably the key reason portfolio managers overall have a hard time beating the market. According to Morningstar, stock funds on average charge shareholders nearly 1.5 percent a year, reducing investment returns by the same amount. These costs are expressed in each fund's expense ratio. Brokerage outlays, which aren't included in this ratio but do eat into returns, average another 0.3 percent or so annually. Adding the two produces 1.8 percent a year in total costs.

And keep in mind that the 0.3-percent brokerage number merely reflects commissions, not other trading costs a fund faces. These consist of two additional components: (1) the *bid-asked spread,* which typically shows up as a difference of ⅛-point between a dealer's "buy" and "sell" prices on a stock, and (2) any price impacts of making large trades in smaller, less-liquid stocks. Although it's impossible to tabulate total outlays precisely, you can safely assume that the typical fund shoulders about 2 percent a year in both operating expenses and trading costs.

The Efficient-Market Hypothesis

The fact that the stock market is at least reasonably efficient works against portfolio managers trying to offset the drag of higher costs. By this, we mean that stocks normally are correctly priced, more or less, so it doesn't pay to spend a lot of time and effort trying to discover undervalued companies. This idea derives from the *efficient-market hypothesis,* a theory that gained credence in the early 1970s after academic studies provided convincing evidence that most managed portfolios lagged behind their benchmarks.

According to the efficient-market hypothesis, a stock is said to be correctly priced when "price" and "value" are one and the same number. That is, whenever something causes a stock to become more or less valuable, its price should react immediately. For example, suppose the shares of ABC Company, which traded for $24 each, suddenly shoot up to a value of $26 in the eyes of security analysts because management just landed a big contract in Europe. It follows that the price should immediately jump to $26. This doesn't always happen exactly as it's supposed to, but the theory holds up pretty well much of the time.

Several factors cause the market to be efficient, meaning that it's hard to locate undervalued stocks:

1. Wall Street has become fiercely competitive, full of many intelligent, highly educated, well-trained professionals using the latest analytical tools.

2. News disseminates rapidly and widely, thanks to advances in communications.

3. News disseminates randomly over time, often in the form of high-impact "surprise" announcements. In other words, you don't know which stocks are going to be the subject of unexpected news stories tomorrow that will move their prices, as in the ABC Company example above. Academics say that prices follow a "random walk" because news is random and prices move in tandem with the news.

4. Many Wall Street pros managing huge sums of money monitor individual companies throughout the day. When big news hits, they act so fast that by the time people on the street learn of the story (perhaps many hours if not days later) the price has already responded.

The efficient-market hypothesis implies that past performance is not a useful predictor of future results, holding risk constant. By "holding risk constant," we mean that more volatile portfolios should outperform more placid ones over long stretches. This is why stocks have fared better than bonds over the years and why small companies have outpaced larger ones.

In its strictest interpretation, the hypothesis implies that even those funds with the best histories would not be expected to stand out in the future, because outstanding returns year after year are more a matter of luck than skill. An influential 1968 study of mutual fund performance by professor Michael Jensen concluded that a fund's past performance was of no value in predicting its future returns. But more recent studies find that past performance can be helpful. In particular, chronic poor performance appears to persist. And even though the market is relatively efficient, pockets of inefficiency can be found, especially among neglected small stocks and under-researched foreign companies.

Buying a Package Deal—Index Funds

Index funds are like traveling to Europe on a carefully orchestrated tour package. You expect to see the major sights and have a generally good time, but you're not as likely to make as many unexpected discoveries, for better or worse, as you would if you really let yourself wander. We can say several good things about index funds, and predictability is one of them. These portfolios provide a way to perform as well as the market—no better, no worse.

An index fund simply attempts to mimic its target benchmark by investing in all the same stocks in the index (or a large sampling if the benchmark is very broad like the Wilshire 5000). Index-fund managers do not attempt to find undervalued stocks. They simply purchase whatever companies are in the benchmark. They normally weight these companies the same as they are in the index, to track performance as closely as possible. For example, if General Electric amounts to 2.7 percent of the value of the S&P 500 index, it would be given the same representation in the Vanguard Index Trust 500 portfolio, which mimics the S&P 500.

Index funds generally remain fully invested, whereas a typical mutual fund might keep 5 to 10 percent of its assets in cash. Consequently, index portfolios should deliver better long-term performance because the stock market trends upward over time.

Index-Fund Features

True index funds exhibit four important characteristics. If you buy a ticket, this is what you can expect:

1. *Low expense ratios.* The portfolio manager does not need to search for promising stocks or sectors because index funds follow a cookie-cutter approach to investing. This saves travel and other research costs.
2. *Low portfolio turnovers.* The manager does not actively trade stocks, rotate among sectors or time the market. Index funds embody buy-and-hold investing all the way.

3. *Tax efficiency.* Because of low turnover, an index fund does not realize as many taxable capital gains that must be passed along to shareholders. Some index funds strive to be even more tax efficient by offsetting realized gains with losses on other holdings.
4. *Total-return predictability.* You're assured of performing nearly the same as the benchmark. No need to worry about being saddled with a laggard manager.

A fund that lacks the above characteristics is not a true index fund. Some portfolios strive to beat a particular index by trying to predict which stocks in the benchmark will deliver the best performance. With these investments, however, you can't assume you'll get predictable results.

Excursion Choices

Vanguard is the pioneer and fund-industry leader in indexing. Introduced in 1976, its flagship Index Trust 500 portfolio counts more than $11 billion in assets. The S&P 500 covers about two-thirds of the total market value of domestic stocks. The Wilshire 4500 Index represents the other third. This slice consists of the medium and smaller issues—everything but the large S&P 500 corporations. Actually, the Wilshire 4500 has grown to more than 6,300 companies. Vanguard's Extended Market Portfolio holds a sampling of 1,400 to 1,700 stocks in the Wilshire 4500, which provides ample representation.

Vanguard now offers more than a dozen index products. All normally stay fully invested in their respective benchmarks. Two of these portfolios take the stocks in the S&P 500 and split them into growth or value. Out-of-favor blue chips that have lower PE and price-book ratios and higher dividend yields represent the value portion. The rest fall into the growth camp.

Because of their lower expenses, index funds can be especially good choices in the bond area, where returns cluster together much more closely than with stocks. Vanguard's Total Bond Market Portfolio includes mortgage-backed securities, Treasuries and corporates. The other bond-index products focus on different maturities of Treasuries and corporates only. All of these choices should handily outperform their more costly peers.

Other fund groups with notable index products include Dreyfus, Schwab, Federated, Dimensional Fund Advisors, SEI and even Fidelity.

AT THE HELM: JOHN C. BOGLE

For a key member of the mutual fund establishment, John C. Bogle is a rebel. But at least he's a rebel with a cause.

Bogle is chairman of the giant Vanguard Group, the second largest fund complex behind Fidelity Investments. Because Vanguard is owned by the shareholders of its many funds, it provides money-management and other services at cost. This allows the company to shave expenses to a minimum, providing Bogle a platform from which to preach the merits of low-cost investing. In recent years, he has railed against rival fund companies that have failed to pass along economies of scale to investors in the form of lower expense ratios. Vanguard has kept up the competitive pressure by introducing more than a dozen index funds.

Bogle founded Vanguard in 1975 and has been at the helm ever since, although he recently passed the torch of daily oversight to new chief executive officer John Brennan. Bogle is a Princeton graduate who was born in the market-crash year of 1929. One of his six children, John C. Bogle Jr., serves as portfolio manager for the Quantitative Group of Lincoln, Massachusetts, where he has compiled a fine record of his own.

In short, many people would probably benefit if they added an index component to their existing stable of actively managed funds. Broad index products work well as core holdings, amounting to perhaps 30 to 50 percent of the total value of your investment portfolio. You get very wide diversification and low expenses. Plus, you don't have to worry about the portfolio manager. You can buy and hold a good index fund for decades.

Tracking the Benchmark

Before investing in an index fund, see how well it has kept up with its target index in the past. With some of the newer portfolios this is difficult to do, but you should at least be able to make some inferences as to how it will behave in the future. Not all index funds track their benchmarks closely.

The following two factors can help you evaluate the performance differential between an index fund and the index itself:

1. *Whether the fund buys the whole universe or samples.* A sufficiently large S&P 500 index fund would normally invest in all 500 companies and weight them correctly, which is known as *complete replication.* However, a Wilshire 5000 portfolio would almost certainly take samples because the Wilshire includes more than 6,800 firms. The sample stocks chosen will determine in part how closely the portfolio tracks its benchmark.

2. *The fund's expense ratio.* The higher the costs, the greater the degree to which a fund trails its benchmark. Higher management and administrative fees lead to greater expenses. Smaller index products may have loftier expense ratios because they don't benefit from economies of scale like bigger funds, which can spread their costs over a wider asset base. Also be aware of temporary fee waivers or special situations where the fund company absorbs some or even all of the costs. These deals can be attractive while they last, but don't get caught by surprise when their time runs out. A major reason for investing in an index fund is a low expense ratio.

Market Timing: No Road to Riches

The most direct way to beat the market is to time it successfully—if you can. The *market timing* concept is simple—shift your assets to stock funds when prices are rising, then to money market portfolios to sidestep any declines. Timers read all sorts of tea leaves, looking for signals of those elusive market turns. Most focus on graphs of trading activity. These show stock-price movements, moving averages of stock prices and trading-volume measures. Extreme market timers shuttle between 100 percent in stock funds and 100 percent in cash, based on their signals.

It's not easy to time the market successfully. Timers risk missing out on stock-market surges by being on the sidelines. Those really big upward stampedes have three things in common: They are unpredictable, infrequent and of limited duration.

If you are sitting at the docks when you should be underway, your long-run returns might never make up for the lost distance. In addition, if your funds are held in taxable accounts, the taxes you must pay on any gains generated by switching from stocks to cash will further reduce your performance. Finally, any transaction costs also will eat into the bottom line. For these reasons, you should steer clear of funds that aggressively try to time the market.

During a European vacation in early 1990, one of us encountered a know-it-all American traveler from San Diego who was convinced the stock market was then overvalued, with the Dow Jones industrial average trading around 2900. This man vowed to refrain from making any equity investments until the Dow ebbed to about 2200. As it turned out, stocks dropped later in the year when Iraq invaded Kuwait, but the Dow fell only to the 2600 level. We don't know if this person stuck with his vow, but if so he missed the subsequent 2,000-point rally. As this episode shows, you don't profit with a timing strategy unless you can accurately predict when to get out of the market, and when to get back in.

We advocate a long-term investment strategy based on asset allocation, in which you maintain appropriate amounts of stocks, bonds and cash. But we're not at all opposed to fine tuning a portfolio in line with the stock market's behavior. We also concede that most investors probably do some modest timing, whether they realize it or not. But we recommend gradual shifts rather than extreme moves. If you hold big cash positions in anticipation of a bear market, you risk missing those infrequent large rallies. You also risk swimming against the tide, as the market's long-term trend undeniably has been up. You want to be on board for the long term!

Breaking the Law of Averages

You can always find superstars—whether they're in sports, movies, politics or finance. As you would expect, a select group of funds have outperformed the market averages and their peers for long periods. Figure 5.3 identifies the 10 funds out of a group of 387 with the highest total returns over a recent 15-year period, based on Lipper data. Their managers have proved that beating the law of averages is possible. Top-ranked Fidelity Magellan scored an amazing 22.73 percent average annual return. Phoenix Growth A, the number 10-ranked portfolio, returned 16.96 percent, well above the 14.13 percent generated by the Vanguard Index Trust 500 over this lengthy period. But the worst three of the 387 funds all had negative total returns. The real

---

TRAVELER'S ADVISORY:
Spotting an Overvalued Market

If the stock market is clearly overpriced, you may wish to scale back on your equity allocation, especially if you're going to have to tap into your portfolio for cash within the next five years or so. One good indicator of an overheated stock market is the relationship between the yield on 91-day T-bills and the dividend yield on the S&P 500. Simply divide the former by the latter. Be especially cautious when this number climbs above 2.0 and dividend yields are below 3 percent. For example, a bearish scenario is when T-bills yield 6 percent and stocks yield 2.5 percent, putting the yardstick at 2.4.

High ratios normally occur in the late stages of an economic upswing, when stocks are peaking and short-term rates are climbing, as the Fed applies the monetary brakes. Higher interest rates put a damper on economic activity, which hurts corporate earnings and slows dividend growth. In addition, a high T-bill/dividend yield ratio implies that investors will transfer dollars from stocks into more attractive money market funds and the like. T-bill yields appear daily in *The Wall Street Journal,* and the S&P 500 dividend yield can be found weekly in *Barron's.*

---

question is whether you can identify today which funds are going to top the list for future periods. Doing this is harder than it seems.

This leads us to conclude that indexing is a sound choice if you want to outperform the average fund over a long stretch. You won't finish at the top of any list, but you won't be near the bottom either. In fact, a good strategy involves splitting your holdings between passive and actively managed funds. Finding a good index portfolio won't take long, leaving you with more time and energy to try to identify the next superstars.

**FIGURE 5.3   Ten Top Performers Over 15 Years
Ended December 31, 1994**

Rank	Fund	Objective*	Average Annual Total Return
1	Fidelity Magellan	G	22.73%
2	CGM Capital Development	G	20.81
3	Merrill Lynch Pacific A	PC	19.25
4	Fidelity Destiny I	G	18.46
5	IDS New Dimensions	G	17.86
6	New York Venture A	G	17.39
7	Janus Fund	CA	17.29
8	New England Growth	G	17.10
9	AIM Constellation	MC	17.08
10	Phoenix Growth A	G	16.96

*CA = capital appreciation; G = growth; MC = mid cap; PC = Pacific region.
Source: Reprinted by permission of Lipper Analytical Services, Inc.

Street Smarts

- Index funds handily beat most rival funds over long stretches. They make good core holdings for lengthy stock-market journeys.
- In shopping for actively managed funds that could beat the market in the future, lean toward portfolios that have reasonable expenses and consistent performance. Also, favor those that normally stay fully invested.
- Avoid moving a large chunk of your assets into cash in an effort to sidestep a bear market. You might miss out on those large, infrequent and unpredictable upward surges.

CHAPTER 6

Getting Your Investments Under Way

Rome wasn't built in a day, and you certainly wouldn't expect to visit it all in a day. The best way to build wealth is gradually over a long period, following a systematic plan. No traveler would enjoy touring the French countryside via high-speed train when a more leisurely mode of transportation will give you much more enjoyment. So too, it's best not to have to hurry an investment plan. Get-rich-quick schemes backfire all too often because they normally involve unacceptable levels of risk.

You can put a fixed amount of cash into your mutual fund monthly or quarterly using an automatic investment plan, a service many fund companies offer. With an electronic linkage between your bank and mutual fund accounts, the money transfers automatically. With systematic investing, the minimum dollar amounts can be as low as $25 or $50, depending on the fund company. You also can elect to have cash withheld from your paycheck, assuming your employer offers that option. Regular investing over many years in good stock funds builds wealth steadily because your money grows exponentially over time.

Dollar Cost Averaging

Mutual fund companies have heavily promoted this investing approach as a sensible, disciplined way to build wealth. You invest a fixed dollar amount on a regular schedule, such as monthly or quarterly. You benefit from market fluctuations because your contributions buy more shares when prices are low and fewer when they are high. An averaging strategy helps take the emotions out of investing, making it less painful to set aside money in bearish environments. The best time to invest is when stocks have been beaten down to bargain levels, when people fear they will fall even further.

But you've got to be able to hang in for a long trip. For best results, follow an averaging strategy for at least ten years—you need to ride through a couple of market cycles. The approach is ideal for tax-deferred retirement plans and other long-term savings programs. Dollar cost averaging actually works best with more volatile stock funds, because some of your fixed investments will be made at times when prices are particularly low.

Dollar cost averaging makes sense with mutual funds rather than individual stocks for two reasons:

1. The transaction costs of investing small, regular amounts are generally less with funds. You face no transaction expenses if you use commission-free portfolios.
2. Individual funds invariably rebound after a sinking spell whereas individual stocks often don't, particularly when a company goes into bankruptcy. This advantage is explained by the wide diversification typical of most mutual funds.

An Averaging Illustration

Figure 6.1 shows how dollar cost averaging might work with a volatile aggressive-growth or sector fund over a three-year horizon. The price or NAV starts at $50, falls to a $25 low in the second year, but ultimately climbs back to $50 in the final quarter. To keep the example reasonably simple, we've assumed that the fund paid nothing in dividends or capital gains.

With dollar cost averaging, your 12 quarterly $1,000 investments buy 383.92 shares at an average cost of $31.26. The $19,196 ending portfolio value exceeds your $12,000 investment, even though the fund's price never got above the initial $50 mark. Of course, you could have done better had you invested the entire $12,000 at the $25 low. You would have acquired 480 shares, and your account would have doubled to $24,000. However, you might not have felt comfortable

FIGURE 6.1   Example of Dollar Cost Averaging at Work

Quarterly Investment	Price or NAV	Shares Bought	Cumulative Shares	Account Value
$1,000	$50	20.00	20.00	$1,000
1,000	40	25.00	45.00	1,800
1,000	32	31.25	76.25	2,440
1,000	28	35.71	111.96	3,135
1,000	25	40.00	151.96	3,799
1,000	25	40.00	191.96	4,799
1,000	25	40.00	231.96	5,799
1,000	25	40.00	271.96	6,799
1,000	28	35.71	307.67	8,615
1,000	32	31.25	338.92	10,845
1,000	40	25.00	363.92	14,557
1,000	50	20.00	383.92	19,196

Three-Year Summary

Total investment: $12,000   Average cost per share: $31.26
Total shares bought: 383.92   Simple average of NAVs: $33.33
Ending portfolio value: $19,196

risking your entire lump sum at a single price. An averaging strategy offers an alternative.

Double Up When Stocks Are Down

Here is a great way to increase your long-run investment returns: Take a deep breath and invest more when prices have fallen. Don't be afraid to commit money to good funds when the seas get stormy. Going back to our illustration, suppose we doubled our investments to $2,000 during each of the four quarters when the NAV was at its $25 low. We would then own 543.92 shares instead of 383.92, and our average cost would be reduced from $31.26 to $29.42.

Bear markets are less frequent and of shorter duration than bull phases, so it's wise to take advantage of them when the opportunity strikes. You could modify your dollar cost averaging strategy to do this. For example, you might decide to double up on your investments when the market has dropped 15 percent or more from its 12-month high. Of course, you've got to keep some extra cash in reserve so you can jump into action when the time is ripe.

TRAVELER'S ADVISORY:
Dollar Cost Averaging in Reverse

Dollar cost averaging doesn't guarantee a profit. If your fund's price is way down at the time you plan to liquidate, you could be stuck with a loss. However, this isn't likely to happen if you've followed the plan for many years because the market's long-term trend is up.

A good strategy is to take your money out bit by bit, using a systematic withdrawal plan. By spreading your withdrawals over the years, you don't risk taking all your money out at a low point in the market's cycle. Plus, your remaining assets continue to grow, while you defer taxes until gains are realized. It's essentially a form of dollar cost averaging in reverse. Chapter 19 takes a close look at withdrawal programs.

FIGURE 6.2   Investing Three Different Ways for 25 Years

$1,000 Annual Investment at	Average Annual Total Return	Final Account Value
S&P 500 low	13.41%	$178,353
S&P 500 high	11.86	138,604
December 31	12.43	160,113

Source: Reprinted by permission of The Vanguard Group.

Buying at Yearly Highs

If you think market timing is important, you may be surprised to learn the results of studies made by Vanguard, American Funds and other companies. Their research has shown that even if you had the extreme misfortune to have invested once a year at the market's annual high, you still would have actually achieved decent returns over time.

Figure 6.2 shows the results of placing $1,000 annually into the S&P 500 index for 25 years beginning December 31, 1969. Investments are made three different ways: at the S&P's yearly high, at its yearly low and on each December 31. The year-end approach is a form of dollar cost averaging. The key point is that the investment results generated by the three methods don't vary that much. In particular, buying at the yearly highs doesn't hurt you all that much, though you certainly wouldn't want to try.

Lump-Sum Investing

Dollar cost averaging is not necessarily the best option if you have a large cash amount to put to work. Suppose you receive $200,000 from your employer's pension plan or an inheritance. You decide to allocate the entire amount to stock funds. Should you invest the whole $200,000 now or dollar cost average into the market by making, say, 12 equal monthly investments?

The answer depends on what the market will be doing over the next year, which no one obviously can know for sure. With dollar cost averaging, you effectively diversify over time and therefore reduce your risk of committing a large sum of money at a market peak. The problem, however, is that you face a high opportunity cost with the uninvested portion of your capital, as stocks have returned far more than T-bills over the long term and can be expected to outperform T-bills in any given year. For this reason, you're likely better off investing the entire lump sum immediately. To do well in the stock market, you've simply got to be in the game for as long as possible, exposing yourself to the possibility of catching the sharp but infrequent rallies that occur. The risk of being out of the market is far greater than most people realize.

That said, dollar cost averaging may still make sense, especially from an anxiety-reducing standpoint. One important consideration is how much you could earn on the uninvested component. If it's one of those rare periods when money market funds are paying double-digit rates, dollar cost averaging becomes even more attractive. But don't spend too much time on the sidelines because you'll do much better over the long haul with stocks. In fact, you might consider averaging into the market over, say, three or six months rather than a full year.

One final consideration is that older investors who receive lump-sum retirement payouts and don't have as long a time horizon may be better off with an averaging strategy. These individuals are not in a position to risk jumping in at a market peak, because they don't have as much time to recoup any major setback. Plus, they may be more conservative investors anyway, so a risk-reducing approach would be suitable.

FIGURE 6.3   Value Averaging Illustration

Account Value	Price or NAV	Shares Needed	Shares Bought (Sold)	Transaction Amount
$1,000	$50	20	20	$1,000
2,000	40	50	30	1,200
3,000	50	60	10	500
4,000	80	50	(10)	(800)

Value Averaging

If dollar cost averaging seems too simple, you might consider a higher-octane strategy to achieve greater returns. *Value averaging,* a newer wealth-building approach developed by Professor Michael Edleson of Harvard University, can lead to a lower average cost and a higher compound growth rate. With value averaging, you work on ways to get your account to grow by a fixed amount, such as $1,000 each quarter. That is, the amounts you invest are not fixed. Rather, you contribute varying amounts, or even sell some shares, depending on price movements. Only if the price remains constant would you buy the same number of shares.

Suppose you want your account to grow by $1,000 a quarter. In the first quarter, assuming an NAV of $50, you would buy 20 shares to bring your account to $1,000. In the second quarter, your target is $2,000. If the NAV has fallen to $40, your 20 shares would be worth only $800, so you must kick in $1,200 and buy 30 shares to raise your stake to $2,000. The further the price falls, the more you invest.

Now suppose the NAV returns to $50 in the third quarter. Your 50 shares are now worth $2,500, which is $500 short of your target account value, so you contribute $500. In the fourth quarter, if the NAV jumps to $80, your holdings amount to $4,800. You now sell $800 worth of shares (10 of your 50) to get down to your $4,000 target. Figure 6.3 contains a recap of the arithmetic.

Value averaging is more complicated than dollar-cost averaging because you must determine how much to buy or sell each period based on the fund's NAV and your current share position. The strategy can also complicate your recordkeeping for tax purposes when you sell shares. However, you can forego the option of selling when the price rises and still derive a good portion of the benefit from value averaging. This may be wise if your fund is in a taxable account and selling would give rise to taxable capital gains.

Street Smarts

- With a good investment plan, time becomes your ally in the stock market because of the market's clear tendency to rise over the years. Mutual funds work better than individual stocks in view of their much greater tendency to rebound from bearish downdrafts.
- Investing a lump sum as soon as possible is often more profitable than dollar cost averaging into the market over, say, a year. But an averaging strategy can help you sleep easier at night.
- Dollar cost averaging is the logical choice for socking away a portion of each paycheck.
- But to maximize your returns, consider value averaging, a more complicated method.

CHAPTER 7

A Growth Odyssey

Growth funds follow the road that points toward capital gains by investing in common stocks with good appreciation potential. By this, we mean companies that generate profit increases of at least 15 percent a year. Dividends generally are a modest byproduct, so don't expect too much in the way of income.

Growth investors should be working with at least a ten-year time horizon. The idea is to take maximum advantage of the stock market's long-term compounding potential, while being able to ride out short-term traumas. And we're not kidding about the trauma part. High-flying growth companies that report disappointing quarterly earnings have been known to lose a quarter or a third of their value in a single day. The diversified nature of mutual funds helps to minimize these occasional shocks, but doesn't prevent them. During prolonged bear markets, growth funds can be expected to decline 15 to 50 percent, depending on the fund and severity of the investment climate.

Who Should Take This Route

Still, growth funds, at least in moderate quantities, make sense for most people. Over time, you can expect them to outperform income-oriented strategies. Obviously, younger investors can usually afford to take more risk in the hopes of earning higher returns. But age isn't the sole determinant here—the importance you attach to growth funds also depends on your time horizon, risk tolerance, income needs and other factors.

Because of their volatility, growth funds aren't good places to put money that might be needed in an emergency or to meet short-term goals. However, even conservative investors should consider small growth holdings—perhaps 10 to 25 percent of their portfolios. Inflation poses the major long-term financial risk, and people are living longer. Today's young senior citizens can plan on living another 20 to 30 years—plenty of time for growth funds to do their jobs.

Making Connections

Growth funds are among the most popular types of mutual funds, with most families counting at least one such product. Because of their good long-term potential and because they are volatile, growth funds are ideal for systematic investment plans such as dollar cost averaging. Most fund groups do allow systematic investing—whether you choose to write a check each month, have your checking account debited or have the money transferred from your paycheck. People who hope to get more compounding bang for the buck can do so by reinvesting their capital-gains distributions, which tend to be larger with growth portfolios. And during periods like the present, when capital gains are taxed at lower rates than dividends for high-income individuals, growth funds can offer some modest tax-sheltering benefits.

Sidetrips

Because of the large number of growth funds—more than 800 are now available—investors have plenty to choose from. For your flagship, you might select a large, well-known portfolio from a family renowned for growth investing. Examples include Fidelity Disciplined Equity and Fidelity Retirement Growth, the Janus Fund, T. Rowe Price Growth Stock, Twentieth Century Growth and Vanguard World U.S. Growth, among no-commission funds. Standout load products include Fidelity Magellan, AIM Weingarten, Growth Fund of America and Putnam New Opportunities A. All of these are multibillion-dollar portfolios from some of the largest mutual fund groups. They make good anchors for growth investors.

As a second or even third growth choice, you might consider a boutique growth fund such as Berger 100, Brandywine, Clipper, Longleaf

---

Traveler's Advisory:
Tracking Management

A brilliant 15-year track record on a growth fund might not mean much if the individual responsible for that showing was given a retirement party and his gold watch last week. Or if she split suddenly to launch her own mutual fund. The person behind your fund obviously can have a major impact on its performance. The prospectus will name the manager and state how long he or she has been at the helm. In addition, Morningstar provides biographical information on the managers of funds in its database. The fund's telephone reps should be able to fill you in on any recent changes. Ideally, you'd like to see the same person in charge for at least five years. Teams manage some portfolios, such as the Twentieth Century funds. In this case you need not be concerned if a team member leaves.

Partners, Oakmark, L. Roy Papp Stock or Yacktman. These products are offered by smaller groups that specialize in growth investing. At some of these companies, the person who owns or controls the fund family is also the portfolio manager. In general, this arrangement benefits shareholders, as entrepreneurs have an added incentive to perform well.

Buying Your Ticket

True growth investors might want to allocate 75 to 95 percent of their overall portfolio to appreciation-oriented funds. In addition to one or two mainstream growth products, complimentary choices include aggressive-growth, mid-cap, small-company and international funds. Also, there's a lot to be said for taking along a spare tire in the form of a bond or money market fund. Including these will dampen your overall volatility and provide a reservoir of cash for taking advantage of buying opportunities.

Vehicles for Transportation

With so many growth funds available, you can bet that there's plenty of diversity within the group. The typical growth fund focuses on larger corporations that are well known on Wall Street. The market capitalizations of these firms run in the billions. Conversely, mid-cap portfolios explicitly target firms worth $600 million to $5 billion or so, and small-company growth funds choose stocks in the range of about $600 million or less. Some small-company managers may still hold onto firms that have grown considerably bigger. This is known in the business as "capitalization creep," and it often occurs as a successful small-cap fund gets larger.

Aggressive-growth (or capital-appreciation) funds often load up on small stocks but they differ because they employ riskier strategies. In their search for maximum gains, aggressive-growth products may concentrate on "hot" industries, they may buy and sell frequently, they might make use of options and they might borrow money to leverage their holdings. Some aggressive-growth managers even sell stocks short to try to capitalize on a price drop. Portfolios in this category can be especially volatile and are not necessarily good candidates for a buy-and-hold strategy.

Growth versus Value

The growth category is sufficiently large to include a number of funds that might be better described as following a value approach. Value managers focus on stocks that are cheap according to yardsticks such as PE, price-book, and price-cash flow ratios (see Chapter 4). They may also look for high dividend yields.

Value investors often focus on companies in cyclical industries that may be at the low point in their profit cycles. Or they could be companies that have fallen on difficult times for a number of reasons. Value funds tend to hold up better during market declines because their stocks already had been beaten down, so they usually won't have as far to fall as traditional growth stocks. Value thus provides an added dimension of diversification when combined with growth because the two styles tend to do well at different times. This can smooth out your ride. Babson, Crabbe Huson, Lindner, Mutual Series, Neuberger & Berman and Royce are among the no-load families known for their value emphasis. Bigger fund groups such as Fidelity, T. Rowe Price and Vanguard also offer some value portfolios.

Compiling Your Itinerary

The following examples provide some suggested allocation ranges to help you build a growth portfolio. You might not want to include all of these categories, especially if you don't have a lot of money to work with or want to keep things simple. Then again, you might want to add other choices, such as specialized international funds or some index funds with your actively managed portfolios. Index funds tend to be above-average performers because of their lower costs and other factors (see Chapter 5). In addition, a closed-end fund or two can add even greater diversity to your mix, if you're inclined to go a bit off the beaten path. Chapter 14 covers these unique investments.

A Compact Growth Package

A 35-year-old single woman has $20,000 to invest, good job security, a growing income and high risk tolerance. She wants to build her positions through dollar cost averaging. She's also willing to keep an eye on what's happening in the financial markets. Even though her portfolio is relatively small, she may want to split the money among several types of funds in the following combination:

20% Babson Shadow Stock (small-cap value)
20% Founders Special (capital appreciation)
25% Berger 100 (mid-cap growth)
25% Scudder International (non–U.S. stock)
10% Scudder Short Term Bond (short-term bond)

An Indexed Core

In contrast, a working couple in their early 40s has $100,000 to invest. They earn good salaries, have two children ages 4 and 6, and are mostly concerned about their youngsters' college education and their own retirement. They too want to invest gradually through dollar cost averaging, and they want to index a large part of their portfolio. Their allocation might look something like this:

15% Warburg Pincus Emerging Growth (small-cap growth)
25% Brandywine (mid-cap growth)
25% Vanguard Index Trust 500 (growth and income)
15% T. Rowe Price International (non–U.S. stock)
15% Vanguard Short Term Corporate (short-term bond)
 5% Vanguard Money Market Reserves Prime (money market)

Blending Growth and Value

A fairly well-to-do couple in their mid-50s have about ten years to go before retirement. They want to split their $500,000 portfolio between growth and value for greater stability. They also want exposure to small-company and foreign stocks because of the potential for earning higher long-run returns. Because they are in a high tax bracket, they have mixed in tax-free funds. Here are their allocations:

10% Montgomery MicroCap (small-cap growth)
15% Mutual Beacon (mid-cap value)
10% Janus (large-cap growth)
10% Neuberger & Berman Guardian (large-cap value)
20% Vanguard International Growth (foreign stock)
20% Vanguard Intermediate-Term Muni Bond (intermediate muni)
10% Vanguard Short-Term Muni Bond (short muni)
 5% Vanguard Municipal Money Market (tax-free money market)

Monitoring Your Growth Portfolio

It's a good idea to reexamine your holdings at least once a year. Check the weightings in stocks, bonds and cash, as well as the percentage allocations to your various funds. Do they still fall within your target ranges? Allocations can change significantly over time with volatile funds. They also can shift if you're dollar cost averaging widely differing amounts in certain funds. But it's all right to tolerate small deviations from your targets, because too many minor adjustments can complicate your recordkeeping and tax preparation.

AT THE HELM: SAMUEL S. STEWART JR.

Relatively few business professors have made a name for themselves as a money manager. Samuel S. Stewart Jr. is one of the exceptions.

Stewart heads the Wasatch Advisors group of funds in Salt Lake City. His flagship Wasatch Aggressive Equity Fund has beaten the market over the years, attracting favorable attention in the process. Yet Stewart continues to spend time in the classroom, teaching classes at the University of Utah. Two of his four research analysts at Wasatch Advisors, which was named after a local mountain chain, are former students.

Stewart seeks out smaller companies that show good earnings potential. Because his shareholder base in and around Utah includes many Mormons, he runs the funds with an eye on avoiding sin stocks. "We'll generally stay away from certain types of stocks such as tobacco, alcohol and gambling companies because we know enough shareholders wouldn't like them," he says.

A solid growth fund can and should be held for many years. Sometimes, however, a core holding will break down. One sign of a possible road hazard occurs when an established manager quits or retires and is replaced by a relative newcomer. At best, this calls the fund's long-term record into question. Another sign is persistent underperformance over a period of, say, 18 to 24 months. If your fund is lagging its growth peers and you can't find a good explanation, it might be time to jump ship. Yet a third yellow flag involves escalating expenses. Not only will this lower your returns but it could hint of more profound problems, like a portfolio that's losing assets fast because its manager has lost his touch or is experimenting with new approaches that don't seem to be working.

Street Smarts

Much like the Rockies in North America or the Andes in South America, growth funds form the backbone of many investment portfolios. Growth managers seek long-term capital appreciation, with only incidental attention paid to dividends. They hope to achieve this by investing in companies showing rising profitability.

However, the growth classification can be misleading as bargain-hunting value funds often are included within the category. There also can be some overlap with small-company, international and similar types of funds, which investors should be mindful of when designing portfolios.

CHAPTER 8

A Growth and Income Package

When most people think about the stock market, they envision its most visible and dominant components—large, well-known firms such as General Electric, General Motors, Exxon and AT&T. These are solid, dividend-paying giants that have grown over many decades. Yet they are too mature to be accurately described as growth stocks. Rather, most of these household names fall into the growth-and-income camp, which emphasizes a mixture of appreciation potential and dividend income. Both the Dow Jones Industrial Average and Standard & Poor's 500 index are primarily growth-and-income indicators.

As you might expect, the growth-and-income route provides a nice compromise. It's less volatile than a pure growth itinerary, but still offers plenty of long-term appreciation potential. The important thing to remember is that you still get a lot more inflation protection than you would with an income-only itinerary.

Who Should Take This Route

Many people, especially those in their mid-40s and older, will find a growth-and-income package attractive. As asset builders, these people still have a basic appreciation orientation, but also want dividend and interest income. The greater stability of the compromise approach may lead to a more restful journey.

Vehicles for Transportation

A variety of fund types can be woven into a growth-and-income portfolio. They don't all have to have the dual income and appreciation attribute. Pure income and pure growth funds can be added in whatever proportions you need to fine tune your portfolio. But the following three categories are staples of a growth-and-income itinerary.

- *Growth-and-income funds* seek capital appreciation and dividends by investing in the stocks of larger companies. The relative emphasis on appreciation or income is usually about equal, but varies somewhat among funds.
- *Equity-income funds,* a category of close cousins, emphasize yield a bit more than their growth-and-income counterparts. They invest heavily in industrial, utility and financial companies—just the types of firms that pay the fattest dividends.
- *Balanced funds* are particularly well-suited for people nearing retirement age. They may be thought of as a special type of growth-and-income product, where the yield derives from both dividend-paying stocks as well as interest-bearing bonds.

You don't have to spend the income produced by your mutual funds. If you reinvest, the heftier dividends typically paid by the above types of funds will compound more quickly. The income also adds a dimension of stability because dividend-paying stocks, and interest-bearing bonds, tend to be less volatile. These investments provide a value anchor during rough weather.

The Growth and Income Tradeoff

You can't get high income and high growth simultaneously from the same portfolio. The more dividends you earn, the less appreciation you'll realize, and vice versa. Be careful not to sacrifice too much appreciation for income, especially if you have a long time horizon and intend to reinvest most of your dividends anyway.

S&P 500-style stocks should be the cornerstone of a growth-and-income portfolio. Many big companies spin off dividends that grow at a rate of 5 or 6 percent annually. You can find a surprisingly large number of companies that have consistently raised their dividends each year for 10 or 20 years in a row. Moody's *Handbook of Dividend Achievers* identifies them. Some portfolios, such as T. Rowe Price

---

TRAVELER'S ADVISORY:
Interest-Rate Risk Impacts Stocks

Growth-and-income investors can't expect a perfectly smooth ride on their moderate route to greater wealth. One of the biggest dangers is interest-rate risk. It affects dividend-paying stocks, such as utilities and financial companies, as well as bonds.

Rising rates hurt dividend-paying stocks because their yields have to stay competitive with those on bonds. For example, a utility stock has an 8-percent yield based on its $8 annual dividend and $100 share price. Interest rates rise sharply, knocking down the stock's price to the point where it yields 10 percent. With a dividend of $8, the price would have to tumble to $80 to yield 10 percent. Utilities, which are heavy borrowers, also incur higher financing costs in times of rising rates, which narrows profits and further reinforces the decline in share prices. Utilities were hit hard by rising rates in both 1987 and 1994.

Dividend Growth and Putnam Dividend Growth, explicitly target these types of stocks. Both funds recently have maintained a particularly large stake in financial companies.

Over time, stock prices should increase in tandem with dividend growth. Conversely, the flow of interest payments from a bond won't ever increase. This makes a compelling reason to allocate a large chunk of your assets to mutual funds holding income-producing stocks, so you can sidestep the corrosive effect of inflation. Of course, higher dividends are not a certainty. Utility stocks took a beating in 1993 and 1994 as investors worried about future dividend growth in an increasingly competitive environment. If investors think dividends won't rise or might even be cut, stock prices will suffer.

Finding Your Flagship

Your flagship mutual fund should combine the qualities of stability, appreciation potential and decent dividend yields. You have plenty of choices from the growth-and-income and equity-income categories, including several index funds. Good candidates among no-load funds include Dodge & Cox Stock, Fidelity Equity-Income II, Gateway Index Plus, Mutual Beacon, Neuberger & Berman Guardian, Schwab 1000, USAA Mutual Income Stock, Vanguard Index 500 and Vanguard Windsor II.

Compiling an Itinerary

To offset inflation, it is important for your growth-and-income portfolio to have a healthy appreciation component. That's why we recommend that you add moderate doses of small-stock and international funds to your core, assuming you're working with a time horizon of at least ten years. However, you would generally give less weight to these categories than would a regular growth investor. And because your portfolio is more conservative, you want to select stock funds that follow more of a value style.

How many funds you hold and the number of categories depend on the amount of money you're working with. A $10,000 investor might own a single balanced fund, whereas a $500,000 portfolio could include a dozen or more fund selections. To be considered "balanced" by the Securities and Exchange Commission, a mutual fund must have at least 25 percent of its assets invested in fixed-income securities. Most target from 30 to 50 percent in bonds, with the remainder in stocks. If you use a balanced fund, find out its bond allocation, and keep this in mind as you build your portfolio.

A Simple Balanced Portfolio

A couple in their late 40s have a modest $40,000 portfolio. They've had some bad experiences with investments in the past so they don't want the volatility associated with a pure growth portfolio. But they also need some appreciation to build their assets. They have no children, are saving primarily for retirement and want to keep their finances simple. They already have parked $15,000 in a money market fund to deal with any short-term cash needs, but they've decided not to include this as part of their long-term asset mix. Here's their allocation:

30% Fidelity Equity-Income II (equity income)
60% Vanguard Wellington (balanced)
10% Vanguard Short-Term Corporate (short bond)

A Portfolio Tilted to Growth

A divorced woman in her late 30s has one child, aged 3. As a single parent, she doesn't feel comfortable with a pure growth portfolio so she decides to include a modest income mix. Her $50,000 portfolio is invested both for her own retirement and her young child's college education. All income and capital-gains distributions are reinvested. She keeps her short-term savings separate from her long-term investments and has enough set aside in a money fund to take care of emergencies. She purchases her funds through Charles Schwab's OneSource (no-fee) program. Her growth-tilt portfolio appears as follows:

5% Hotchkis & Wiley Small Cap (small-cap value)
5% Benham Gold Equities Index (gold index)
20% Schwab 1000 (growth-and-income index)
20% Neuberger & Berman Guardian (large-cap value)
10% Schwab International Index (non-U.S. stock index)
25% Benham GNMA Income (mortgage-backed bond)
15% Benham Treasury Note (short Treasury)

A Portfolio Skewed to Income

A retired California husband and wife in their early 70s want to minimize risk on their $1-million portfolio. They've made their money and don't want to take any unnecessary chances. To keep their investments reasonably simple, they prefer to stick with just a few families and funds. A large portion of their portfolio is in a taxable account, so municipal-bond investments are important.

20% AARP Growth & Income (mid-cap growth and income)
20% Dodge & Cox Stock (large-cap growth and income)
10% Dodge & Cox Balanced (stock and bond)
5% Vanguard Tax-Free CA Insured Long-Term (long muni)
35% Vanguard Tax-Free CA Insured Intermediate-Term (intermediate muni)
10% Vanguard Tax-Free CA Money Market (tax-free money fund)

Know Your Bond Weighting

The proportion of bond securities for growth-and-income investors will typically range from about 25 to 50 percent. Keeping track of this percentage is important because bonds will exert a drag on performance over time. Yet the amount may be higher than you think because conservative equity-oriented funds could have significant fixed-income stakes. The higher this percentage, the less you will need to invest in pure bond funds.

AT THE HELM: R. LYNN YTURRI

Bankers have a reputation for being mediocre money managers, but don't tell that to R. Lynn Yturri. An Oregon native who now lives in Arizona, Yturri runs two value-oriented stock portfolios for the One Group, a family of funds from Banc One Corp. in Columbus, Ohio. His One Group Large Company Growth Fund has been among a mere handful of bank-sponsored funds to enjoy a top five-star rating from Morningstar. He also has achieved solid results with the somewhat more conservative One Group Income Equity Fund.

Yturri is a top-down investor who analyzes the big picture first. "We look at demographic, political, economic and technological changes, collected in research from various sources, and try to narrow these to a few investment themes," he says. One recent such theme was a belief that oil stocks were poised for an extended rally.

A history degree from the University of Oregon in 1964 helped to lay the foundation for his broad stockpicking approach.

Street Smarts

Appreciation and dividends represent the two paths to profit in the stock market. A growth-and-income strategy seeks to generate returns from both components. This dual approach tends to offer a smoother ride than what investors would experience with a pure growth orientation. Risk can be cut further by incorporating bonds into the equation, as balanced funds do. Like a package vacation tour, a growth-and-income itinerary doesn't make sense for everybody. But as a compromise, it's not a bad way to go for most people.

CHAPTER 9

The Income Route

Not everyone should have a jumbo slice of his or her investment pie in the stock market. This is especially true in the mid-1990s, because the probabilities are low that the performance of stock funds during the next decade or so will be anywhere near as good as the 13.4 percent average annual return spun off by the well-diversified funds in Lipper's general-equity group from 1982 through 1994.

Income investors are primarily asset consumers rather than builders. They normally have considerably shorter time horizons than growth seekers. Many are retired and require a flow of cash from their portfolios to meet monthly expenses. Income investors tend to invest prudently. They often have a lot of time to travel, but not much time to make up for large portfolio losses.

Bonds and bond funds normally compose the core of an income portfolio, though dividends also can be collected from stocks. In fact, many older investors make the mistake of limiting their focus to fixed-income securities. Even individuals in their 80s should consider maintaining 15 to 20 percent of their nest egg in stocks to obtain modest inflation protection. Besides a "cracked" nest egg, which can result from big-time speculations, the greatest risk you face is outliving your assets by being too conservative and harboring too much in low-yielding products such as money market funds.

Who Should Take This Path

Age is often the single most important determinant of portfolio structure. As we've said earlier, a simple guideline is to invest a percentage of your portfolio in fixed-income securities about equal to your age. The remainder, 100 minus your age, would be in equities. That means a 60-year-old person would allocate about 60 percent to bond holdings and 40 percent to stocks. Of course, this is only a rough benchmark because the optimal asset allocation will vary according to other personal circumstances.

Like growth, income can be pursued in various ways. Examples include high-yield bonds (which are prone to credit risk), Treasuries, corporates and municipal bonds (interest-rate risk), and foreign issues (currency risk). More aggressive holdings such as high-yield and international funds normally lead to greater income, but can result in uncomfortably high volatility.

Although we don't recommend a big stake in aggressive holdings for older investors, don't avoid them entirely because the name of the

---

AT THE HELM: ROBERT L. RODRIGUEZ

It's a lot harder for a talented manager to add value with bonds than with stocks. But Rodriguez has that Midas Touch with his FPA New Income Fund, which has delivered high returns with low volatility. New Income invests heavily in U.S. government securities, but also allocates a slice of its assets to the realm of high-yield bonds and convertibles, areas where Rodriguez cherry picks exceptional values. He describes his style as contrarian and eclectic.

Rodriguez was Morningstar's 1994 portfolio manager of the year. He joined Los Angeles-based First Pacific Advisors in 1983. An alumnus of the University of Southern California and a fan of its football team, Rodriguez enjoys theater, racquetball and racing cars. In addition to FPA New Income, Rodriguez manages FPA Capital Fund, a brilliant performer in the equity arena.

game in asset allocation is diversity. A large, well-diversified income mix should have at least modest exposure to junk and foreign bonds as well as to high-quality domestic issues.

Withdrawal Plans

Even if you're an asset consumer, you might need to build stock fund investments into your income-generating equation. Perhaps you expect to live to a ripe old age. And you might want to leave a nice sum to your heirs. If so, stock funds are the key to making your wealth grow.

Enter the *withdrawal plan*. This arrangement allows you to receive regular monthly or quarterly checks from your fund holdings. If you expect to be pulling out money over a decade or longer, a conservative stock fund can lead to better results than a bond product because of the greater appreciation potential. Growth-and-income, equity-income and balanced portfolios all are good withdrawal-plan candidates. Chapter 19 takes a close look at withdrawal plans.

Compiling Your Itinerary

Despite what you might think, the bond market is hardly a monolith. A wide variety of bond-fund categories are available, characterized by different maturities and types of securities held. The short-term portfolios are considerably less risky than the long-term funds, but generally produce lower returns. The intermediate portfolios offer a nice compromise. In terms of security types, funds can be broken down in many ways: corporate, high-yield corporate, U.S. government, mortgage-backed, foreign, flexible and municipal. You likely would want a few of these categories for diversification purposes, and maybe stakes in all.

Spreading Your Bets

Want a simple ticket for high income while holding volatility to a reasonable level? Allocate equal amounts to these three types of bond funds: U.S. government, high-yield corporate and foreign. Each group responds differently to changing economic conditions, so you get a well-diversified mix. For example, as the U.S. economy grows stronger, junk bonds tend to perform well even though Treasuries may get hammered by rising interest rates. The opposite could be true as economic conditions deteriorate and rates gradually decline. Foreign bonds, in turn, would do well when the dollar weakens, while the domestic investments could fare better at other times.

Finding Low-Cost Products

Families offering a choice of good, low-cost bond products include Benham, Dreyfus, Fidelity, Hotchkis & Wiley, Scudder, Strong, T. Rowe Price and Vanguard. An important decision is whether you want taxable or tax-exempt portfolios. Chapter 10 covers the latter.

Less is more when it comes to bond investments. It's generally a good idea to shop for the lowest-cost income funds because bond-fund returns are more homogeneous than those of stock portfolios—there simply isn't as much opportunity for a truly exceptional manager to add value. In addition, bond returns are lower than those of stocks, so expenses play a larger role in determining how much flows to the bottom line.

If you're prepared to invest $10,000 to $50,000 or more in a fixed-income fund, take a look at the Fidelity Spartan, T. Rowe Price Summit and Vanguard Admiral portfolios. All feature exceptionally low expense ratios. By excluding the smallest shareholders, these funds cost less to operate. A low-cost bond fund is like a cheap airline ticket: a good deal.

A Withdrawal Program in Action

A recently retired couple in their early 60s have set up a withdrawal plan using stock funds. Because the dividends from their bond and equity holdings will meet a good part of their needs, they will begin with a modest withdrawal rate. The bulk of their $700,000 portfolio is invested in conservative stock funds. Notice also the 15-percent position in a high-yield fund for aggressive income.

20% Columbia Balanced (balanced)
15% INVESCO Strategic Utilities (utility stock)
30% USAA Mutual Income Stock (equity income)
15% Vanguard Fixed Income High Yield Corporate (high-yield bond)
10% Strong Advantage (general corporate bond)
10% Vanguard Money Market Prime (money fund)

A Mixed Income Portfolio

Another couple in their 60s want to diversify into three distinct areas: U.S. Treasury securities, high-yield corporates and foreign bonds. They realize that the returns in these diverse markets are not very highly correlated, which means at least one of the three may be doing reasonably well if the others are not. They also have 35 percent of their portfolio invested for stock income.

They already have an adequate amount of cash set aside to meet emergency needs and foreseeable expenses over the next five years, so they have decided not to include a money market fund as a part of their long-term portfolio. Most of the assets in their $600,000 portfolio are tax-deferred IRA rollovers.

20% Fidelity Equity-Income II (equity income)
15% INVESCO Strategic Utilities (utility stock)
10% Fidelity Spartan Ginnie Mae (mortgage-backed bond)
20% Fidelity Spartan High-Income (high-yield bond)
15% Scudder International Bond (foreign bond)
10% Vanguard Admiral Long Term U.S. Treasury (long Treasury)
10% Vanguard Admiral Short Term U.S. Treasury (short Treasury)

TRAVELER'S ADVISORY:
Bond Funds on Steroids

The vast majority of bond funds are conservatively run and won't play any games with your money. If they do use derivatives, they employ them prudently and in moderation. But beware of those muscle-flexing exceptions. Any mutual fund that generates returns much higher than those of its peers must be taking on big risks.

Street Smarts

Asset consumers typically look less to stocks and more to bond funds for the bulk of their portfolios. The latter pay higher yields and bounce around less severely—important considerations for conservative individuals. Because bond returns tend to cluster together in a fairly narrow range, low expenses become especially critical. A low-cost income portfolio makes an excellent value, comparable to a heavily discounted airline ticket. However, no investors should completely ignore stock funds, which generate superior returns over time. Stock funds can also make sense as key components in a systematic withdrawal plan.

CHAPTER 10

The Path to Tax-Free Income

Over the past decade and a half of unprecedented growth in the mutual fund business, nothing has been more remarkable than the surge in municipal-bond and tax-exempt money market portfolios. These investments have gone from about 3 percent of the overall fund market in 1980 to 16 percent in 1995. They were aided by tax-law revisions in the mid-1980s that made competing investments such as limited partnerships less attractive. Muni-bond funds stepped into the vacuum in a big way to satisfy investors seeking relief from taxes.

Today, many types of municipal funds are available—national, single state, high-yield and insured portfolios, further categorized by their holdings of short, intermediate and long-term bonds. Though their risk levels vary, all share the common denominator of tax-free interest.

Who Should Consider This Route

But as great as all this sounds, muni-bond funds aren't for everybody. Extremely conservative individuals might not be able to tolerate a muni fund's price fluctuations, modest as they may be, while growth-oriented investors will have little need for bond products generally. Even some mainstream income investors may find that government, corporate or foreign bond funds offer better yields after taxes.

Calculating Taxable-Equivalent Yields

To decide where you stand on this last point, you need to know your marginal tax bracket and then do a little arithmetic. You will want to calculate your taxable-equivalent yield, which will help to determine whether you should be looking at national or single-state muni funds, or none at all. Find this yield by dividing the yield on a municipal investment by (1.00 *minus* your federal tax bracket).

For example, if the muni portfolio yields 6 percent and you are in the 36-percent federal bracket, your taxable-equivalent yield would be 9.38 percent [0.06 ÷ (1.00 − 0.36)]. If you can't find taxable bond funds of similar risk that yield 9.38 percent or more, take the muni. As you can see from Figure 10.1, you don't need to be in the top brackets to benefit from tax-exempt bonds. As long as your federal rate is 28 percent or more, give them serious consideration.

State and Territory Allocation Percentages

If you invest in a regular or national muni fund, you will be holding bonds from all around the country. The fund company will provide you with information on the percentage of its holdings in each state at tax time, because the amount for your state will also be exempt from state taxes. If a New York resident has a national portfolio with 5 percent of its assets in New York, that share of income would be double exempt. In addition, if the fund has investments in U.S. territories such as Puerto Rico and Guam, the income from those issues also would be double tax free.

FIGURE 10.1   Taxable-Equivalent Yields

Tax-Exempt Yield	Federal Tax Bracket				
	15%	28%	31%	36%	39.6%
4.0%	4.71	5.56%	5.80%	6.25%	6.62%
5.0	5.88	6.94	7.25	7.81	8.28
6.0	7.06	8.33	8.70	9.38	9.93
7.0	8.24	9.72	10.14	10.94	11.59
8.0	9.41	11.11	11.59	12.50	13.25

Taxable-Equivalent Yields on Single-State Funds

You can find the taxable-equivalent yield on a single-state fund by dividing the fund's yield by:

(1.00 – federal bracket) *times* (1.00 – state bracket)

This assumes that muni interest is tax exempt in your state and that you deduct state taxes on your federal return. With a 36-percent federal and an 8-percent state tax rate, a 6-percent yield on a single-state muni fund provides a 10.19 percent taxable-equivalent yield:

$$\frac{0.06}{(1.00 - 0.36)(1.00 - 0.08)}$$

Be familiar with your state's tax laws. The District of Columbia and a couple of states exempt interest on all munis from taxation, not just local issues. A few other states, including Florida, Texas, Nevada and Washington, have no state income taxes. Florida does, however, impose a small intangibles tax on certain out-of-state investments. This, combined with Florida's large retiree population, has made the Sunshine State the third-largest muni-bond market, behind California and New York.

Single-State versus National Portfolios

The single-state format often offers a better taxable-equivalent yield in high-tax states like California, Massachusetts, New Jersey and New York. The disadvantage is less diversification, which may subject these funds to somewhat greater risk, especially in smaller states. For this reason, you might consider an insured single-state portfolio, if you feel compelled about getting double-exempt income. Even people who live in larger states might find insured portfolios attractive. For instance, fear of earthquakes may be sufficient justification for investing in an insured California fund.

If you live in a state that has a relatively low tax rate (or no taxes), you're better off with a national fund. Conversely, if you live in a high-tax state and have a large amount invested in muni-bond funds, consider allocating some of that money to a national portfolio for the added diversification. This is especially important if your state is having budgetary problems.

Muni Gains and Losses

Only the dividend income from your muni fund is entitled to tax exemption. Any capital gains passed through to shareholders are taxable, whether received in cash or reinvested in additional shares. Long- and short-term capital gain distributions are reported to the IRS and to you on Form 1099-DIV. Many investors paid taxes on their muni-fund profits during the long bull market of the 1980s and early 1990s because a sizable portion of their returns consisted of capital gains. In addition, if you sell muni-fund shares at a higher price than you paid (including shares acquired by reinvesting any distributions), you will have a taxable gain. Conversely, losses would be deductible. But if a fund incurs losses in excess of its gains, they must be retained and carried forward to offset future profits, benefiting investors at that time.

Retirees living on modest incomes must make one more calculation to determine whether muni-bond funds would make sense. If you're receiving Social Security benefits, you need to combine your municipal-bond interest with your adjusted gross income and one half of your Social Security income to determine your "provisional income." A higher level of provisional income subjects a larger amount of your Social Security benefits to taxation. Under current law, as much as 85 percent of Social Security benefits may be taxable, and muni income might push certain people into the higher bracket.

Note: Never put muni bond funds into an individual retirement account. Income generated by investments held in an IRA is automatically tax-deferred, while income from a muni fund is not ordinarily taxable. This would result in an unnecessary duplication of tax-sheltering benefits. In addition, when you ultimately removed the muni from the IRA, all income and gains would become taxable.

What Funds Own

When you examine the holdings of a muni-bond fund, you'll note several kinds of securities: *Municipal notes* typically mature in one year or less, whereas *municipal bonds* come due in as many as 20 to 30 years. *General obligation (GO) bonds* are backed by the full faith, credit and taxing power of the issuer. In contrast, *revenue bonds* depend on the income earned by a specific project or authority, such as

---

TRAVELER'S ADVISORY:
Individual Munis versus Bond Funds

Should you invest directly in muni bonds or use a fund? This question is relevant only if you plan to allocate at least $100,000 to municipals, know how to shop for the best deals, and plan to hold your bonds until maturity. Municipals typically trade infrequently and have wide bid-asked spreads, making them costly for small investors to sell before maturity. It may be difficult to find a buyer for just a few bonds unless you're willing to accept a lower price. One drawback of funds is that they pass along taxable capital-gain distributions. With individual bonds, you realize taxable gains only when you sell.

---

tolls collected on a road or user fees for water. GOs yield somewhat less than revenue bonds because they are more secure. The largest amount of municipal debt is found in the revenue-bond arena. *Industrial-development bonds* are a type of revenue issue backed by the credit of a private company.

Zero-coupon munis do not make periodic interest payments, but instead are sold at deep discounts from their face or maturity values. Because zeros don't pay income, their prices can be highly volatile. A municipal-bond derivative, the *inverse floater,* bears an interest rate that moves inversely to market rates. As interest rates rise, the yield on an inverse floater falls, and vice versa. Inverse floaters can produce eye-popping returns during extended periods of falling rates, but they are very risky due to their inherent leverage.

A number of muni funds hold *nonrated issues.* These are typically smaller, less liquid bonds that are not graded by the rating agencies because it would not be worth the cost to the issuer to pay for this feature. Nonrated issues do not necessarily carry greater credit risk. They may represent good investments for talented fund managers able to pick them. Nonrated issues can range in quality from triple-A to speculative.

Also, you will notice that a number of funds hold bonds issued by the U.S. territories of Puerto Rico, the Virgin Islands and Guam. The yields on these bonds are generally tax-free to all U.S. residents, which makes territory issues especially attractive to managers of single-state funds who may want to diversify a bit.

Duration and Interest-Rate Risk

For many people, the most important consideration in selecting any bond fund is its *duration,* a measure of interest-rate sensitivity. When interest rates rise, portfolios with the highest duration numbers get hit the hardest. Duration is the best indicator of fixed-income volatility. Telephone reps at major fund groups increasingly can provide up-to-date duration numbers.

Durations of eight years or more reflect high interest-rate risk. Here's how to interpret the numbers: If general interest rates increase by one percentage point (say, from 6 percent to 7 percent), a portfolio with a duration of ten years would decline in value by roughly 10 percent. Conversely, if the portfolio had a duration of only three years, it would fall by just 3 percent. If you're concerned about interest-rate risk, stick with short-term funds with low duration numbers. Intermediate-term portfolios can be suitable if you can live with a moderate amount of volatility. The accompanying table shows typical duration and maturity ranges for the three basic groups of bond funds.

Maturity Objective	Duration Range	Maturity Range
Short term	1–3 years	1–3 years
Intermediate term	4–6 years	4–10 years
Long term	7–10 years	10–30 years

Long-term funds are suitable only if you are prepared to hold for the long haul and don't mind the ups and downs. Intermediate-term funds may offer a fairly attractive return with significantly less volatility. With either type, you might want to dollar cost average. That way, you will buy more shares when interest rates rise and prices fall, thereby making the ride psychologically smoother.

Credit Quality

Moody's, Standard & Poor's and other credit rating agencies rate muni bonds just like they do corporate bonds. Bonds in the top four categories (triple-A, double-A, single-A and triple-B) are considered *investment grade.* Categories below triple-B are *speculative.* Muni funds generally invest in obligations rated single-A or better. Insured munis have been given a triple-A mark.

Credit risk is important with high-yield muni portfolios. These funds differ in aggressiveness, but they don't assume as much credit risk at their corporate counterparts because there aren't as many troubled municipalities. A relatively small proportion of sub-investment grade debt is typically found in their portfolios. Most high-yield issues are single-A and triple-B bonds. The prospectus of a high-yield fund should provide a summary breakdown of the holdings by letter-rating category.

Insured funds hold bonds that are protected against credit risk and thus may appeal to people who want the extra margin of safety, although it probably isn't necessary if you're investing in a well-diversified portfolio. Because the coverage carries a cost, insured funds might yield 0.1 to 0.4 percentage points less than otherwise comparable funds—a difference that can add up over the years. More important, insurance protects you against default risk only, not interest-rate risk, which is normally the bigger danger. Insurance is generally more appropriate for people who buy individual bonds because funds are diversified and monitored by a professional manager.

A Word on Expenses

Management fees and other ongoing costs (including any 12b-1 fees) can significantly reduce returns on muni-bond funds. An expense ratio of, say, 1.5 percent is equivalent to an annual charge of $15 for each $1,000 invested. It's thus imperative to search for the lowest-cost funds because bonds, on average, generate lower total returns than stocks. Expenses will probably be even more significant during the next decade, because returns likely will be slimmer than they were over the past decade or so.

The average muni-fund expense ratio recently stood at about 0.8 percent, according to Morningstar. For best results, try to find a muni fund with a ratio that's below 0.5 percent. Vanguard, T. Rowe Price, Strong, Benham, Fidelity, Scudder and USAA are good places to start your search. Not just expenses, but also commissions can exert a drag on performance. Pure no-load investing really makes sense in the tax-exempt bond arena.

AT THE HELM: JAMES M. BENHAM

W hen the topic turns to income funds, James M. Benham, chairman of the Benham Group, stands out. In 1972, this former bank examiner and Merrill Lynch broker founded one of the nation's first money market funds. Reflecting its chairman's skittishness over the nation's economy and banking system, the Benham Group continued to add money market and bond funds, of both the taxable and tax-free varieties, over the years. It didn't introduce its first mainstream stock portfolio until 1990.

By 1995, 90 percent of the Benham Group's $11 billion in shareholder assets under management were held in income funds. At Twentieth Century Mutual Funds, an equally high percentage was invested in stock funds, which explains why these two no-load families decided to join forces that year, creating the nation's fifth-largest commission-free fund group.

Benham attended Michigan State University on a music scholarship and marched with the school's band in the 1956 Rose Bowl. He continues to play jazz on the trumpet and fluegel horn, and he has participated in the recording of three compact discs.

Street Smarts

The lure of tax-free income for investors is as strong as the attraction of a top resort or national park for tourists. Municipal-bond funds have boomed in recent years as the number of competing tax shelters dried up. Muni funds vary in terms of credit risk and interest-rate exposure. In addition, some portfolios pay income that skirts state as well as federal taxes, whereas the remainder avoid federal taxation only. The diversity of muni funds has created all sorts of niches for investors.

CHAPTER 11

Exploring All-in-One Funds

If you like to travel light, consider buying an all-weather fund. These products offer one-stop diversification for people able to afford only a single investment. They also can serve as a nice portfolio core for more affluent individuals who want to simplify their holdings. With all-weather funds, there's little excess baggage.

These portfolios combine as many as six or seven market sectors under one roof. They include both asset-allocation and balanced funds. The so-called "life-cycle" funds offer an asset-class mix geared to your age. Some all-weather portfolios gain their needed diversification by holding stakes in other mutual funds, whereas most invest in individual stocks and bonds. In most cases, the intent is to provide a smooth ride for shareholders.

Spreading Risk for a More Pleasant Trip

Asset allocation, the central theme of *Building Your Mutual Fund Portfolio,* aims to offset possible weak performance in one security group with stronger returns in another, leading to greater overall stability. For example, foreign stocks and bonds perform very differently from their domestic counterparts in some years. That's why international diversification is a key ingredient of most asset-allocation programs.

96

Money market securities also play a part in all-weather portfolios, despite their low long-run average returns. That's because T-bills and the like sometimes do very well on a relative basis. For instance, in 1981, when inflation was unusually high, T-bills returned 14 percent when the S&P 500 slumped by 5 percent. In 1994, money funds outperformed both their stock and bond counterparts. If inflation becomes a major problem, cash will rule until consumer and wholesale price increases are brought under control.

Some all-weather investors mix in a little gold as an insurance policy. This asset tends to shine when stocks and bonds are crumbling. In theory, gold stocks should be able to lower a portfolio's volatility because their prices often move counter to those of other investments. But the metal has been a poor long-term performer. According to Lipper Analytical Services, gold funds returned 6.3 percent annually over the 15 years ended December 1994. Energy or natural-resources funds have fared better than gold investments while providing an inflation hedge.

Asset-Allocation Funds

These extra-diversified portfolios spread money across several investment classes, including stocks, bonds and cash. Most have a global orientation. Individual funds within this category can vary markedly from one another. Asset-allocation products have the following distinguishing traits:

- *The kinds of stocks held.* Does the fund invest in small as well as large companies, or does it focus exclusively on the latter? Do gold stocks play a significant role?
- *The types of bonds owned.* Can the fund invest in a broad range of bond groups or is it more focused?
- *The amount of flexibility.* To what degree does the manager change the asset mix? How frequently are reallocations made, as evidenced by the portfolio turnover?
- *The foreign exposure.* What percentage of the portfolio's assets is normally allocated to foreign markets? Does the fund invest in emerging as well as developed nations?
- *The use of derivatives.* To what extent does the manager use options and futures?

It's an understatement to say that asset-allocation funds are difficult to run. With certain portfolios, separate managers handle separate classes of securities, and an allocator decides which percentages to invest in each. The prospectus may set allowable ranges for holdings of stocks, bonds and cash. Managers then make gradual reallocations as market conditions change, moving perhaps 10 or 20 percent of the portfolio each time.

Sample "neutral" weightings for several no-load portfolios appear in Figure 11.1. The neutral mix indicates what each fund considers normal. All these funds can include foreign stocks and bonds, except for Vanguard Asset Allocation, which sticks pretty much to stateside issues. Though the allowable asset-class ranges of some portfolios are wide, managers typically make gradual adjustments and normally don't get close to the extremes of zero or 100 percent.

A few asset-allocation funds hardly vary their weightings. An older portfolio, USAA Investment Cornerstone, has maintained fairly specific weightings with a little leeway to vary its mix. It normally invests as much as 10 percent in gold stocks and between 22 and 28 percent in four other groups: value stocks, foreign stocks, real estate stocks and U.S. government bonds. If stable allocations sound appealing, look at this fund, which returned 12.3 percent annually for the ten years ended December 1994.

Ensuring a Smoother Ride

Keep these four points in mind if you're ready to climb aboard an asset-allocation fund:

1. Look for funds that make gradual reallocations. Avoid aggressive market timers who make big bets that could sour. A turnover of 150 percent or more is a red flag.

FIGURE 11.1   Neutral Mixes for Selected Asset-Allocation Funds

	Stocks	Bonds	Cash
Crabbe Huson Asset Allocation	55%	35%	10%
Fidelity Asset Manager	40	40	20
Fidelity Asset Manager Growth	65	30	5
Fidelity Asset Manager Income	20	30	50
Fremont Global	60	36	4
Strong Asset Allocation	40	40	20
Vanguard Asset Allocation	55	40	5

AT THE HELM: ROBERT A. BECKWITT

Holding degrees from Princeton and Massachusetts Institute of Technology, Beckwitt uses his quantitative background extensively as portfolio manager of the $11-billion Fidelity Asset Manager fund, the largest of the asset-allocation products. He has been at the helm since the fund was introduced in 1988. Beckwitt also manages two offshoot allocation portfolios with more than $3 billion combined.

As an asset allocator, Beckwitt works with Fidelity analysts who supply lists of potential stocks and bonds to buy. He takes positions in a range of securities, including volatile high-yield bonds and emerging-market stocks. He uses options and futures to a modest extent as defensive tools.

In addition to his duties as a fund manager, Beckwitt is chief investment strategist for Fidelity Portfolio Advisory Services, which provides individualized help for affluent investors. In his leisure time, he enjoys playing the piano.

2. Watch out for overly cautious funds that always hold large positions in U.S. Treasury bonds and precious metals. Their long-run returns could disappoint you.

3. Choose funds with a proven manager who's been at the helm for several years. Top-quality management is essential, especially because you might be placing a large chunk of your wealth into a single all-weather portfolio.

4. Consider hedging your bets by going with two asset-allocation funds, especially if you're investing a large dollar amount.

Balanced Funds: A Standard Package

Balanced funds follow a simpler approach compared with their asset-allocation brethren. They split their holdings between stocks and bonds, typically favoring the former by a 60 to 40 ratio. Some

---

POINTS OF INTEREST:
Income Funds

Income funds are close relatives of balanced funds. Both invest in stocks as well as bonds. But income funds' primary objective is income, which means they tend to emphasize bonds over stocks, the reverse of balanced funds. Plus, the stocks they do own may well be characterized by their dividend yields rather than appreciation potential.

---

also include modest holdings of cash, and others may toss in some convertible bonds and preferred stock for good measure. Most balanced products are conservative and hold large, established companies and investment-grade bonds. The more aggressive might mix in some smaller stocks or bonds with lower ratings. Increasingly, balanced funds have been dabbling in foreign stock and bond markets to try to enhance their returns. This trend makes sense.

A balanced fund could serve as a complete portfolio for those who want something less volatile than a traditional equity fund that still offers appreciation potential. The category delivered sparkling returns for most of the 1980s and early 1990s thanks to strong bull markets in bonds as well as stocks. The long, downward drift of interest rates propelled the funds on a low-turbulence ride. But you can probably look for more modest returns in the future.

Contrary to what you might think, there is a definite positive correlation between bond and stock returns because interest rates and inflation are dominating factors and often push both assets in the same direction. But holding both can lead to less volatility because they generally do not move to the same extent. Balanced-fund managers do what they can with just the two main investment categories. The people who run asset-allocation funds have more tools at their disposal and thus enjoy far more leeway.

Each balanced portfolio has its own unique personality, and the best way to understand these funds is to study them in the pages of *Morningstar Mutual Funds* or *The Value Line Mutual Fund Survey*. If you're shopping for a balanced fund, here are some no-load names to keep in mind: CGM Mutual, Dodge & Cox Balanced, Fidelity Balanced, T. Rowe Price Balanced, Vanguard Balanced Index and Vanguard Wellington.

Doubling Your Diversification

So-called *funds of funds* don't buy individual stocks or bonds at all. They merely invest in other mutual funds of varying types. Consequently, they tend to behave much like asset-allocation portfolios. They also appeal to first-time investors or those with limited assets looking for one-stop diversification.

However, funds of funds can be rather costly to own because they typically impose two layers of fees—those of the underlying funds as well as one for the overall portfolio. This can take a big bite out of your long-run returns.

There are a few exceptions, though. Vanguard Star invests in seven other Vanguard funds—four equity, two bond and one money market—and it doesn't charge an overall fee. Shareholders merely pay a pro-rated slice of the underlying funds' expenses, as they would if they held each individual portfolio. Similarly, T. Rowe Price Spectrum Income and T. Rowe Price Spectrum Growth invest in other T. Rowe Price funds, without charging an additional fee.

Life-Cycle Funds

Age is a key determinant of a person's asset mix, so mutual fund companies have begun to trot out new products geared to the life-cycle concept. In 1994, Vanguard introduced a new twist on the "fund of funds" idea with four Star LifeStrategy portfolios geared to people in different age brackets. The lineup includes LifeStrategy Growth, Moderate Growth, Conservative Growth and Income. Each of the four invests in other Vanguard portfolios, with a 30-percent stake in Vanguard Asset Allocation as an anchor. The most aggressive of the four, LifeStrategy Growth, targets people younger than 50. It has 45 percent of its assets in Vanguard's Total Stock Market portfolio, which is indexed to the Wilshire 5000. The most conservative, LifeStrategy Income, is designed for those 75 and older. All LifeStrategy funds feature very low expenses. Wells Fargo Bank offers a similar design with its five Stagecoach Lifepath Portfolios.

Fitting All-Weather Funds into Your Plans

Generally, asset-allocation, balanced and funds of funds are appropriate for individuals who either want or can afford to invest in a single product only. These people may be looking for convenience or a hub for their portfolio of individual stocks and bonds or more specialized mutual funds. The one-stop products are like major cities to which the cheapest flights connect. Once you land, you can rent a car and head in any direction you like.

All-weather funds also are an appealing option for parents saving for a child's college education who want a single, broadly diversified and stable place to accumulate the cash. If the child is young and you're looking at 10 to 15 years or more to build up assets, consider a stock-oriented portfolio such as T. Rowe Price Spectrum Growth or Vanguard Star LifeStrategy Growth.

But as good as multi-asset portfolios are, they become less appropriate for larger investors already spreading their money across, say, eight or more different funds. The larger your portfolio and the more involved you are with it, the more advisable it becomes to build your own investment mix. This way, you can pick the very best funds you can find for each component—U.S. stocks, foreign stocks, taxable and tax-exempt bonds and so on. Also, you could use index funds to minimize costs, if you're so inclined. So you would essentially be building your own asset-allocation or balanced portfolio, readily adjustable as your circumstances change.

Street Smarts

- All-weather funds pack maximum diversification for investors seeking one-stop convenience. Their broad asset mixes make for smooth rides overall.
- The category includes asset-allocation, balanced and income portfolios and so-called funds of funds. Of these types, the asset-allocation format is the most flexible.
- Many people could find all-weather funds attractive, and in this sense the portfolios are like big foreign cities to which most vacationers fly to take advantage of the best air-fare values. From there, you can head in any direction you choose.

- On the other hand, if you have the time and interest to build your own mutual fund portfolio, you're probably better off bypassing the all-in-one packages. That way you can get just what you want by choosing the best funds in each category and weighting them as you see fit.

CHAPTER 12

Small Stocks Enhance Your Journey

It's not enough to own stock funds in your account. You should also spread your bets among different types of equity products. Just as natural disasters, political unrest, crime or other problems can make certain travel destinations less appealing, you never know which equity groups will be in or out of favor at any moment.

Small stocks, foreign stocks and big U.S. blue chips each have their day in the sun. Mixing them in the right proportions can lead to higher returns with only a negligible change in your portfolio's risk. Small U.S. stocks and foreign shares both have outperformed the most established American companies, as represented by the S&P 500, over long stretches. And although they can be quite volatile, combining small stocks into a diversified portfolio can lead to a smoother ride.

A T. Rowe Price Associates study shows that over the 20 years through 1994, you would have earned a 15.1-percent annualized return by investing 20 percent of your equity holdings in foreign stocks, 15 percent in small companies and the remaining 65 percent in the S&P 500. That compares with a 14.5-percent yearly return for the S&P 500 alone, yet the overall risk, as measured by standard deviation, was slightly greater for the all-S&P portfolio.

Small-stock and foreign categories fluctuate more than blue chip American companies and can underperform for several years, so use them to supplement your holdings of S&P 500-type companies without dominating your allocation. This chapter sizes up small-stock funds and

Chapter 13 analyzes foreign-equity portfolios. Together these two areas are crucial legs on a profitable journey.

Getting Extra Mileage with Small Stocks

Small stocks are good candidates for at least a tiny slice of the investment pie in all but the most conservative portfolios. Over many decades they have generated noticeably higher returns than their larger brethren. The "small-stock premium" implies that small-cap mutual funds should play an important role for individuals below age 55 or so who are trying to build their nest eggs over a long time horizon.

Although most small-stock funds don't have multidecade histories, Acorn (which is currently closed to new investors) and Pennsylvania Mutual both have been around for more than 20 years and have built impressive records. From its June 1970 debut through December 1994, Acorn returned 16.3 percent yearly. Pennsylvania Mutual, part of the Royce Funds, earned 16.3 percent from its June 1973 inception to year-end 1994.

Here are some reasons why selected small stocks can deliver outsized returns:

- These companies have greater growth potential because they are compounding their profits, sales and assets from a smaller base. It's possible for a firm with $50 million in sales to double that within a few years, but virtually impossible for a corporation with $10 billion in sales to turn the same trick.
- Small companies typically specialize in making only one or two products or providing a limited range of services. They often have greater flexibility than larger firms because of their reduced scale, narrower business focus and lean managements.
- At smaller corporations, top executives frequently hold a significant amount of a firm's stock and thus have added incentive to see that the business prospers and grows.
- Small firms generally have limited international activities and consequently don't face adverse fluctuations in earnings from foreign operations or currency factors.

Putting the Dangers in Perspective

Before investing in any small-cap fund, you should understand the many risk factors. A fund's prospectus might warn that small companies may lack depth of management or be unable to generate sufficient financing. Small businesses also can face devastating competition from corporate titans. The shares of small stocks normally lack liquidity, and transaction costs are relatively high. All this points toward the need for a competent fund manager overseeing a diversified portfolio to control risk. Mutual funds are ideal for minimizing the dangers relating to individual companies.

Still, the small-stock market can run hot or cold for several years at a time, and all such mutual funds will feel these swings. The big danger of small-stock funds is that they could significantly underperform their large-cap cousins for seven or more years. Consider them very long-term investments that shouldn't dominate your stock allocation— even if you're young and have a time horizon of several decades.

The "Small-Firm Effect"

This phenomenon is one of the most important anomalies to the efficient market hypothesis (see Chapter 5). For a market to act in an efficient manner, you need a large number of analysts following stocks and prices on a regular basis. But many small companies are neglected by Wall Street researchers because it isn't practical for a brokerage's large institutional customers—a primary source of the firm's revenues—to take meaningful positions in small stocks. Even if such a company delivered scintillating returns, it would still have a minuscule impact on a huge portfolio. Because thousands of small firms are unknown "shadow stocks," they could be inefficiently priced.

But market inefficiency is a two-edged sword: You can lose as well as profit. You should thus expect to see a fairly large disparity between the returns of the best and worst managers of small-stock funds, and sharp variations among the companies themselves.

How Small Is Small?

A company's size is customarily defined in terms of its *market capitalization* or "cap" (the price per share times the number of shares outstanding). The researchers who initially identified the superior performance of smaller firms defined "small" as those firms falling within the bottom 20 percent of businesses on the New York Stock Exchange. The upper boundary of this measure, which was $144 million as of year-end 1994, changes as prices rise and fall.

By Wall Street's broader standards, small companies can range up to about $600 million. For example, the market capitalizations of stocks in the Russell 2000—a popular index—range from about $60 million to nearly $600 million.

Maneuvering Through Back Alleys

Before investing in a small-cap product, check its total assets. With this type of mutual fund, unlike many others, size does seem to make a difference. When assets exceed $250 million to $300 million or so, it becomes increasingly difficult for a fund to function as a true small-cap portfolio. An $80-million fund might invest $400,000 in a promising small firm. Conversely, an $800-million competitor would need to invest ten times more, or $4 million, to give that stock the same 0.5-percent weight. Because small stocks are illiquid, it's hard for a large mutual fund to buy or sell a meaningful amount of shares without moving the price. A $4-million stake in some tiny companies would be neither practical nor prudent.

Small portfolios are easier to maneuver, and their holdings can be limited to several dozen of the manager's favorites. Large rivals that hold hundreds of stocks could wind up with superfluous diversification.

Spotting a Fund's True Stripes

Fund names and labels can be misleading. With some small-stock portfolios, you might discover that the average holding has a capitalization of $1 billion or more. Companies of this size wouldn't give you a strong exposure to small stocks. To help determine a fund's true colors, Morningstar calculates the median market capitalization of the portfolios it tracks, and Value Line provides a weighted-average cap number. The methods used by the two fund researchers thus differ, but they both provide the information you need.

The average median market cap for the small-stock funds in the Morningstar database was $500 million at this writing, or about 3 percent of the $15 billion median market cap of the big-cap dominated Vanguard Index Trust 500 portfolio. Funds that target the smallest firms have median market caps below $200 million. Babson Shadow Stock, Evergreen Limited Market, Heartland Value, Lindner/Ryback

---

TRAVELER'S ADVISORY:
Should You Buy a New Fund?

New small-stock funds that are members of respected families often do exceptionally well during their first year or two, if the market cooperates. One reason is that they start out small and can build the portfolio exclusively with the manager's prime choices yet grow at a healthy rate thanks to the family's solid reputation. Some new portfolios have performed spectacularly well because fund groups often nurture their youngest family members by stuffing them with the choicest stock pickings.

But don't buy a new stand-alone fund. It may have a difficult time attracting the money needed to reach a cost-effective size. It's a lot safer to stick with new members of well-established families.

Small-Cap and Montgomery MicroCap, for example, all fit into the micro-cap category. At the other end of the range, some small-company funds have median market caps above $1 billion.

Small-Stock Cycles

Small stocks go through extended periods when they either beat or lag the S&P 500. Such cycles average five to seven years. If you're planning to make a big investment or redemption in a small-cap fund, it pays to determine where small stocks are in their cycle.

An easy way to gauge this is to check the average PE of the T. Rowe Price New Horizons Fund—the granddaddy of small-cap portfolios—relative to the PE of the S&P 500. If the PE on New Horizons is 30 when the multiple on the S&P 500 is 20, the relative PE would be 1.5 (or 30÷20). This represents a normal reading. The relative PE has ranged from about 1.0 to 2.0, with an average around 1.4 or 1.5. When the ratio drops close to 1.0, small stocks represent excellent value. When it nears 2.0, the sector is overheated. Small caps generally sell at higher multiples than their far bigger cousins because they typically offer more exciting growth potential.

In addition to studying New Horizons, you can compare the PEs of most small-stock portfolios against the PE of the S&P 500. Morningstar and Value Line supply this information. Don't invest a lot of money in small-cap funds when they are pricey.

Sorting Out the Portfolios

The small-stock sector can be broken down into several key categories. Here are some of the major ones:

Growth. Most small-cap portfolios take this orientation. Their managers seek companies whose earnings are expected to ratchet upward at a high rate. These stocks generally carry above-average PEs and therefore possess above-average risk. But even here, funds differ in their volatility. Founders Discovery, Meridian and PBHG Growth are three examples of this large category.

Aggressive Growth. In general, the average capitalizations of stocks in aggressive-growth portfolios are significantly higher than those of true small-cap funds. But a number of funds labeled as aggressive growth do target small caps. These managers sometimes place big bets on sectors such as technology and health care in their quest for maximum capital gains. They may turn their holdings over rapidly and make use of options and short selling. Kaufmann and Wasatch Aggressive Equity are small-cap funds with an aggressive-growth flavor.

People who cannot weather choppy seas should not buy an aggressive-growth product. American Heritage is a good illustration of how turbulent the investment waters can be. This portfolio plunged 31 percent in 1990, but then rebounded, returning an astounding 97 percent in 1991, 19 percent in 1992 and 41 percent in 1993 under celebrity manager Heiko Thieme. With a 49-percent average annual return for the three years through 1993, American Heritage earned the number one ranking of all funds for that period. But the days of glory came to a screeching halt in 1994, when Thieme's portfolio tumbled a gut-wrenching 35 percent.

Value. An increasing number of small-cap funds are taking this orientation. They look for firms that are cheap in terms of their PE ratios and other valuation yardsticks. FPA Capital Fund, a load product, has built an outstanding record under manager Robert L. Rodriguez, who focuses on small and midsize companies selling at bargain levels. Fidelity Low-Priced Stock and Royce Equity-Income are other solid choices in the value area.

A fund's composite PE tells a lot about where it falls within the range from pure growth to pure value. The style boxes in Morningstar and Value Line also provide revealing clues. Some small-cap funds, such as T. Rowe Price OTC and Vanguard Index Trust—Small Cap Stock, blend the two approaches.

Index.   Several small-cap index funds also are available. Some argue that an index portfolio doesn't make as much sense for small stocks because astute managers should be able to profit from potential inefficiencies in underfollowed companies. However, because transaction expenses are relatively high for small stocks, the index approach offers a cost advantage. Besides, many actively managed portfolios are

---

AT THE HELM: CHARLES M. ROYCE

Charles M. Royce has built a solid record as a small-cap investor. In his spare time, he enjoys restoring old houses and traveling. Royce's flagship Pennsylvania Mutual Fund has appeared three times on the *Forbes* mutual fund honor roll. A staunch believer in market inefficiencies, Royce has devoted his energies to the small-stock arena because of the opportunity to earn higher long-run returns. In contrast to the more popular growth style of selecting small stocks, Royce opts for a traditional value approach. He favors the latter because growth seekers often overpay for anticipated earnings increases that don't materialize.

Royce and his staff manage nine open-end and two closed-end funds. All focus on small companies and search for underpriced assets. Royce is a firm believer in performance-based management fees and uses them in his two closed-end funds, Royce Value Trust and Royce OTC Micro-Cap. Managers should be paid only if they do well for shareholders, he says.

bound to underperform their peers and the Russell 2000, an index that represents small stocks. Examples of index funds in this category include Gateway Small Cap Index, Schwab Small-Cap Index and Vanguard Index Trust—Small Cap Stock.

Mixing Growth and Value

Besides spreading your nest egg across big, small, U.S. and foreign stocks, it's advisable to have mutual funds representing both the growth and value camps. Just as small stocks go through periods when they beat or trail big stocks, value shares often lead or lag growth companies for many months if not years. An especially logical pairing might include a small-cap value fund and a large-stock growth fund in the same portfolio, or perhaps a small-cap growth fund and a big-stock value fund.

Here's a breakdown you might consider for the stock portion of your portfolio:

30% large-cap growth
30% large-cap value
10% small-cap growth
10% small-cap value
20% international

Taking the Middle Road

No discussion of small stocks would be complete without mentioning medium-size (mid-cap) companies. These investments have enjoyed better long-term returns compared with large caps, but with less volatility than small firms.

The S&P 400 MidCap index has been tracking these companies since June 1991, resulting in increased interest in the category. Utility, financial, service and technology shares are well-represented in the midsize arena. The stocks have market values ranging from around $600 million to more than $5 billion.

Medium-size firms offer several attractions:

- They have survived their formative years and can point to proven operations and concepts. They face less risk of going belly up than a small company.

- They are run by seasoned managements and generate a more dependable earnings stream than the typical small company. Usually, medium-size firms offer multiple products or services, which lessens business risk.
- They are more apt to have the financial resources to sustain growth, and their balance sheets are generally healthier than those of the typical small firm.
- They still can look forward to better earnings potential than blue chip growth companies.
- The shares of midsize companies generally feature greater liquidity than those of small firms, which leads to lower transaction costs and makes them appealing to large institutional investors.

In general, mid-caps tend to follow a price cycle similar to that of small-caps, but their up and down moves are less pronounced. Your portfolio could include both categories. Growth investors need exposure to small stocks, but if you're uneasy about this end of the market, you might opt for a mid-cap fund.

Mid-Cap Portfolios

Lipper Analytical Services tracks about 100 mid-cap portfolios. Federated Index Trust Mid-Cap and Dreyfus Peoples S&P MidCap both target the S&P 400, for which the median size of stocks is about $1.5 billion. Brandywine, Fidelity Mid-Cap Stock, IAI Midcap Growth, IAI Regional, Lindner, Nicholas, T. Rowe Price Mid-Cap Growth and Twentieth Century Ultra Investors are examples of competing mid-cap portfolios.

Most funds targeting this sector do not have "mid-cap" in their names, so you need to check with Morningstar, Value Line or the fund company to be sure that a portfolio you're looking at has this orientation. As you might expect, different managers define midsize companies differently. Fidelity Mid-Cap Stock, for example, targets companies in the $50 million to $8 billion range, whereas T. Rowe Price Mid-Cap Growth tends to shop in the $300 million to $4 billion group.

Street Smarts

- Small stocks historically have traveled a greater distance in the market than the big blue chips, so adding an appropriate mutual fund can boost the performance of your overall portfolio.
- Small-stock funds should be bought and held for a long time— ten years or more.
- Dollar cost averaging—the strategy of making small monthly or quarterly investments on a continuing basis—is often the best way to go. The greater volatility of small-cap funds gives them a special advantage under an averaging program because more shares are acquired when prices fall further.
- Small-company funds with assets less than $300 million or so are more nimble and better able to negotiate narrow byways. But some products within this category invest in much larger stocks, so you have to check around.
- Small-stock funds promise higher returns over the long run, but there are no guarantees. You also need large-cap portfolios to round out your holdings.
- Investors not willing to commit to small-stock investments should instead consider a less-adventurous alternative, the mid-cap funds.

CHAPTER 13

Traveling Abroad Can Be Profitable

The world is at your fingertips. International investing has never been easier and more cost effective. That's fortunate because non–U.S. stock markets have performed quite well over longer stretches. For the decade ended December 1994, Morgan Stanley Capital International's EAFE index generated a 17.6-percent annual return versus 14.4 percent for the S&P 500. The EAFE represents more than 1,100 companies in Europe, Australia and the Far East and is the most widely followed overseas benchmark.

Many tried-and-true foreign-stock portfolios have compiled impressive records. Some examples, with annualized returns for the decade ended December 1994, appear in Figure 13.1. T. Rowe Price International appeared on *Forbes'* honor roll five consecutive years, and Templeton Foreign made the honor roll two years running. All of these funds handily beat the 14.4-percent yearly S&P 500 return over the decade.

Of course, past results can't be projected into the future with certainty. That's why we recommend that you allocate assets. Nevertheless, the long-term outlook for foreign stocks in both developed and emerging economies is bright. And with roughly two-thirds of the world's stock values outside the United States, fund managers have a wide spectrum of companies and markets from which to choose.

Lowering Risk with International Diversification

Mixing foreign stocks into a purely domestic portfolio can calm overall volatility and increase returns. Why? Because markets perform differently. One country's exchange might be up 30 percent in a year when another's remains flat or tumbles 25 percent. The degree of association between stock returns in the United States and other developed markets, such as Germany and Japan, is often fairly low. Emerging markets—such as Argentina, China, India, Taiwan, Malaysia, Mexico and Zimbabwe—typically have the weakest association with ours and with one another.

Some researchers report that the correlations between the world's major stock markets gradually have crept up over the years because of better communications ties and the increasing degree of economic interdependence. But the vastly different results in the U.S. and Japanese markets in recent years show that diversification still offers important benefits. Even so, it's a good idea to allocate at least a tiny part of your foreign stock exposure to emerging nations, where prices move much more independently of our own.

Selecting Your Sidetrips

Just as you can divide a city like Jerusalem or Paris into distinct neighborhoods, foreign stock funds can be grouped into various subcategories, depending on the range of markets in which they invest and other considerations. Here's a look at the leading classifications.

Global and International.   *Global* portfolios invest in both U.S. stocks and foreign equities from a range of countries. A global manager normally allocates at least two-thirds of the money to foreign markets, but the non–U.S. exposure varies widely among funds and can change to reflect world market conditions. Conversely, *international* funds usually invest exclusively in an assortment of foreign markets, with no American exposure.

Because of their broader diversification, global and international portfolios generally are better choices for most people than the more narrowly focused single-country or regional funds. However, if a global product keeps a large proportion of its money in stateside stocks, it may not offer the foreign exposure you need.

FIGURE 13.1   Foreign-Stock Portfolios and Yearly Returns

Fund	Yearly Return*
T. Rowe Price International Stock	18.0%
Templeton Foreign	17.7
EuroPacific Growth	17.6
Vanguard International Growth	17.2
Vanguard/Trustees' Equity International	16.8
Scudder International	16.2
Average International Fund	**15.7**

10 years ended 12/31/94
Source: Reprinted by permission of Lipper Analytical Services, Inc.

Most international funds invest virtually all their assets in large, developed markets like Germany, France, Japan and Britain. Some also may move in and out of the more volatile emerging economies, with a moderate portion of their assets. A manager who is bullish on emerging markets might put 25 percent of the portfolio into this realm. When the outlook clouds, he or she could cut back or might even pull up stakes completely. Check to see whether an international fund has the flexibility to invest in emerging markets.

Index Portfolios.   These products offer a low-cost, passive approach to gain exposure to many larger, well-established companies around the world. The Schwab International Index Fund tracks the performance of Schwab's proprietary index of 350 dominant foreign corporations. Its expense ratio has been running a modest 0.9 percent.

The European and Pacific portfolios of the Vanguard International Equity Index Fund track Morgan Stanley Capital International's Europe and Pacific indexes, respectively. Their expense ratios have been near 0.3 percent recently. Each invests in a wide sample of stocks. Because of Japan's large market weighting, the Pacific portfolio recently had about 80 percent of its assets there. A drawback to holding this fund is that you have big country risk because of the high Japanese stake. You could approximate the EAFE by allocating roughly 55 percent and 45 percent of your foreign investments to the Pacific and Europe portfolios, respectively.

Small-Company Funds.   A handful of portfolios focus on small to medium-size foreign stocks. Founders Passport, Montgomery Inter-

---

TRAVELER'S ADVISORY:
The International Domino Effect

International diversification doesn't always calm a portfolio. That's because the correlation of price movements in major world stock markets increases markedly during severe traumas, such as the bear routs of 1973–1974 and 1987. Heavy selling produces a domino effect, where all of the world's major markets plunge together. Cash is the only safe haven in times like these. But most of the time, world markets are less correlated, and international diversification does its job well.

---

national Small Cap, T. Rowe Price International Discovery, Scudder Global Small Company and Tweedy Browne Global Value belong to this group. As discussed in Chapter 12, fledgling companies often have above-average growth potential. In addition, the small-firm effect exists in foreign markets. And because the prices of second-tier foreign firms do not normally move in sync with small stateside stocks, they provide added diversification. Of course, small-stock portfolios—whether they consist of domestic or international companies—can be volatile. These funds best serve investors with very long time horizons.

Emerging Markets. Capitalism is flourishing. Stock exchanges in developing countries are attracting growing attention, and new ones have been established in former Communist nations to accommodate state-owned industries that are privatizing. Emerging markets represent less than one-tenth of global stock values, yet they promise exciting growth opportunities. A major reason for the excitement is that more than three-quarters of the world's population reside in these countries. Industries that are mature in the United States and other developed economies—such as banking or cement—offer strong potential in developing nations.

Despite the potential, don't go overboard with your investments in emerging markets. One way to lessen risk is to own a fund with exposure to several emerging countries in different regions of the world. Among broader developing-nations funds, Montgomery Emerging

Markets represents a more or less pure play in this area, whereas Lexington Worldwide Emerging Markets earmarks a portion of its assets to more established countries. Both are no-commission investments. You could also purchase shares in an assortment of single-country closed-end funds. Either way, you would want to limit your emerging-markets stake to between 10 and 40 percent of total foreign holdings, depending on your comfort level.

Vanguard International Equity Index Emerging Markets is a passive fund that tracks stocks in a dozen developing countries. This fund represents a low-cost way to gain exposure to these nations, because most actively managed competitors have higher expense ratios. In addition, the Vanguard fund is probably more diversified than the typical rival in total stock holdings. A possible drawback is that the 12 markets it tracks are among the more established in the category and thus would

AT THE HELM: J. MARK MOBIUS

J. Mark Mobius is the quintessential foreign-fund manager, if not the consummate global citizen. An emerging-markets specialist for the Franklin/Templeton Group, Mobius was born in New York, but educated at universities in Massachusetts, Wisconsin, New Mexico and Japan. He received a doctorate in economics and political science from M.I.T. in 1964.

Mobius has lived in Hong Kong since 1965, but also maintains an office in Singapore. And he's on the road constantly, seeking out promising companies in nations as varied as Russia, Argentina, India and Vietnam. "I spend about 80 percent of the time traveling, and each year I visit about 30 countries, very often more than once," he says.

Mobius joined Templeton in 1987 as managing director of its Far East division. He oversees more than a dozen foreign-flavored mutual funds, in addition to closed-end portfolios and pension money. To American mutual fund investors, he's most closely associated with the Templeton Developing Markets Trust, which he personally manages.

tend not to offer the most dynamic growth opportunities. The Vanguard portfolio is intended for long-term investors. Shareholders face a 2-percent fee to purchase shares and a 1-percent charge to redeem. These fees are paid directly to the fund for the benefit of continuing investors to defray the high costs of buying and selling emerging-markets stocks.

Regional Funds.   These portfolios focus on a group of countries within a defined geographic area—namely East Asia, Latin America or Europe. Scudder Latin America and T. Rowe Price New Asia are two of the many examples. Chapter 14 discusses a number of regional closed-end funds. The main point to remember about all regional funds is that they can be a lot more volatile than broadly diversified global or international products.

Single-Country Funds.   Because of their narrow focus, the single-country portfolios are generally the riskiest of all stock funds. A country fund ordinarily should account for no more than 5 to 10 percent of one's equity allocation. Most members of this group are closed-end, so we will say more about them in Chapter 14. However, several open-end funds focus on Japan, a handful track Canada and a few others follow a limited number of other countries.

The ecstasy and agony of speculating big time in one country was well illustrated by the plunge of the Japanese market. For the two decades ending in December 1989, Japanese stocks generated average annual returns more than twice those of U.S. equities. The Tokyo Stock Exchange's Nikkei index reached an all-time high near 39,000 at the end of 1989, but then the bubble burst. By August 1992, it had tumbled to nearly 14,000. This was worse than anything experienced in the United States since the infamous 1929–1932 bear market. The irony is that Japan rates as a fairly low-risk foreign nation.

Markets can crash suddenly due to scandals, political upheaval or other problems. In emerging markets, dangers include unstable governments, economies based on a handful of commodities or industries, and runaway inflation. Stock-market risks include illiquidity and volatility. In addition, some developing economies can be plagued by extreme currency fluctuations and sudden devaluations, as occurred in Mexico toward the end of 1994.

As we noted earlier, you can lower country risk by investing either in a fund that holds stock from many nations or in an assortment of single-country portfolios. So too for currency risk.

Dangers of Changing Your Money

You can do very well with foreign securities when the dollar depreciates and other currencies gain. But when the greenback rises, your foreign returns get stung. Funds that invest mainly where the local currency is not linked to the dollar—such as Europe and Japan—face this double-edged sword. It is, of course, the same risk that confronts tourists visiting foreign countries.

Suppose you invest in a Japanese fund that returns 25 percent in yen during a year, but the dollar gains 15 percent relative to the yen at the same time. Your return in dollars would be only 10 percent. Conversely, if the dollar loses 15 percent, your return jumps to 40 percent.

Should you worry about foreign funds because of this danger? Over the short haul, yes, because near-term fluctuations in exchange rates are very difficult to predict. But currency risk generally doesn't pose much of a problem for long-term investors using well-diversified global and international funds. That's because the favorable and unfavorable fluctuations should more or less balance out over time. Such fluctuations don't represent the major component of long-run returns.

Fund managers can reduce the threat posed by adverse currency swings by *hedging* or initiating an offsetting position in currency futures, options or forward contracts. But a hedge can lower returns if the manager guesses incorrectly. Also, hedging increases costs because—like other forms of insurance—it must be paid for. That's why many managers do not hedge more than 25 percent of their assets, if at all. Equity funds tend to use the strategy less than fixed-income portfolios, so check the prospectus or call the company. If you have a light or moderate stake in international markets, lean toward those funds that do little or no currency hedging.

Know Your International Exposure

You may have a bigger international stake right now with your domestic funds than you think. A number of U.S. equity managers have raised their foreign allocations in recent years. The average foreign exposure of U.S. diversified stock funds is less than 10 percent, but it's not at all uncommon to see a domestic stock fund with more than 20 percent of its assets invested abroad.

You can check a fund's international exposure by referring to the percentage allocation to foreign markets provided by Morningstar and Value Line or by reading shareholder reports. You may notice some "ADRs" or "ADSs" listed among the fund's holdings. These are American Depositary Receipts and American Depositary Shares, which represent ownership in foreign companies that trade in U.S. markets. Your fund might also have positions in U.S. multinationals such as Caterpillar and Xerox, with strong overseas business franchises. This too leads to a more globalized portfolio.

Tips for International Investors

You can easily achieve international diversification through mutual funds. However, there are a range of foreign-flavored portfolios, and not all will work for your goals. Here's a list of tips to keep in mind:

- Plan on allocating between 10 and 40 percent of your equity holdings to foreign-stock funds. The amount depends on factors such as your time horizon and risk tolerance.
- Lean toward an international fund rather than a global product to maintain better control of your non–U.S. exposure. With a global fund, the manager can drastically alter the domestic/foreign split, which would change your overall allocation.
- Check the percentages that multinational funds have invested in different regions and countries—know where your money is going. You can find these weightings in fund shareholder reports, or call the company for a more recent breakdown.
- Consider a mix of international portfolios to smooth your overall volatility. You might hold one that focuses on large stocks and another targeting smaller issues or emerging markets.
- Consider regional or single-country portfolios to concentrate your exposure in areas with extraordinary potential, such as Southeast Asia. But remember that focused funds can be more volatile. Keep these investments to 10 percent or less of your total stock allocation.
- Avoid funds that do a lot of currency hedging—a costly practice. By investing in both foreign and domestic stocks, you automatically diversify your currency risk anyway.
- Evaluate the performances of individual foreign-stock portfolios

against their peers and appropriate market benchmarks. For example, compare Japanese funds with one another and the Nikkei average. A broadly diversified international product should be pegged against the EAFE index.

- Seek out fund companies with a network of analysts who know their markets and visit companies. Look for managers with good track records who think independently. Franklin/Templeton, G.T. Global, T. Rowe Price and Scudder are among the larger fund complexes noted for their international expertise.

- Pay close attention to expenses, which tend to run fairly high on foreign funds because of the added costs of researching companies around the globe and heightened trading costs in many markets. T. Rowe Price International, Scudder International, Vanguard International Growth and Vanguard/Trustees' Equity International are pure no-load foreign funds that have achieved commendable long-term performance with reasonable expenses.

CHAPTER 14

Exploring the World of Closed-End Funds

At one time you could tour Europe on $10 a day, or other parts of the world for even less. This was the era of the truly great travel bargains, which are fast disappearing with increased development, commercialism and economic interdependencies around the globe.

Fortunately, you can still find bargains in the investment world from time to time. All you need to do is shop in the realm of closed-end funds. These portfolios are a bit more complicated than regular mutual funds, which are known as "open-end" funds because they stand continually ready to sell and buy back their shares. But because closed-end funds are diversified and professionally managed, they have many of the same desirable attributes. In fact, most closed-end portfolios are run by companies that also offer mutual funds, such as Alliance, Fidelity, Gabelli, Franklin/Templeton, Merrill Lynch, Putnam, Salomon Brothers and Scudder.

The closed-end format preceded open-end funds as the original type of investment company. In fact, closed-end portfolios were more numerous during the roaring bull market of the 1920s. However, they were highly leveraged and volatile and consequently fell fast and hard when the market crashed in 1929. They then remained an obscure investment vehicle for years, but have enjoyed a huge renaissance starting in the 1980s. Today's closed-end funds are much safer than their predecessors of the freewheeling 1920s because—like mutual funds—they are highly regulated. The Investment Company Act of

1940 and the Securities Act of 1933 are two of the major laws regulating both categories.

All told, there are now more than 500 closed-end portfolios with more than $125 billion in assets, representing about 6 percent of the fund universe. Many investment categories are available, especially single-country, regional, municipal bond and a wide assortment of taxable-bond portfolios.

The Closed-End Way

When a new closed-end portfolio debuts, management sells shares through an initial public offering (IPO), just like a corporation would issue stock. The fund is offered to investors at a price that includes underwriting fees of 7 percent or so. It then trades like General Motors or any other stock and its market price bobs up and down based on demand and supply. Most closed-end issues change hands on the New York Stock Exchange. In fact, about one in six stocks listed on the Big Board is a closed-end fund. Others trade on the American Stock Exchange and a few in the Nasdaq market. Share prices appear daily in the regular stock tables.

You buy and sell closed-end investments through your broker, paying the usual commission. One of the most important differences between open- and closed-end portfolios is that the fund company won't redeem your closed-end shares at NAV as you're accustomed to doing with mutual funds. Nor will it issue new shares—you must buy what's already available in the market.

The fact that closed-end managers work with a fixed number of shares has important implications. In theory, a closed-end fund should perform better than an equivalent open-end product because its manager can be more long-term oriented, for the following reasons:

1. Closed-end managers don't face tidal waves of new shareholder money in overheated bull markets, which could cause them to invest in overpriced securities or sit on a pile of cash.
2. Closed-end managers don't need to worry about wholesale redemptions by nervous investors in bearish environments. Heavy selling by shareholders in regular mutual funds could force managers to dump underpriced securities when they should be buying instead.

Because they work with a stable pool of capital, closed-end managers can invest more heavily in illiquid, volatile securities, such as micro-cap stocks or issues traded in emerging foreign markets. This explains why single-country funds typically adopt the closed-end structure.

In addition, because closed-end products need not maintain a cash buffer to meet shareholder redemptions, they can adopt a posture that is truly close to being fully invested. An open-end fund may keep 5 percent of its assets in cash, whereas a comparable closed-end portfolio might maintain only 2.5 percent.

Understanding Discounts and Premiums

Closed-end funds have two separate prices—a net asset value and a market price. The two rarely match up. When the market price is less than NAV, the portfolio trades at a *discount;* when the price exceeds NAV, it sports a *premium*. Discounts and premiums are calculated as follows:

Discount (Premium) = (Share Price – NAV) ÷ NAV

Here's an example:

	NAV	Market Price	Premium (+) or Discount (−)
Fund A	$10	$8.50	−15%
Fund B	10	12.50	+25

Discounts and premiums are reported weekly in *Barron's, The Wall Street Journal,* and a few other newspapers, along with each fund's NAV and 52-week market return. An increasing number of closed-end portfolios compute their NAVs daily and quote them to interested investors by phone. The larger fund companies have toll-free 800 numbers. Daily NAVs are useful during fast-moving markets, especially if you're planning on buying or selling a fairly large number of shares.

But purchasing closed-end portfolios at bargain prices isn't as easy as it seems. If you buy in at too narrow a discount, you face the danger of the discount deepening, which would adversely affect your return. As a general rule, try to buy equity funds at markdowns of 10 percent or more, but the relevant number also depends on each fund's historic trading range.

Closed-end share prices often fluctuate up and down more than their NAVs, so some advisers advocate short-term trading. But this requires that you keep close tabs on premiums and discounts for individual funds and their peers. You also have to pay brokerage commissions on your purchases and sales, which will eat into your returns if you trade too frequently. For most closed-end shareholders, it's best to be a long-term investor.

Most closed-end funds allow you to reinvest your dividend and capital-gains distributions at little or no cost. When the fund trades at a discount, dividends are normally reinvested at the market price— rather than at the NAV, as with mutual funds. Reinvestment at a discount thus enhances your overall return.

In short, the discount is the number one advantage of closed-end funds for most people. But unless you can find good portfolios trading at attractive markdowns, you're probably better off sticking with mutual funds.

Market Sentiment

So what causes closed-end funds to trade at discounts or premiums?

Just like PE ratios on ordinary stocks, valuations expand and contract with changes in investor psychology and the general level of stock and bond prices. Keep in mind two important points:

- *Premiums tend to occur during periods of euphoria and greed.* This is the time to stay away from closed-end funds. Why pay a markup when you can purchase excellent no-load funds at NAV? If you do buy at a premium, your risk increases. If anything, this is a good time to consider selling.
- *When greed turns to fear and nervous sellers outnumber buyers, premiums quickly shrink and turn to discounts.* Funds that already had been trading at markdowns slump to deeper ones. This is a great time to buy top-quality portfolios. In effect, you're really getting a "double discount" because the market is already cheap.

Other Factors

But investor sentiment isn't the only variable that determines a portfolio's discount or premium. Here are five more:

1. *Nature of the portfolio*. Stock funds tend to trade at wider discounts than bond products, which are more stable and produce a regular income stream. Investors are willing to pay for these attributes.
2. *Performance and management*. Funds that have sparkled under the direction of talented managers generally sell at smaller discounts or fatter premiums. Poor performers often wallow at hefty markdowns.
3. *Expense ratios*. High expenses lead to bigger discounts. As with mutual funds, you also need to examine the cost characteristics of closed-end portfolios.
4. *Liquidity*. A portfolio that trades 100,000 shares a day is far more liquid than one that averages less than 5,000. Funds that trade infrequently sell at wider discounts.
5. *Price supports*. Managers don't want their funds to trade at deep discounts. Consequently, they frequently try to support the price in various ways. For example, they might buy back some of their shares in the market when prices dip.

POINTS OF INTEREST:
Year-End Markdowns

Closed-end funds are owned largely by individual investors, primarily in taxable accounts. Investors who have suffered a loss during the year often sell their shares in November or December to realize a deduction for tax purposes. This is especially prevalent at times when the market has done poorly, but it occurs every year in at least some funds. In particular, new portfolios have a tendency to slip to discounts after a few months, when the investment bankers stop supporting their prices. December represents the best time of the year to go bargain hunting for closed-end funds.

On Safari with Country Funds

One of the most popular uses of closed-end products involves investments in single countries. Many funds target emerging nations such as China, Korea, the Philippines, Brazil and Mexico. Others focus on more developed markets. Either way, the stable asset base of the closed-end structure is ideal for a single-country focus.

These funds offer convenient access to their respective nations. The facts that they are regulated by the SEC and trade in the United States provide significant advantages. But while country funds can offer the highest potential returns in the closed-end arena, they also have the greatest risk and should be purchased only by sophisticated investors who fully appreciate the economic and stock-market conditions of the target country. Single-country funds are more volatile, so they should account for a maximum 10 percent or so of an individual's stock allocation.

For something a bit tamer, go with a closed-end regional portfolio. Compared with their single-country relatives, regional funds provide an added dimension of diversification, with holdings spread over an assortment of nations in Europe, Latin America or Asia. By investing in the right three regional funds, you can pretty much cover all the major stock markets outside the United States.

Keep these points in mind when considering foreign closed-end investments:

- *Know the fund's premium and discount history.* Valuations on volatile single-country products can range from discounts in excess of 20 percent to premiums higher than 50 percent. Try to buy at a deeper than normal markdown. Also, compare discounts and premiums on competing funds of the same type—such as the Emerging Germany, Germany and New Germany portfolios.
- *Stick with funds that remain fully invested.* A 10-percent cash position is considered normal for a country fund. Avoid those that retreat heavily to the sidelines because their market might take off suddenly, catching them flat-footed.
- *Diversify among countries.* If you decide to go for single-country funds, try to reduce your stock market and currency risks by buying into at least three or four nations.
- *Opt for open-end funds when comparable closed-end products trade at rich premiums.*

Searching for Tax-Free Yields

Municipal-bond funds now constitute the largest segment within the closed-end universe. Their prices stay in a narrower range, from discounts of 10 percent or so to premiums around 10 percent, depending on investor sentiment, the outlook for interest rates and specific characteristics of the portfolio.

Closed-end muni funds have several favorable attributes compared with their open-end relatives:

- They appeal to traders who like to watch for opportunities to pick up shares at a good discount and sell at a premium.
- They can outperform regular mutual funds during favorable climates. Closed-end managers don't need to worry about shareholder redemptions, so they need not maintain a cash cushion for this purpose.
- They also may perform better during weak markets, as their managers are not forced to sell bonds at unfavorable prices to meet shareholder redemptions.
- They can score better gains during periods of falling or flat interest rates through the use of borrowing or leverage—an option not normally practiced by regular mutual funds. (However, if interest rates rise sharply, as they did in 1994, leveraged muni investors face increased risk.)

Analyzing Closed-End Funds

The process for selecting closed-end portfolios isn't much different than for regular mutual funds. You want to look at portfolio holdings, expense ratios, turnover, past performance, management tenure and the like. The main difference with closed-end funds is that you need to examine the discount (or premium) and give high weight to that variable when making your buy or sell decision.

Another difference you will observe is that both "market-price" returns as well as NAV returns may be reported. The NAV performance is generally recognized as the more important of the two because it reflects the results achieved by the portfolio manager, independent of fluctuations in discounts and premiums. The manager doesn't have control over changes in investor sentiment, although a

---

TRAVELER'S ADVISORY:
Relating Discounts to Expenses

Would you prefer stock-fund A with a 10-percent discount or B with a 25-percent markdown? Before snapping up the latter, evaluate its discount in comparison with its expense ratio. A deeply discounted fund is no bargain if outrageously high expenses eat into its returns. To check this out, simply divide the discount by the expense ratio. Suppose A has a 0.5-percent expense ratio and B's is 3 percent. The "expense-adjusted discounts" would be 20 and 8.3, respectively. The higher this yardstick, the better. At a minimum, look for a value of at least 10. In our illustration, A passes with flying colors and B fails, assuming that the two are reasonably comparable in other respects.

---

good track record can result in a narrower markdown or a premium. Market-price returns reflect the behavior of premiums and discounts over time.

Mutual fund investors are accustomed to gleaning a prospectus, but closed-end funds normally issue this document only when they have their initial public offering or raise additional capital through a rights offering. So you can't request a prospectus from them as you would from a mutual fund. However, you can find ample information and numbers to study in the annual and semiannual shareholder reports.

Closed-end funds are stocks, so you also can find useful profiles of them in such widely available publications as *Standard & Poor's Stock Reports* and *The Value Line Investment Survey*. See Appendix 2 for other sources of information.

Know Your Rights

Unlike open-end funds, closed-end portfolios do not enjoy an ongoing influx of new investor money after they go public. However, in recent years many funds have chosen to sell new shares to existing investors via *rights offerings* to raise additional capital.

Investors normally receive one right for every share they own. They can then use the rights to buy new shares usually at a discount to the fund's market price.

If you own a fund that has a rights offering, take appropriate action—either by subscribing to new shares with your rights or selling them if they are *transferable* (or tradable in the market). If they are *nontransferable* and you don't want to increase your investment in the fund, you should subscribe to the shares anyway, but immediately turn around and sell them, locking in the difference between the market price and the lower subscription price. This allows you to capture the value of your rights. Those who hesitate lose out as the rights have a life of just several weeks, after which they expire worthless.

Should You Follow the Closed-End Route?

Closed-end portfolios add a dimension of diversification for investors. With good timing and selection, you should be able to improve your overall performance. But buy these products only when you are satisfied that they offer value. Watch for these four pitfalls:

1. *Initial public offerings.* Closed-end fund IPOs are executed at a premium to NAV, which includes an underwriting spread or markup of 7 percent or so on stock funds. After a few months, the shares of equity funds normally slip to a discount. Don't lose money by buying on the IPO—wait for the discount.

2. *High premiums.* Hot single-country portfolios can trade at steep premiums of 25 percent or more. A high markup can quickly diminish or even compress to a discount if an exotic foreign market takes a tumble. The higher the premium, the greater your risk.

3. *Discounted funds with problems.* Although buying funds at large discounts (especially in bear markets) may be wise, don't let the markdown be your sole criterion. Weigh other factors such as performance and expenses. A fund with a 20-percent discount might have a 3-percent expense ratio and a terrible record.

4. *Complex products.* Some closed-end funds use strategies that may not be totally clear to you. For example, many municipal-bond portfolios leverage their holdings with borrowed cash. Never invest in anything you don't understand.

AT THE HELM: DOUGLAS G. OBER

Ober has been managing Adams Express, a closed-end fund, since 1986. He got his start as an aeronautical engineer, then transferred his skills with numbers into banking and ultimately into the investment business.

Preservation of capital is the primary objective for Adams Express, which scores highly in down markets. The portfolio sports an amazingly low 0.3-percent expense ratio—something you'd expect to find in an index product. The fund, which began in 1929, charges no management fee. Ober targets medium-size stocks, blending the growth and value styles. He often uses convertible securities, which provide additional income and protective features. A buy-and-hold investor, Ober keeps his stocks for about five years on average. He also manages Petroleum & Resources, a closed-end sector fund that started in 1929.

Narrowing Your Destinations

We can't give you an unconditional list of recommended buy candidates because the appeal of individual closed-end funds changes from week to week as their discounts fluctuate. However, several solid domestic stock portfolios are worth keeping an eye on. If you can find any of them at deeper than normal discounts, consider adding them to your holdings.

The Pre-Depression Funds

Among our favorites are a handful of conservatively managed domestic stock funds that trace their beginnings to the late 1920s. They tend to have low expense ratios and modest portfolio turnovers. They certainly have served the test of time and make sensible core investments, especially when they can be had at double-digit discounts. Incidentally, these pre-depression funds, like solid mutual funds, can be excellent holdings for an IRA. They also can be used as gifts to minors. The pre-depression funds are: Adams Express (NYSE: ADX), Central

---

TRAVELER'S ADVISORY:
Placing Limit Orders

Be a penny pincher when you trade closed-end shares. Use *limit orders* to get a better execution. This is an order to buy or sell at a specified price or better. It can be entered either as a day order (which expires at the end of the day) or as a good-till-canceled order.

Suppose Fund A is quoted at 10 bid, 10⅛ offered. You could save $200 on a 1,600-share trade by placing a limit order and hoping the price drops to 10 rather than accepting the current asked price of 10⅛, which is what you normally would pay if you place a market order. You need patience, especially on less liquid issues, and you run the risk of never seeing your order filled if the price moves higher. But limit orders can save you cash and are often worth the wait.

Securities (AMEX: CET), General American Investors (NYSE: GAM), Salomon Brothers Fund (NYSE: SBF) and Tri-Continental (NYSE: TY). For further information on these and other products, see *Morningstar Closed-End Funds* or *Standard & Poor's Stock Reports*.

Small-Cap Portfolios

Closed-end funds are excellent vehicles for investing in the less liquid small-stock sector because their managers work with a stable pool of cash and therefore can be long-term oriented. Here are some choices: Morgan Grenfell Smallcap (NYSE: MGC), Royce OTC Micro-Cap (Nasdaq: OTCM) and Royce Value Trust (NYSE: RVT).

Street Smarts

- Adventurous investors should consider straying from the beaten path with closed-end funds. These vehicles trade like regular stocks, which opens the possibility that their shares could slip to discounts or jump to premiums. During bearish phases, prices frequently slide to bargain levels. And you often can spot good values during the year-end tax selling season, when investors dump shares to realize losses.

- Do your homework. The two most popular closed-end categories are country funds and municipal-bond portfolios. Both groups are complicated and require careful study.
- Generally, closed-end stock funds represent a better deal than their bond counterparts. The best place to invest if you want to give closed-ends a try is within the plain vanilla domestic equity group.

CHAPTER 15

Perusing the Sector Funds Menu

Sector or industry-specific portfolios sit on the edge between investing and speculating. These funds dominate the monthly and quarterly lists of best and worst performers. They have explosive profit potential, but carry above-average risks. They can round out a well-balanced portfolio, but can't replace one. They make interesting side-trips, but shouldn't become the main excursion.

Gold or precious-metals portfolios are the most notorious. With the exception of a few periodic surges in years such as 1986, 1987 and 1993, they have been chronic losers. Then there are the health-care funds, which rated as the top mutual fund group for three straight years from 1989 through 1991, but then fell hard. Even utility portfolios—once considered an excellent choice for widows and orphans—were hit hard in 1993 and 1994 by the double whammy of higher interest rates and deregulation fears.

Well-diversified stock funds generally spread risk better than sector funds, but the latter at least offer better diversification than individual stocks. That's one reason to consider a sector portfolio. Here are some others:

1. *As a trading vehicle.* In your quest for fast profits, you can actively buy and sell sector funds like individual stocks.
2. *To obtain concentrated exposure to a promising industry or theme.* A modest investment in one or more sector funds can

augment a broadly diversified portfolio, providing a nice kicker if the right funds are used at the right time.

3. *As a way to generate income.* Both utility and real-estate portfolios pay above-average dividends.

4. *To gain inflation protection from investments in real-estate or natural-resources funds.* Gold products also are a possibility here, but their long-term record has not been encouraging.

There are various ways to select sectors. A value investor might buy a stake in an industry that has been beaten up and appears due for a rebound. Undervalued stocks tend to cluster within specific industries. Conversely, growth players might search for hot industries on the move. They don't mind paying above-average prices for exceptional profit potential.

Narrowing the Field

The characteristics and risks of several popular industry groups are outlined here. Keep in mind that substantial differences can exist among portfolios within any one category, depending on management style, the use of cash or hedging techniques, and other factors.

Financial Services.   These portfolios hold the stocks of banks, other lending institutions, brokerages, leasing outfits, insurance firms and mutual fund companies—all of which are sensitive to changes in economic conditions and interest rates. Fidelity Select Financial Services and INVESCO Strategic Financial Services are examples of funds that own various firms within the sector. Fidelity Select Brokerage & Investment Management and Fidelity Select Insurance target narrower subgroups.

Health Care.   These funds invest in pharmaceutical companies, medical-equipment manufacturers, hospitals, home health-care agencies and the like. The graying of America should lead to continued strong demand for this sector, though companies in the medical industry must deal with government regulations, which could affect them adversely. Also, many products or services could be subject to rapid obsolescence.

INVESCO Strategic Health Sciences and Vanguard Specialized Health Care target the sector broadly. Fidelity Select Biotechnology has a narrower focus. Closed-end investors might want to look at H&Q Healthcare and H&Q Life Sciences, which both trade on the New York Stock Exchange.

Natural Resources. These commodity-oriented portfolios target companies involved in oil and natural gas, metals and minerals, and paper and forest products. Resource funds tend to perform best in inflationary times, especially when oil prices advance sharply. T. Rowe Price New Era is one of the oldest and largest products of this type. Petroleum & Resources is a closed-end portfolio with a long history that trades on the New York Stock Exchange. Fidelity Select Industrial Materials is another possibility. Some funds in this group are pure energy plays, including INVESCO Strategic Energy and Vanguard Specialized Energy.

Precious Metals. The stocks of gold-mining companies are the primary focus here. Buying gold via mutual funds is a simple way to participate in an anticipated rally in the metal. Speculators move in and out of funds and stocks quickly, so these products exhibit far more volatility than the metal itself. Further exaggerating the moves of mining companies is their earnings leverage. Because mining costs are largely fixed, a big percentage of any gold-price rise goes to a firm's bottom line. Gold sometimes moves inversely to the prices of stocks and bonds and occasionally performs very well during highly inflationary, tumultuous times. But the price of the metal is very unpredictable. Some choices include Benham Gold Equities Index, INVESCO Strategic Gold and Vanguard Specialized Gold & Precious Metals. ASA Limited is an NYSE-traded closed-end fund that targets South African gold issues.

Real Estate. Real estate rates as a major asset class to which countless homeowners don't have adequate exposure because they typically aren't diversified by geographic markets and property types such as apartment complexes, retail centers, industrial parks and office buildings. The mutual fund route is a great way to include a small slice of real estate in your investment pie, and it offers you the ability to hold real estate within an IRA.

Such funds do not invest directly in land and buildings. They primarily purchase real-estate investment trusts (REITs), along with other stocks in the industry such as home builders. *REITs* are pooled investment vehicles similar to closed-end funds. They trade like any other stock on an exchange such as the NYSE. Like mutual funds, REITs are not taxed on their income, provided they follow IRS guidelines and distribute at least 95 percent of it to shareholders. *Equity REITs,* the largest category, own real property directly and receive rental income in return. REITs are now available for every major property type located in virtually every region of the country.

Real-estate funds typically diversify their holdings across state lines, and a few take a global slant. Funds that have large REIT holdings tend to generate good income, but can be volatile. As REITs typically are small, it's not unreasonable to think of real-estate funds as high-yielding portfolios of small stocks. Fund groups offering real-estate portfolios include CGM, Cohen & Steers, Columbia, Crabbe Huson, Evergreen, Fidelity and Franklin/Templeton.

Technology.   This broad category is most closely identified with computers and, to a lesser extent, telecommunications and medical technology. Favored stock picks include many small growth firms that feature high return potential and considerable risk. Fidelity Select Technology, INVESCO Strategic Technology and T. Rowe Price Science & Technology are among the choices in this area, although many small-company and aggressive-growth funds typically have a noticeable technology flavor.

Telecommunications.   These funds stock up on companies that provide telephone, cellular and cable service, as well as communication equipment. Worldwide funds such as GT Global Telecommunications and Montgomery Global Communications are more diversified than the typical sector portfolio because of the variety of companies in this industry. These investments are not your typical single-industry sector products subject to wide volatility. Growth investors with lengthy time horizons can use them as specialized holdings. Global managers seek to capitalize on two movements: the installation of basic telephone services in emerging nations and the rapid growth of sophisticated equipment and services in developed economies. Emerging Markets Telecommunications, which recently had heavy exposure in Latin America, is a closed-end fund that trades on the NYSE.

Utility.   The largest sector-fund category, utility portfolios are usually fairly stable. Many utility stocks fluctuate only about half as much as the overall market. These portfolios might own a combination of

---

AT THE HELM: ROBERT H. STEERS

Steers is chairman of New York City-based Cohen & Steers Capital Management, which manages about $1.3 billion in real estate securities. Before founding the firm in 1986, he was affiliated with National Securities & Research Corporation, where he introduced the country's first real-estate mutual fund.

With colleague Martin Cohen, Steers runs two closed-end real-estate funds—Cohen & Steers Realty Income and Cohen & Steers Total Return Realty—in addition to the no-load, open-end Cohen & Steers Realty Shares. The open-end fund recently was the only real-estate portfolio tracked by Morningstar to enjoy a five-star rating. "This is the beginning of the trend toward the securitization of real estate," says Steers. "REITs are poised for the greatest growth in their history, and the industry will increase from a $50-billion market cap in 1995 to nearly $200 billion by the end of this decade."

---

electric, natural gas and telephone companies. But most emphasize electrics and are yield-oriented.

Even though utility funds ordinarily are sedate, they can be volatile, especially during periods of rising interest rates such as 1994. Increasing rates depress high-yielding stocks as well as long-term bonds; whereas declining rates lead to attractive gains. Utility funds do well in a sluggish, low-inflation economy.

Many solid no-load choices are available from companies such as Benham, Dreyfus, Fidelity, INVESCO, Lindner, Rushmore, Strong and Vanguard. A load product, Franklin Utility, ranks as the nation's oldest utility portfolio. Templeton Global Utilities is a notable closed-end fund that trades on the American Stock Exchange.

The Fidelity Select Group

Fidelity Investments deserves special mention regarding sector portfolios. Fidelity counts three dozen funds in its Select sector group.

A unique feature of each is that they are priced hourly so that short-term traders can move in and out quickly, getting transactions executed at any of several possible prices during the day. The funds charge a 3-percent front-end load, although the fee is reduced for large purchases starting at $250,000. You also face a 0.75-percent redemption fee if you sell before 30 days. Some Select portfolios can even be sold short, allowing you to speculate on price declines. This makes them another oddity in the mutual fund business.

Seven Tips for Sector-Fund Investing

Because of their risk characteristics, industry-specific portfolios are best used sparingly. Nevertheless, if taking a concentrated bet appeals to you, keep these suggestions in mind:

1. *Check the portfolio and compare it with its peers.* Major differences can exist among funds investing in the same sector.
2. *Limit any investments in volatile sectors to 5 to 10 percent of your overall stock allocation.*
3. *Don't buy late.* If a sector becomes pricey following a period of brilliant performance, don't expect the trend to last for much longer.
4. *Don't overpay.* Some smaller portfolios have expense ratios well above 2 percent. This is too much to pay because sector-fund managers do a lot less to earn their fees, as they don't have to determine industry selection, weighting and rotation.
5. *Watch portfolio turnover.* Some sector funds run up turnovers of 200 percent or more. Shareholders must absorb the high resulting transaction costs.
6. *Avoid active switching.* It often leads to poor long-run results, and you may face additional transaction expenses.
7. *Don't buy a sector fund and forget about it.* Watch the narrower, more volatile portfolios closely. Keep up with industry developments.

CHAPTER 16

Incorporating Tax Planning in Your Itinerary

Careful tax planning can help you squeeze extra mileage out of your wealthbuilding journey. Although tax considerations are secondary to your investment's overall performance, they certainly impact the bottom line. A small improvement in your compounding rate resulting from more tax-efficient strategies can make a huge difference in how fast your capital grows over many years.

You may be subject to taxes when you hold investments that produce taxable income, net realized gains or both. In accordance with Subchapter M of the Internal Revenue Code, fund companies are not subject to taxation themselves on their net dividend and interest income and net realized gains. Rather, they funnel profits through to investors, who pay any applicable taxes on their share of the distribution. At least 98 percent of a mutual fund's net investment income and net realized capital gains must "flow through" to shareholders each year. This gives rise to a potential annual tax liability for those who hold their funds in an unsheltered account.

If a fund never sold any securities, it wouldn't generate capital gains to distribute. But funds do liquidate positions, creating potential tax liabilities for shareholders. How a fund treats these gains or losses for tax purposes depends on its holding period, not yours. If you recently bought a fund that distributed long-term capital gains, the amount would be taxable to you even if you had held the position for just a few days.

Here are four ways to ease the tax bite if you own shares within an ordinary taxable account:

1. Use the most advantageous cost basis when you sell your shares.
2. Realize capital losses to offset ordinary income and capital gains.
3. Buy funds *after,* not before, they have gone *ex-distribution.* If you buy shares on or after the "ex" date, you no longer are entitled to the distribution, but you pay a lower price because the NAV has been reduced by the amount of the payout.
4. Invest in tax-efficient funds.

Finding Your Cost Basis

Whenever you sell mutual fund shares, you need to calculate a *cost basis* so that you can determine your realized gain or loss. Your basis is essentially the dollar amount of your investment on which you wouldn't owe taxes when you eventually sell. It is thus one of the most important things to keep track of for tax purposes. It includes the cost of shares acquired directly and through reinvested dividends and capital-gains distributions. Whenever you reinvest such proceeds, you are purchasing more shares. Some people don't realize this and needlessly pay taxes twice. First, they paid taxes in the year of the distribution. Then, if they do not add the amount of the payout to their cost basis, any capital gain would be larger by the amount of the reinvested distribution, resulting in a higher tax bill. The tax accounting for funds gets complicated, especially if you do a lot of buying and selling. So it's vital to keep careful records on all reinvestments over the years. Of course, if you don't reinvest your distributions, they don't become a part of your cost basis.

When you redeem shares, you either sell all or a portion of your holdings. Figuring the basis is simpler when you sell the entire lot at once: Merely total the cost of all shares sold. For example, if you redeemed at once all 3,600 of your shares of ABC Fund in Figure 16.1, your cost basis would be $39,875, the total of all purchases and reinvested distributions. You report a gain if the proceeds from the sale exceed your cost basis. Conversely, you have a loss if the latter exceeds the former.

When you sell a portion of your holdings, calculating an appropriate basis gets more complicated. It's important to figure the gain or

FIGURE 16.1   ABC Fund Transaction Logbook

Date	Shares	Price	Value	Type of Transaction
Jan. 20, 1991	1,000	$10.00	$10,000	Initial purchase
Dec. 15, 1992	150	11.00	1,650	Capital-gains distribution
June 10, 1993	1,000	11.50	11,500	Subsequent purchase
Dec. 15, 1993	200	10.50	2,100	Capital-gains distribution
July 20, 1994	1,000	11.75	11,750	Subsequent purchase
Dec. 15, 1994	250	11.50	2,875	Capital-gains distribution
Totals	**3,600**		**$39,875**	

Average cost = $11.08 ($39,875 ÷ 3,600 shares)

loss using the IRS-approved method that would result in the most favorable tax consequences. Suppose that on August 31, 1995, you sold 1,000 of your 3,600 shares of ABC at $12.50 each, for total proceeds of $12,500. What is your basis and realized gain? You can use one of three general methods to determine this.

1. First-In, First-Out (FIFO).   Under this approach, any shares sold are assumed to come first from the earliest acquisition, then from the next oldest purchase, and so on. In our example, on August 31, 1995, you sell the 1,000 shares that you had originally acquired at $10 a share on January 20, 1991. In this case, the $10,000 you paid is your cost basis. Subtracting your $10,000 basis from the $12,500 sales proceeds equals a $2,500 gain ($12,500 proceeds − $10,000 basis = $2,500 capital gain). FIFO is the approach you must use when you don't elect to follow one of the other IRS-sanctioned methods.

2. Specific Identification.   This tax-smart method allows you to pinpoint the shares sold to minimize your taxable gain (or widen your loss). These normally would be your most costly shares. But exercise care with this approach. If the IRS decides to investigate, you need to be able to produce adequate documentation of what you did. Before selling, you must tell your fund company that shares acquired on a specific date (or dates) are to be sold. Then, you must make sure that the company sends you satisfactory written documentation clearly identifying the shares that were sold. (Not all fund companies are equipped to do this, so make sure yours can handle such a request if you want to use the specific-identification method.)

For example, you decide to sell the 1,000 shares of ABC purchased on July 20, 1994, at $11.75. Subtracting the resulting $11,750 basis from your $12,500 sales proceeds yields a $750 gain ($12,500 proceeds − $11,750 basis = $750 capital gain). That's far below the $2,500 FIFO profit.

3. Average Cost.   As the name implies, this popular method requires that investors calculate an average cost for all their holdings in a specific fund. Many fund companies now show these calculations on shareholder statements. The average cost is simply the total of all your purchases and reinvested distributions, divided by the number of shares you own. The average cost works out to $11.08 for ABC Fund. Subtracting the $11,080 average cost basis on 1,000 shares from our $12,500 sales proceeds yields a $1,420 profit ($12,500 proceeds − $11,080 basis = $1,420 capital gain). This number falls between the gains derived by the specific-identification and FIFO methods. This average-cost approach works well when you're making systematic redemptions through a withdrawal plan. (We've illustrated the so-called "single-category" average cost method because it's the simplest and most commonly used. Larger, more active investors might prefer the "double-category" approach. Consult your tax adviser or IRS publication 564 for details.)

Once you adopt a certain cost-basis method on a particular fund, stick with it unless you obtain written permission from the IRS to change. However, you are free to use different approaches for different funds.

Tax-Free "Step-Up" in Basis

Admittedly, it's a small consolation. But at the time of a share-holder's death, mutual funds and other securities that make up the deceased investor's estate are eligible for a *tax-free "step-up" in basis*. This feature of the tax law can be very attractive for your heirs.

For example, the cost basis of an index fund is $50,000, but its fair-market value at the time of death is $90,000. Using the step-up, the new basis becomes $90,000. So your estate and heirs could escape from paying taxes on $40,000 worth of unrealized gains. Your heirs would have the option of establishing the value of the basis as of either the date of death *or* six months thereafter. The higher of the two is normally the better choice. The opportunity to reduce potential taxes makes the step-up in basis a very attractive provision for all parties concerned—except the IRS.

TRAVELER'S ADVISORY:
Avoid Wash Sales

The IRS will not allow you to deduct a loss on the sale of fund shares or other securities if you purchased substantially identical ones within 30 days before or after the sale. If, for instance, you sell 10,000 shares in ABC Small-Cap Fund to take a $3,000 loss and want to reestablish your position, you need to wait at least 31 days before doing so to avoid a so-called "wash sale."

If you don't want to wait 31 days, you can stay clear of the wash-sale rule simply by purchasing a similar fund at any time. With more than 6,000 mutual funds available, you can easily find good substitutes for any type of portfolio.

Appreciation-oriented funds that pay little or no income dividends are good investments if you want to incorporate the tax-free step-up strategy into your estate planning. Even better, you can take advantage of the automatic tax-deferral feature of index funds (see Chapter 18). If you decide not to leave your appreciated investments to any beneficiaries, you still will benefit by postponing the day of reckoning with the IRS through the build up of unrealized profits. Incidentally, variable annuities, also covered in Chapter 18, don't qualify for any tax-free step-up in basis.

Realizing Losses

No one likes losses, but sometimes they're inevitable. Fortunately, tax laws can ease the sting of market setbacks, as you can use a loss to offset either income or gains. Under current tax laws, you can use realized *net capital losses* (that is, total capital losses in excess of total capital gains) to offset ordinary income up to $3,000 a year. Suppose you have $10,000 in net capital losses. This means $3,000 could offset income in the current year, and the remaining $7,000 could be carried forward to shelter realized gains and ordinary income in future years.

Don't Buy a Tax Liability

One additional tax warning concerns year-end payments to share-holders. Mutual funds generally distribute any net-investment income and realized capital gains in December. In years when the stock market has done particularly well, the size of the capital gains can be quite large. Suppose ABC Fund with a $10 NAV distributes $1 of long-term capital gains. When ABC announces this payment, it goes *ex-distribution,* and the NAV falls by $1, plus or minus any market fluctuations that day. If you invested $10,000 in ABC at a $10 NAV before it went ex-distribution, you would receive a $1 long-term capital gains payment for each of the 1,000 shares. Assuming you were in the 28-percent federal tax bracket, you would owe $280 in taxes to Uncle Sam. However, if you had waited a few days, you could have invested at $9, obtained 1,111 rather than 1,000 shares for your $10,000 and would not have faced the $280 tax liability.

Avoiding the trap of buying a distribution can help minimize your tax bite. If you're thinking of investing in a fund toward the end of the year, be sure to call the company to find out when it will go ex-distribution and what the payout will amount to. Some funds declare semi-annual distributions, so this too is worth checking.

If you do buy shares before a distribution, it's not the end of the world. You will essentially get a benefit when you ultimately sell corresponding to the size of the distribution you paid taxes on when you bought the fund. Still, it's nice to minimize your tax bite in the current year.

Getting the Most Mileage from Tax-Efficient Portfolios

Some funds tend to spin off smaller amounts of income and gains than others. In fact, new research shows that the relative performance rankings of mutual funds can change markedly when after-tax returns are used. The differences become especially significant when returns compound over long periods. In an extreme case a portfolio might be ranked as "good" on a pre-tax basis yet "poor" after tax, or vice versa.

Tax-Adjusted Returns

Tax-efficiency has received lots of attention recently, and fund trackers such as Morningstar and Value Line now report *tax-adjusted*

FIGURE 16.2   Tax Efficiency of Selected Large Stock Funds*

Fund	Obj.**	Pre-Tax Return	Tax-Adj. Return	Tax Efficiency
Twentieth Century Ultra Investors	AG	18.78%	17.00%	90.0%
Vanguard Index 500	GI	14.05	12.17	86.6
Fidelity Magellan	G	17.95	14.88	82.9
Washington Mutual Investors	GI	13.87	11.35	81.8
Investment Company of America	GI	14.37	11.58	80.6
Janus	G	15.13	12.12	80.1
Fidelity Puritan	B	13.70	9.96	72.8
Income Fund of America	I	12.11	8.65	71.4
Vanguard Windsor	GI	13.28	9.19	69.2

Source: Reprinted by permission of Morningstar Inc. (225 W. Wacker Dr., Chicago, IL 60606).
*Average annual total returns for ten years ended 12/31/94.
**Fund Objectives: AG = aggressive growth; B = balanced; G = growth;
* GI = growth and income; I = income.*

returns for individual portfolios. To calculate its tax-adjusted results, Morningstar assumes that income and capital-gains distributions were taxed at the maximum respective federal rates each year (state and local taxes are ignored) over the time span used.

Here's an example. A fund has a 20-percent annualized pre-tax return during a five-year period. Over this time, it paid out income and capital gains, which were taxed each year. Knocking off the appropriate amount of taxes nets a 16-percent annualized tax-adjusted return. (The computation excludes any capital-gains tax effect from selling the fund at the end of the five years.) Finally, the fund's tax-adjusted return is expressed as a percentage of its pre-tax gain. This percentage depicts its *relative tax efficiency.* In our example, the relative efficiency is 80 percent (16 percent divided by 20 percent). The highest would be 100 percent, which some municipal bond funds have achieved.

The pre-tax and tax-adjusted returns for selected large stock funds appear in Figure 16.2. Your own pre-tax and after-tax results depend on when you make your initial and subsequent investments and on your personal tax circumstances. If you invest primarily in IRAs and other sheltered accounts, this and other tax angles would be significantly less important.

Funds such as Twentieth Century Ultra that pay little or no dividends tend to be more tax-efficient than more income-oriented rivals. A growth fund holding smaller stocks would be more efficient than an

---

POINTS OF INTEREST:
Charting the NAV

A rough-and-ready way to tell how tax-efficient a fund has been is to see to what extent, if any, its NAV has grown over the years. Growth funds that hold on to appreciated stocks and pay little or no income dividends can enjoy dramatic increases in their NAVs over time, because they don't pay out most of their gains and virtually all of the return comes in the form of appreciation. Conversely, income-oriented funds that realize and distribute their capital gains and pay relatively high current dividends may exhibit only a slight growth in NAV.

---

equity-income, balanced or corporate-bond fund, for example. Another factor is portfolio turnover. Even though Vanguard Index 500 has somewhat of an income tilt, it still scores highly in tax efficiency because of its minuscule turnover rate, which was 6 percent in 1994.

Is tax-efficiency something to pay attention to in the selection process? It is if you're trying to decide between two funds and need something to break a tie. However, it can be hard to identify those funds that will be efficient in the years ahead. Just like past performance, past tax efficiency is not necessarily indicative of future results. Nevertheless, it's generally smart to hold your least-efficient funds such as large-stock value portfolios within your IRA or tax-deferred retirement accounts. If the efficiency angle intrigues you, carefully consider index funds for this purpose, as discussed in Chapter 18.

Turnover Counts

Many fund managers churn their stocks at a fairly rapid rate. It's not uncommon to see 200-percent or even higher portfolio turnovers. As we saw in Chapter 4, the *portfolio turnover ratio* represents the percentage of a fund's holdings sold annually. It seems logical to assume that funds with lower trading activity are more tax-efficient. In fact, the findings of some researchers indicate that turnover must be less than 10 percent to significantly lower the tax bite. Index portfolios—many of which have minuscule turnovers of 5 percent or so—seem to be your best bet in that regard.

But turnover as an indicator of tax efficiency can be deceiving in several ways. Portfolio managers who don't trade much may have sizable amounts of built-in unrealized appreciation. When they do liquidate positions, the capital-gains distributions will be high. Also, a low-turnover stock fund could be more income-oriented, making the fund less tax-efficient in that sense, especially as income is taxed at the individual's highest rate rather than the capital-gains rate. Finally, a high turnover fund that emphasizes growth stocks with accelerating earnings and revenues may cut its losses quickly on picks that don't pan out, leading to lower capital-gains distributions and thus lower potential taxes.

However, all other factors being equal, investing in funds with relatively low turnovers still makes sense. These portfolios might not be more tax-efficient, but they certainly will have lower transaction costs and a longer-term orientation.

Capital-Gains Vulnerability

Looking to the future, Morningstar provides a "potential capital gain exposure" figure for funds it tracks. This number expresses a portfolio's unrealized capital gains as a percentage of assets. *Unrealized capital gains* are simply paper profits that could become tax liabilities when the holdings are sold. For some stock funds the potential capital-gains exposure exceeds 20 percent; a few even have readings higher than 40 percent. The larger this number, the greater your potential tax bill. However, some managers hold on to stocks with large embedded gains for years or even decades. But if a change occurs in the fund's management, objectives or philosophy, an increase in liquidations could lead to sizable distributions, possibly resulting in more taxable realized capital gains for you.

Loss Carryforwards

Conversely, you can find some funds that have *capital-loss carryforwards*. Funds do not distribute net realized losses to shareholders. Rather, they hang onto them to offset realized gains in future years. This can give investors a nice tax shelter until the loss carryforward is used up. The danger here is that funds with histories of losses may not be the best investments. You need to ask yourself whether the setbacks resulted from bad management or simply from a market or sector that performed poorly. Tax efficiency should not be the tail that wags the portfolio dog. As noted, it's best viewed as a tiebreaker when choosing among funds.

Street Smarts

To minimize the tax bite on investments not held within sheltered retirement plans or variable annuities,

1. Track your cost basis carefully so you don't overpay taxes on reinvested shares.
2. Choose an appropriate method to figure your cost basis when selling only some of your shares.
3. Don't create a tax nightmare by frequently selling bits and pieces of your funds at different prices. The exceptions here are money market funds because they maintain a stable NAV of $1.
4. Lean toward tax-efficient portfolios such as growth-stock funds with low turnover rates.

CHAPTER 17

Tax-Favored Retirement Vehicles

Inflation and taxes are two of the biggest bandits along the road to wealth. Like a pickpocket in a bus depot or airport, both can dip into your nest egg and leave you with surprisingly little money. To come out a financial winner over the long haul, you've got to overcome these two obstacles. The best way to do that is by making growth and tax deferral top priorities in your itinerary.

To maximize the long-run value of your retirement assets, you need to invest as much as you comfortably can in stock funds, including international and small-company products. At the same time, you need to organize your investments to minimize the impact of taxes. The best way to deal with taxes legally is to postpone paying them for as many years as possible. Fortunately, you have several ways to do this.

As discussed in Chapter 10, municipal-bond funds offer tax-free income but they don't provide the all-important growth dynamic of stocks. In addition, municipal-bond funds are suitable only for investments involving *after-tax dollars*. But you can sock away *pre-tax dollars* in a *qualified retirement plan* such as an employer-sponsored 401(k) or 403(b). That is, you lower your overall tax bite each year because your taxable income is reduced by the amount invested. For example, if you're in the 36-percent tax bracket, putting $1 into a pre-tax plan costs you only 64 cents in take-home pay. A so-called qualified retirement plan satisfies conditions spelled out in the Employee Retirement and Income Security Act (ERISA).

Individual Retirement Accounts (IRAs)

An IRA is a great way to start investing for the long term. Even though IRAs are the most widespread retirement plans, they nevertheless have been greatly underused. IRA investments dropped sharply after 1986, the final year when all workers could deduct as much as $2,000 in annual contributions. Any individual still can set aside as much as $2,000 each year in an IRA, but the contributions might not be deductible. The relatively low annual limits work best for younger people with modest cash amounts to invest but a lengthy savings horizon.

With IRAs, you must choose your investments. Mutual funds, banks and brokerages offer IRAs, so you have plenty of choices. You can open several different IRAs over the years if you want, but it's best to limit the number to keep things simple and hold custodial fees down.

Deductible versus Nondeductible

You might not be able to write off the amount of your IRA investment, so your IRA contributions won't necessarily reduce your taxable income, dollar for dollar. This depends on your personal situation and

---

TRAVELER'S ADVISORY:
Charting Nontaxable Amounts

Good financial housekeeping pays. Many of us have made both deductible and nondeductible IRA contributions over the years. When you withdraw cash from an IRA, your tax bill will be lower on the nondeductible contributions. It is thus important to keep good records so you don't end up paying taxes again on your after-tax investments down the road. Keep a running list of, and be able to document, your nondeductible amounts. When you make nondeductible investments, you're supposed to file IRS Form 8606 with your tax return. To help keep things simpler, we suggest that you segregate your nondeductible IRAs in accounts separate from your deductible ones. If you've done your homework carefully, you won't pay taxes on the after-tax amounts.

can change as tax laws change. To determine the current rules and how they affect you, check with your tax adviser, mutual fund company, bank or broker.

Tax-Deferred Growth

Regardless of whether or not you can take advantage of a write-off, all IRA investments grow *tax-deferred*. This means you don't have to worry about paying taxes on income and realized gains until you start to withdraw money, normally in retirement years.

How worthwhile is tax-deferral? Suppose you put $2,000 at the start of each year into an IRA, investing in an equity-income fund that has a 10-percent pre-tax and 7.5-percent tax-adjusted return, based on your tax bracket. In 25 years, you would have $216,364 in an IRA versus $146,152 in a taxable account. The difference was paid to Uncle Sam each year. So it's often a good idea to contribute to an IRA even if you must sock away nondeductible dollars. As the time horizon lengthens, tax-deferred compounding becomes an increasingly powerful force.

The Advantage of Starting Early

As with any long-term savings plan, it's best to begin an IRA as soon as you can. Alan, who is 23 years old, contributes $2,000 to his mutual fund IRA at the beginning of each of the next five years. He invests in a growth fund that returns 10 percent annually. After making five contributions, Alan stops investing and simply lets his nest egg compound tax deferred, as seen in Figure 17.1. Bob, Alan's friend who is the same age, waits until he is 28 before making any contributions. Then he invests $2,000 a year in the same fund, which continues to return 10 percent annually.

Will Bob catch up with Alan? Yes, as you can see in Figure 17.1. But Bob doesn't achieve this until 15 years after Alan made his first investment, when both men are 37. Also observe that Alan put away a total of only $10,000 over five years, whereas Bob needed to contribute $20,000 to reach the same final amount. If the growth rate for both men is increased, it would take Bob even longer to catch up with Alan. The lesson is simple: Start early, and let time work for you.

Incidentally, you can spread your IRA investments out over the year by using an *automatic investment plan* linking your bank account and mutual fund. For example, $166.66 invested monthly beginning

FIGURE 17.1   Tracking Alan and Bob's IRAs

Investor Age	Alan's Contributions	Alan's Year-End Value	Bob's Contributions	Bob's Year-End Value
23	$2,000	$2,200	$-0-	$-0-
24	2,000	4,620	-0-	-0-
25	2,000	7,282	-0-	-0-
26	2,000	10,210	-0-	-0-
27	2,000	13,431	-0-	-0-
28	-0-	14,774	2,000	2,200
29	-0-	16,252	2,000	4,620
30	-0-	17,877	2,000	7,282
31	-0-	19,664	2,000	10,210
32	-0-	21,631	2,000	13,431
33	-0-	23,794	2,000	16,974
34	-0-	26,173	2,000	20,782
35	-0-	28,791	2,000	25,159
36	-0-	31,670	2,000	29,875
37	-0-	34,837	2,000	35,062

in January equals $2,000 for the year. Many people find it easier to set the money aside in small increments than to come up with the $2,000 all at once. You need to save less than $6 a day to fully fund an IRA.

Selecting a Highway for Your IRA

In your IRA portfolio, emphasize equities as much as possible for maximum long-term growth. Stock funds are multiyear investments, after all, and so are IRAs. In addition, consider putting less tax-efficient funds into your IRA, including those that pay greater dividends such as equity-income and utility portfolios. Older investors who will be withdrawing money from their IRAs within a few years should emphasize more conservative stock and bond funds anyway.

An important advantage of IRAs is that you can choose from a range of investments, including several thousand mutual funds. Another benefit is that many fund families have lower minimum investment requirements for IRAs than they do for ordinary accounts. In many cases, a fund company that would normally insist on a $5,000 or $10,000 minimum will let investors in for $2,000 through the IRA back door.

If you want to hold funds from several different families, consider setting up an IRA with a discount brokerage such as Charles Schwab or Fidelity Investments. This will simplify your paperwork and allow you to move easily between families. It will also greatly reduce and maybe even eliminate those $10 or $20 per-account IRA fees. You also can use closed-end funds when your IRA is set up with a brokerage. Closed-end products selling at big discounts and paying large distributions are ideal for retirement investing.

Moving Your IRA

All IRAs must be established with some financial firm, such as a bank, brokerage or mutual fund family, acting as custodian. To change custodians without incurring a tax liability or IRS penalty, you have two options:

- *Indirect Rollover.* Under this option, your old custodian sends the IRA money to you, and you then must deposit it with a new firm within 60 days. The advantage of this method is that you can use the money for as long as 60 days if you need it. This makes a nice short-term loan, but be sure to reinvest the cash before your 60 days expire to avoid a substantial IRS penalty. You are allowed one such rollover every 12 months.
- *Custodian-to-custodian transfer.* This is a more efficient way to move an IRA. You simply go to your new custodian, fill out a couple of forms and request that your IRA be moved from your old custodian. The new firm takes care of all of the details—you don't even need to contact your former company. There is no limit on the number of custodian-to-custodian transfers you can make, although it's generally best to pick a good investment and stay put.

Direct Rollovers

If you've built up a tidy sum in a company retirement plan and leave your employer, you face some choices about what to do with the money. You may be able to leave the savings with the employer, assuming the company permits this. Staying put makes sense if the plan features a good selection of funds and special advantages such as an attractive borrowing option, which an IRA doesn't offer. But you also may choose to take control of the money yourself and move it into an IRA with a mutual fund family, bank or discount brokerage. This is often wiser because you can invest the cash exactly as you choose. You can park your nest egg for as long as you like in a money market fund with your new IRA custodian if you need time to choose your long-term investments.

It may make sense to open a separate or *conduit IRA* for a lump-sum rollover from an employer plan, to keep it apart from any other IRAs you may have. Why take this extra measure? Because someday you may want to roll the balance back into a future employer's plan, which you can't do if the account is mixed with other IRA money.

IRA Withdrawals

In general, IRA investing is fraught with tax obstacles, including the following:

- *If you withdraw money before age 59½, you incur a 10-percent penalty, unless you do so because you have become disabled.* In this sense, an IRA offers a form of disability insurance. As another option, you will not be liable for the 10-percent penalty if you *annuitize* your payments. That is, if you agree to

---

TRAVELER'S ADVISORY:
Avoiding Hazards En Route

Whenever you switch out of an employer retirement plan to an IRA, be careful of dangers in the form of a 20-percent withholding and a tax on premature withdrawals. To avoid these, make sure your former employer cuts a check payable to the future IRA custodian (with you named as beneficiary) and sends the balance from your account directly to that company. This is known as a transfer or *direct rollover.* Conversely, if the check is made payable and sent to you as part of a regular rollover, the IRS requires your old employer to withhold 20 percent of the amount distributed.

withdraw equal amounts each year based on your remaining life expectancy.

- *When you do make withdrawals from an IRA, the total amount is taxable to the extent you invested pre-tax dollars.* Conversely, only the earnings and appreciation would be taxable if you didn't deduct your contributions years earlier.
- *When you withdraw money, everything is taxed as income.* This means that appreciation, which would ordinarily be taxed at the more favorable capital-gains rate, will be subject to the rate on ordinary income—a major disadvantage for those in top tax brackets.
- *The best strategy is to leave money in an IRA to continue tax-deferred compounding for as long as possible.* However, you must begin withdrawing money by April 1 following the year in which you reach 70½. You must follow a schedule of minimum annual withdrawals based on your remaining life expectancy to avoid paying a penalty.
- *A 50-percent penalty applies on any "excess accumulation."* This is the difference between what you withdrew each year upon reaching 70½ and the amount the IRS determined you should have received. The systematic-withdrawal plans offered by mutual fund companies are a convenient way to receive your

---

POINTS OF INTEREST:
The "Back-Ended IRA"

At this printing, potential changes were in the works for IRAs. The so-called "back-ended IRA," popularly known as the "American Dream Savings Account," had gained strong support in Washington. Investors in a back-ended IRA would not be taxed on withdrawals of principal or earnings if the amounts remained in the account for at least five years or qualified as "special purpose distributions" for the purchase of a first home or for meeting college costs or medical expenses. But back-ended IRA contributions would not be deductible, so you could sock away after-tax dollars only. For further details, consult your mutual fund company, bank, brokerage or tax adviser.

IRA funds when you begin taking distributions. More on these plans in Chapter 19.

- *Finally, be aware of a 15-percent tax on annual "excess distributions" or withdrawals from IRAs and other tax-deferred retirement plans that exceed $150,000 in any one year.* You must total the withdrawals made from all your retirement plans to determine whether they exceed this limit.

401(k) Salary-Reduction Plans

Perhaps you have more than $2,000 to invest in an IRA. Perhaps you are getting close to retirement and need to contribute a lot more each year to meet your goals. As a supplement, consider *401(k) plans,* which more companies now offer for employees. The amount you contribute to a 401(k) doesn't show up in your gross salary, which means you pay taxes only on the amount that's left—a nice benefit. If you work for a nonprofit organization such as a public school, you can use a *403(b) plan,* which works in basically the same way.

The maximum amount you can invest in a 401(k) plan adjusts annually for inflation. Employers often limit your contributions to 15 percent or less of your gross income, so you might not be able to reach the IRS limit anyway. Typically, companies offer at least three to six investment options, including mutual funds, which means you don't have the unlimited range of choices you would have with an IRA. At the minimum, a good plan will allow you to select from among a money fund and a handful of stock and bond portfolios. You decide how to allocate your cash, and you can change your mix from time to time.

One particularly attractive feature of a 401(k) plan is that your employer may kick in some money with each contribution you make—perhaps 25 cents, 50 cents or even more for each dollar you invest. Employers do this to maintain good relations with employees and to encourage participation in the retirement plan. Be sure to take maximum advantage of this free money if you can. Incidentally, you can generally borrow against your 401(k) balance, although that depends on the plan's design. Check with your employer's benefits office for details about your plan and its features.

When you leave the company, you can transfer your 401(k) holdings directly into a conduit IRA as explained earlier, or you may have the option of putting the sum into your new employer's 401(k). Also, you may be able to leave it with your old employer, depending on the plan's policies.

Options If You're Self-Employed

Suppose you work full-time for a company and participate in its retirement plan, but you also have a side business. Or perhaps you have a small business and don't work for anyone else. In both instances you're eligible for a *simplified employee pension plan* (SEP-IRA). These plans allow participants to make tax-deductible investments and benefit from tax-sheltered compounding. They're popular among small businesses and sole proprietors looking for an economical program that's easy to set up and administer.

SEP-IRAs are like IRAs in the sense that they're self-directed and you can select from a range of mutual funds or other investments. You can sock away a lot more money with a SEP-IRA, however. If you have employees, all of them normally are required to set up an IRA, into which you as employer make contributions. They also can make their own contributions. In any year that you invest for yourself, you also must make contributions for your employees.

The SEP is by no means the only long-term investment option for a self-employed person. If you're looking for a program that offers more flexibility and allows larger annual contributions, ask the retirement-plan representatives at major mutual fund companies, brokerages or banks for details on other options. These include "profit-sharing," "money-purchase" and "paired" plans.

Street Smarts

- The best way to stretch your investment dollars is to shelter them from taxes in retirement accounts.
- Whether deductible or not, IRAs offer valuable tax-deferred compounding.
- Even better are employer-sponsored programs such as 401(k) plans, which feature current tax savings on investments along with free money in the form of employer matching contributions.
- You can maximize your investment mileage with a combination of sheltered accounts and tax-efficient growth-stock funds in taxable accounts.

CHAPTER 18

Variable Annuities and Other Tax-Efficient Packages

Some travelers like to make an extra effort, prolonging a standard package tour with some additional sightseeing on their own. So too with retirement planning. If you already have invested the maximum in an IRA and company-sponsored plan, you still have a few more options. To sock away more dollars for retirement, consider variable annuities and index funds. Both are supplemental means of achieving tax shelter.

How Variable Annuities Work

Mutual fund companies have teamed up with insurers to offer *variable annuities,* an increasingly popular product among middle-class investors. Variable annuities feature tax-deferred growth with a nominal death benefit and protection from the risk of outliving your nest egg—two insurance features. These attributes are combined with the mutual fund hallmarks of diversification, professional management, different investment choices and switching privileges.

In contrast to *fixed annuities,* which generate set yields like a certificate of deposit, the variable products generate returns that fluctuate over time. The tax-deferred nature of annuities makes them appropriate for people in the 28-percent or higher federal tax brackets. But variable annuities are more costly and less liquid investments compared with mutual funds. They are best not used until you have contributed all you can to your IRAs and company retirement plans.

Variable annuities have two distinct parts:

1. A stable of mutual funds, which are similar to the kinds of stock and bond portfolios with which you are already familiar.
2. An insurance wrapper that provides both a minimal death benefit should the contract owner die prematurely and guaranteed lifetime payments for a designated beneficiary.

The Subaccount Connection

Technically, the insurance company owns the underlying mutual funds. As a *contract owner,* you own a portion of a *subaccount,* which is used to buy an interest in the mutual fund that you select—say, an international stock portfolio. The typical annuity offers seven to ten subaccounts or fund categories, and the numbers are growing.

The subaccount forms part of the insurance company's *separate account,* which serves to channel investor money into a specific portfolio. This arrangement is necessary for a variable annuity to maintain its tax advantage. Because the separate account is independent of the general assets of the insurer, the money you allocate to the annuity is "walled off." This means your cash could not be subject to any claims of the insurance company's creditors, as are assets in the *general account.* The risk you bear reflects fluctuations in the market value of your holdings, not the insurer's creditworthiness.

Variable annuities sell *accumulation units,* which are similar to the shares of a mutual fund. Unlike a fund, a variable annuity distributes no income or capital gains so the accumulation-unit value builds up over the years. Unit prices and recent total returns for variable annuities can be found weekly in *Barron's* and quarterly in *The Wall Street Journal* under the names of their respective insurers.

Flight Insurance

A variable annuity provides a *minimal death benefit* that protects your beneficiary against any principal losses during the *accumulation phase,* when your account value builds up through portfolio earnings and any additional investments. If you die before payments begin in the *distribution phase,* your designated beneficiary would receive a death benefit equal to the amount of your total contributions (less any withdrawals) or your account's current surrender value—whichever is higher.

People generally don't purchase a variable annuity for its token death benefit. Anyone who does is reading from the wrong travel brochure. An annuity is more mutual fund than insurance, and its most important insurance attribute is tax-deferred compounding, not the death benefit, which should never be confused with life insurance. Over time, the death benefit will become irrelevant, because the value of your holding will surpass the amount you invested.

No Contribution Limits

In contrast to other retirement choices, variable annuities feature a major advantage in that the IRS imposes no limit on the amount you can contribute. You can make lump-sum investments, dollar cost average or do both. However, your contributions are not deductible, so in this sense a variable annuity bears similarities to a nondeductible IRA.

You can allocate cash among the subaccounts as you see fit and transfer money tax-free from one portfolio to another, subject to the group's switching policies. For example, you will face no switching limitations in Scudder Horizon, a no-load variable product offered by Scudder and Charter National Life Insurance Co. Horizon's investments consist of balanced, growth-and-income, capital-growth, bond, international and money market portfolios.

Horizon also offers *fixed-rate accounts* that provide a guaranteed yield and guaranteed return of principal over periods of one and three years. As entities separate from the variable annuity, fixed-rate accounts are similar to CDs, although they are not federally insured. You might use this option to lock in a fixed yield when interest rates are high. Or it could be appealing if you worry about stock and bond volatility. Because the fixed-rate option is a part of the insurance company's general account, not a subaccount, the insurance company bears the market risk, not the investor. That's why it's important to go with an insurer with a reasonably high credit standing. Because a fixed-rate account is a conservative way to invest, it is not the first place to consider. But if you do plan to use this option, make sure the yield is competitive.

A Close Look at Costs

Variable annuities have received a negative reputation for their higher ongoing expenses compared with mutual funds. The added charges pay for the insurance components. But costs vary widely among the different companies, so do some careful comparison shopping. Look at the fee tables in several prospectuses, and you will see charges listed that you would never face with an ordinary mutual fund.

Typically, annuity expenses and their usual annual ranges break down as follows:

- *Mortality and expense (M&E) risk:* 1.25 percent a year. This category consists of insurance-related charges. The *mortality* portion of the M&E fee covers the death benefit and the lifetime annuity; the *expense risk* portion guarantees that the ongoing charges will never exceed a specified amount. Higher insurance costs should entitle you to enhanced death benefits, but they don't always.
- *Insurance-company administration:* 0.15 percent. This charge covers costs such as recordkeeping and the printing and mailing of prospectuses by the insurance company.
- *Distribution:* 0 to 0.4 percent. Relatively rare now, distribution costs will probably become more common. Like the 12b-1 fees on some mutual funds, these expenses cover marketing outlays and are used to compensate salespersons.
- *Management fees and administrative costs:* 0.5 to 1.2 percent a year. These correspond to the same charges in a mutual fund. Costs vary by portfolio type and fund family. The 1.2-percent number is the typical upper limit for an international portfolio.
- *Contract maintenance charge:* $25 to $40 a year. This cost weighs more heavily on small accounts as a proportion of dollars invested.

All told, these various charges represent a modest drag compared with regular mutual funds. On a $10,000 investment in a typical domestic-stock subaccount, the annual expenses would total about 2 percent as opposed to 1.4 percent for a comparable mutual fund, according to Morningstar.

In addition to the ongoing outlays, most variable annuities impose a *surrender charge* similar to the back-end load or contingent deferred sales charge assessed by some fund companies for early withdrawals.

The amount levied depends on how long you have held your contract. In a typical case, the outlay might run 7 percent if you redeem in the first year, declining by one percentage point annually until it disappears. However, most variable annuities will allow you to withdraw as much as 10 percent of your balance each year without any surrender penalties.

Just because most annuities carry high surrender charges doesn't necessarily make them bad because these products should be held for the long term anyway. Be aware, however, that the surrender charge may be *stepped-up,* resetting the clock every time you add money to your contract. The stepped-up charge is definitely a red flag and something to avoid if possible.

Economy-Class Tickets

The variable annuities in Figure 18.1 offer relatively low costs and a variety of portfolios, including several stock choices. These annuities have no surrender charges with the exception of Fidelity, which has a charge that begins at 5 percent and drops by one percentage point annually over a five-year period, but it's not stepped up. In addition, these choices have significantly lower insurance expenses than the average product offered by a salesperson.

Destination: Growth

Your riskiest investment money belongs in your variable annuity. The higher long-term returns on aggressive-growth, small-stock and interna-

---

TRAVELER'S ADVISORY:
Excess Baggage

Some people roll distributions from employer plans into an IRA that contains a variable annuity. This is basically putting one tax-sheltered investment vehicle inside another—generally not a good idea. You're better off rolling your pension into a regular IRA mutual fund that doesn't have the higher costs associated with variable annuities.

tional funds should help offset the greater costs to a larger extent. Also, it doesn't make much sense to invest in money market and bond funds for long periods in general and particularly within annuities because the higher annual costs can take a big bite out of the modest returns generated. If you want income, you may be better off with a municipal-bond fund, for which you needn't be concerned about premature-withdrawal penalties. However, a high-yield bond portfolio could be a good choice for a portion of your annuity allocation.

The key with a variable annuity is to stay put for as many years as possible so that the advantages of tax deferral outweigh the higher costs by a wide margin. Ideally, you would compound your money on a sheltered basis for at least 20 years before making withdrawals. With most annuities, you can maintain your holdings until you reach age 85, and even longer on some newer contracts.

If you take money out before age 59½, you face a 10-percent IRS early withdrawal penalty on accumulated gains, with some exceptions. The penalty would not apply, for example, if you become disabled. After age 59½, you can take a lump-sum distribution or *annuitize*— that is, establish one of several plans for receiving periodic payments. It's generally not advisable to take a lump sum, but rather you should withdraw money gradually so that you can continue the tax-deferred compounding for as long as possible. As an alternative both to taking a lump sum or annuitizing, you can simply withdraw money from your annuity whenever the need arises in retirement.

FIGURE 18.1   Selected Low-Cost Variable Annuities

Annuity	No. of Funds	Annual Insurance Expenses	Minimum Initial Investment	Toll-Free Number
Fidelity Retirement Reserves	10	1.00	2,500	800-544-2442
Janus Retirement Advantage	8	0.85	1,000	800-504-4440
T. Rowe Price No-Load Variable Annuity	5	0.55	10,000	800-469-5304
Schwab Investment Advantage	16	0.85	5,000	800-838-0650
Scudder Horizon Plan	6	0.70	2,500	800-225-2470
USAA Life Variable Annuity	8	1.05	1,000	800-531-8000
Vanguard Variable Annuity	7	0.53	5,000	800-522-5555

Cash-Withdrawal Options

If you choose an annuitization plan after age 59½, you have some flexibility. A given product may offer either fixed or variable annuitization, or a choice between the two. In the variable situation, the size of your payments will depend in part on your investment performance.

Here are four common annuity-payout options:

1. *Fixed period.* You receive monthly, quarterly, semi-annual or annual payments over a predetermined period of years.
2. *Lifetime income.* As the name implies, the cash stream, which begins when you annuitize, stops when you die. There won't be any balance left for your heirs. In part, the M&E fees pay for the lifetime-income guarantees provided by the insurance company. This option, which appeals to many single individuals with limited income, generally furnishes more cash than the other lifetime plans. The risk is that you could die much earlier than anticipated and the balance in the account would go to the insurance company.
3. *Life with period certain.* This option can offer you greater peace of mind. You receive income for the rest of your life, but in the event that you die before receiving a minimum number of guaranteed payments, your beneficiary gets the remaining balance. Life with period certain is probably the most popular option for this reason, but its payments would generally be smaller than those on a straight lifetime plan.
4. *Joint and survivor.* Popular with couples, this option produces a stream of payments until the last spouse dies. When one person dies, the survivor receives a predetermined percentage of the original payment, such as 50, 67 or 100 percent. A life with period certain option also is available with the joint and survivor plan. This can be beneficial for heirs if both parties die prematurely.

During the so-called distribution phase, all earnings received will be taxed at your ordinary income rate, rather than the 28-percent capital-gains rate. This is a negative for people in higher brackets and will become an even bigger drawback if the maximum capital gains rate is reduced further, as expected. In addition, if you die your variable annuity would pass to your heirs, but they would not benefit from the tax-free step-up in basis discussed in Chapter 16. This means your heirs would have to pay taxes on all accumulated annuity earnings and gains. For this reason, an index fund or individual stocks could be preferable.

Doing Your Homework

Analyzing a variable annuity is similar to researching a regular mutual fund, but you should do a more thorough job because you're dealing with a far more complex product and making a long-term commitment. You want an annuity that offers a sufficiently wide assortment of stock portfolios with respectable performances and low costs.

Read the prospectus and shareholder reports carefully. *Morningstar Variable Annuities/Life,* published biweekly, covers several dozen variable annuities in depth and features full-page profiles on each subaccount. Also, find out about your state's laws. A handful of states impose *premium taxes* on variable annuities ranging up to 3 percent.

Changing Contracts

Unlike diamonds, variable annuities don't last forever, and you don't even have to stick with one until retirement age. By using a so-called *1035 exchange,* you can move your nest egg from one annuity group to another without tax consequences. When making a 1035 exchange, you must transfer the entire cash value from your old contract to your new annuity. You may incur a surrender charge when you leave your existing group. A 1035 transfer normally takes between three and eight weeks, depending on the company sending the money. (Excluding mail time, your assets normally earn interest and dividends during this period.) Also keep in mind that you normally have ten days after receiving a newly issued contract to make sure it's what you expected. This is known as your *free-look period.* If you're dissatisfied for any reason, you can immediately cancel with no surrender charges.

Alternative Accommodations: Variable Life

Variable annuities are sometimes confused with *variable life* contracts, a not-so-distant relative. A hybrid of insurance and mutual funds, variable life products work much like annuities but with a far greater insurance component. Essentially, you're buying life insurance and investing the cash value of your policy in mutual funds or subaccounts, as with variable annuities. You may be allowed to decide how the cash value will be allocated among available portfolios and when to switch among your options. In contrast with the minimal death benefit of a variable annuity, the death benefit in a variable life policy can be many times the amount of money you've invested. Actually, the death benefit depends in large part on the performance of your selected investment portfolios, giving the policy speculative overtones.

With variable life, your annual premiums are fixed. Conversely, *variable universal life* combines the flexible premiums allowed under the highly successful universal life with the investment selection you get with variable life. Some insurance companies allow you to negotiate a schedule of premium payments. In the future, your premiums could be fully covered by the earnings on your subaccount. Because both premiums and investments can change, this is a highly malleable product. Make sure you understand the market-related risks if you expect to count on it for your family's insurance protection.

Like variable annuities, variable life and variable universal life offer tax-deferred compounding until your money is withdrawn. Following the Tax Reform Act of 1986, these products remain among the few tax-advantaged investments left. They are significantly more complex than variable annuities, but may offer some advantages to astute, affluent investors. Specifically, if certain conditions are met, you can borrow a large percentage of the cash value of your policy tax free and at a low cost. If you have questions on these insurance products, contact a knowledgeable agent or financial planner in whom you have confidence.

Tax-Efficient Index Funds

As discussed in Chapter 5, index funds rank among our favorite investments because they will predictably beat most actively managed funds with their low costs and fully invested portfolios. An added plus, of which many people are unaware, is their tax efficiency.

We've already discussed municipal-bond funds as income vehicles to hold outside your tax-sheltered retirement plans. However, it's important to have an equity component for long-term growth. Index funds can fill the gap. The very low portfolio turnovers on these investments—often less than 5 or 10 percent—reflect the fact that they don't sell off holdings often. This means they don't realize and distribute much in the way of taxable gains.

A true index fund will sell securities in only two situations:

1. To remove a stock that has been dropped from the index, which happens once in a while.

2. To raise cash to meet redemption requests, which occur in a market downturn. True index funds stay close to 100 percent invested to track their benchmarks as closely as possible, so a prolonged slump could entail a fair amount of selling.

Some index portfolios have been introduced with a specific goal of being tax-efficient. Essentially, they try to control their capital gains a little more than a regular index product would, by giving their managers more leeway. When selling securities, the manager may offset a gain by realizing a paper loss on another position, for instance. Or the manager could build in a little cash as a cushion for redemptions. A tax-managed fund would not parallel the performance of its benchmark as closely as a pure index portfolio.

The Vanguard Tax-Managed Fund consists of three low-cost portfolios, of which you can select any or all. The Growth & Income Portfolio targets the S&P 500, the Capital Appreciation Portfolio invests in a sample of low yielding stocks from the Russell 1000, and the Balanced Portfolio maintains an approximately equal split between an actively managed mix of intermediate-term municipal bonds and a passive compilation of Russell 1000 stocks. These three portfolios may appeal to long-term investors who want the most tax-efficient index route possible.

A further way Vanguard attempts to minimize taxes on these funds is by charging a 2-percent redemption fee for shares held less than one year and 1 percent for investors selling within one and five years. These charges are used to discourage short-term trading, which could force the fund to unload shares and realize and distribute capital gains. The money from the fees goes back into the portfolios and helps to cover redemption-related transaction costs, including tax expenses.

Other tax-efficient index portfolios include Schwab 1000 and Schwab Small-Cap Index. These funds attempt to match the investment performance of the 1,000 largest domestic companies and the second 1,000 largest firms, respectively. The two portfolios impose a 0.5-percent redemption fee on shares sold within six months of purchase.

POINTS OF INTEREST:
Mixing Stocks and Funds

One reason to own individual stocks together with mutual funds involves tax deferral. You can hold stocks for many years with minimal tax consequence—you need to be concerned about dividends only. With a buy-and-hold strategy, any appreciation goes untaxed until you ultimately sell the stock, when you would pay taxes at the generally more favorable capital gains rate. To minimize the tax bite on income over the years, lean toward quality stocks that pay small dividends.

Street Smarts

IRAs and company retirement plans go only so far in providing tax shelter because of limits on the amount of cash that you can invest in these vehicles. For additional relief, consider variable annuities and even variable life contracts—diversified investment portfolios in an insurance wrapper. For a simpler sheltering angle, lean toward index funds, which don't pass much in the way of taxable gains to shareholders because they hang on to most holdings for many years. Taxes can crimp an investment plan, much like bad weather can spoil a vacation. But unlike the weather, you can do something about the tax bite on a portfolio.

CHAPTER 19

Navigating the Investment Waters in Retirement

You want your voyage through the seas of your golden years to be as smooth as possible. Because a reasonably healthy 65-year-old can now expect to live for 20 years or more, and a younger retiree can spend as many as 30 or so years in retirement, your income needs to last.

The typical retiree should aim for a low-volatility investment mix that generates growth and income. That's a tall order to fill because the journey to growth is inevitably a rocky one. Nevertheless, the appreciation component is necessary because today's longer life spans mean that people have a much lengthier investment horizon.

The long-run total return on large stocks has averaged about 10 percent; 60 to 70 percent of that consists of growth and the other 30 to 40 percent, income. Bond and cash investments provide more income but little or no growth. To achieve both along with low volatility, a retiree has to put together an appropriate mix of funds from all three categories.

Mapping Out Your Itinerary

The portfolios of retirees can differ considerably. Here are four important questions you need to consider:

1. *What's your time frame?* A healthy 55-year-old couple obviously needs a radically different asset mix than an 85-year-old man or woman.

2. *What's your primary objective: growth, income or some combination?* Younger retirees may opt for conservative growth if they have sufficient income and liquidity from other sources.
3. *What's your risk tolerance?* Older individuals tend to be far less accepting of volatility than younger ones. Review Chapter 2 to evaluate your risk tolerance.
4. *Do you want to expand your portfolio for your heirs?* Even if you have ample income and liquidity to meet day-to-day and emergency needs, you also may want to continue to build up a

---

TRAVELER'S ADVISORY:
Don't Neglect Estate Planning

Your estate includes everything you own—all the wealth you have worked so hard to build over the years. If you die without an estate plan, you could saddle your heirs with complex legal problems and tax burdens. In addition, your assets might not be distributed as you had intended. Many middle-class people have sufficiently small estates so they don't need to worry about estate taxes. But when such taxes are triggered, the bite begins at 37 percent and up to 55 percent for multimillion-dollar fortunes.

A careful estate plan will minimize taxes and allow you to pass property to your intended beneficiaries. Many people include their mutual funds and other assets in a *revocable living trust,* a highly flexible arrangement that allows wealth to pass to heirs without going through probate. You can use a living trust in conjunction with various tax-reducing techniques to minimize the estate tax bite. In addition, you can distribute the assets from a trust as gifts to your loved ones over the years if you so choose.

Estate planning is a highly personal and complex process. IRAs, charitable gifts, wills and living trusts each involve different legal twists and turns. In addition, your mutual fund accounts must be titled correctly if you hope to bequeath assets as intended. View estate planning as getting ready for the last stop on the investment road.

large chunk of assets by investing in growth-oriented stock funds.

Finding the Right Bond Investments

Because interest-rate risk can pose big problems, we advise retirees to stick with intermediate rather than long-term bond portfolios. The former likely will deliver 80 percent or more of the return with only two-thirds to half the volatility. Always check the durations of your bond funds to make sure that they are not too lengthy. Duration is the best gauge of a portfolio's interest-rate sensitivity and usually can be obtained by asking a fund company's telephone reps. To play it safe, stick with bond funds that have durations under 8. Chapter 10 covers duration and interest-rate risk.

Also keep in mind that high-yield bond funds have less interest-rate risk than government and muni-bond portfolios because the prices of lower-rated bonds depend more on the financial health of the issuer and the strength of the economy. Junk bonds do particularly well when the economy is in an expansion phase, even though interest rates may be creeping upward.

Tax-exempt funds play a big role in the portfolios of many older individuals. Retirees often invest heavily in bonds, so they should devote special care to determining their split between taxable- and tax-exempt products. Review Chapter 10 to figure out your taxable-equivalent yields.

Mortgage-Backed Portfolios

Mortgage-backed securities, such as Ginnie Maes, also are popular with retirees because they provide high monthly payouts at relatively low risk. The American Association of Retired Persons (AARP) hired Scudder to manage a special stable of conservative portfolios under the AARP banner with individuals older than 50 in mind. By far the most popular AARP portfolio is the GNMA & U.S. Treasury Fund. Each payment on a mortgage security consists of principal, in addition to interest, so it's important to realize that these investments are self-liquidating.

Mortgage-backed portfolios tend to do best in a stable interest-rate environment. During a sustained period of declining rates, this group is plagued by *prepayment risk,* as homeowners refinance their mortgages. This results in early repayment of principal to bond holders, who must reinvest their proceeds at lower yields. Conversely, when rates rise these portfolios are subject to a moderate amount of interest-rate risk.

Are Short-Term Bond Funds the Way To Go?

During times of rising interest rates, investors in money market funds and T-bills can do very well because maturing short-term debt instruments can be rolled over into newly issued securities bearing higher yields. In fact, cash represents the perfect short-term inflation hedge (although it does terribly in this regard over the long run). The shorter the maturity, the better if rates are rising sharply. Federal regulations require a money market fund to keep its average maturity to 90 days or less, even though it may own some investments that come due as far off as 13 months. This does not mean the fund will liquidate in 90 days, of course, as maturing holdings are continually reinvested.

However, if any rise in rates is gradual, short-term bond funds can do even better. Short-term portfolios generally offer significantly higher yields while exposing you to a modest amount of interest-rate risk. So unlike a money fund, they can generate small gains and losses. Short-term funds invest in government, corporate and municipal IOUs with maturities beyond 13 months.

Before you invest in a short-term bond product, call the fund company and ask for the duration, which normally ranges from one to three years for funds in this category. If interest rates shoot up a full percentage point—a fairly substantial rise—a short-term portfolio with a duration of one would decline about 1 percent; a duration of three would lead to a 3 percent fall.

The best short-term bond and money funds have no sales charges and have rock-bottom expense ratios, because their yields are typically slim to begin with and every bit of economizing makes a difference. If you're uncertain about the direction of interest rates—which you should be because they're extremely difficult to predict—it's best to hold both money market and short-term bond funds. Retirees often keep a larger slice of their nest eggs in the former, so it's important to be aware of the possible advantages you can gain by raising your stake in the latter.

Finding the Right Stock Funds

A big challenge for many retirees is simply getting used to owning volatile investments. These people should consider conservative stock selections, such as those in the equity-income or growth-and-income categories. Examples include AARP Growth & Income, Fidelity Equity-Income II, Lindner and T. Rowe Price Equity-Income.

Utility and energy funds also make worthy choices. Utility funds generally are dependable income producers, although they expose you to interest-rate risk much like long-term bonds. Still, we favor them over bond funds because they offer the growth characteristic of stocks. Utilities can raise the rates consumers are charged so that they can gradually increase their dividends to help investors keep pace with inflation.

A portion of your stock allocation might go into an index fund like the Vanguard Index 500 or the Vanguard Index Total Stock Market portfolios. Balanced funds, which hold a mix of bonds and stocks, also fit nicely in retiree portfolios. Good choices here include Dodge & Cox Balanced, Vanguard Balanced Index, Vanguard Wellesley Income and USAA Balanced, which takes the unusual approach of holding municipal bonds for its fixed-income component. The Balanced portfolio of Vanguard's Tax-Managed Fund is a tax-efficient choice that invests in municipal bonds in addition to a passively managed mix of stocks.

International diversification also rates as an important feature for retirees, although you probably would not want a direct stake in an emerging-markets fund. A solid foreign-stock product that emphasizes larger non–U.S. companies—like T. Rowe Price International, Scudder International or Warburg Pincus International Equity—would round out a portfolio nicely.

But be careful of volatile aggressive-growth, sector and single-country funds. Such products are best avoided, as you may not have time to recoup large losses. Even people in their 20s and 30s who invest in these types of funds should limit their allocation to a modest amount.

Systematic Withdrawal Plans for Smooth Sailing

How can retirees collect income while keeping their portfolios on a growth track? One way is by investing a substantial amount in conservative-stock funds and setting up a systematic withdrawal program.

These plans are useful if you want to receive regular monthly or quarterly checks. The specifics of withdrawal programs depend on a variety of factors such as your age, total investments, other sources of income and whether you want to preserve a substantial nest egg for your heirs.

For people who expect to be drawing out money over a decade or longer, the use of conservative equity funds can lead to the best results. In fact, withdrawals over an extended period can seriously deplete a bond fund. For bond investors, it's better to cash only the monthly dividend checks and not disturb the principal.

Growth-and-income, equity-income and balanced funds with 50 percent or more of their holdings in stocks make ideal withdrawal-plan candidates because they tend to be the most stable categories in the appreciation arena. Because such income-oriented equity products may not yield sufficient dividends to meet your needs, you may have to dip into the principal. But your capital can still grow if your withdrawal rate is not excessive.

Volatile aggressive-growth and sector funds such as gold portfolios don't make good candidates for withdrawal plans, despite their appreciation potential. These choices can plunge as fast as they can surge. Withdrawing money after your account has taken a dive obviously can lead to problems.

Crunching the Numbers

When establishing a withdrawal program, you need to come to grips with three factors that will influence the amount of money you can take out:

1. Your fund's expected total return
2. Your anticipated rate of inflation
3. Your target withdrawal percentage

The best way to plan your future withdrawal stream is to make some projections, perhaps with the help of a computerized spreadsheet. You can get a good estimate of how long your capital will last under different assumptions by figuring annual redemptions, even though you may want to take out cash more frequently. It's critical to stick with realistic assumptions—you don't want to deplete your nest egg too soon.

A Couple's Spreadsheet

Suppose a husband and wife in their early 70s have $500,000 invested in an equity-income portfolio. They want to cut back gradually on their stock allocation over the next decade by making systematic annual withdrawals. They assume the following conditions:

- Inflation of 4 percent
- A portfolio that returns 10 percent
- An initial withdrawal rate of 12 percent

Money will be taken out at the beginning of each year, with the first withdrawal occurring immediately. Each subsequent withdrawal will be increased by the 4-percent inflation factor. Figure 19.1 traces year-by-year their rising cash outflows and declining balances. As you can see, the couple's capital will last for a little more than ten years. Of course, their fund could return much less than 10 percent over the next decade, in which case they would run out of cash sooner.

How Long Will Your Money Last?

If the rate at which you take out cash exceeds your fund's total return, you eventually will run out of money. Figure 19.2 shows roughly how many years your principal will last given various annual returns generated by your fund and different withdrawal rates. To be as conservative as possible, we recommend that you use the projected *real return,* which is simply the anticipated performance in today's dollars (the *nominal return*) minus the expected inflation rate.

The numbers in the body of the table are conservative estimates because they assume beginning-of-year withdrawals. The first annual

FIGURE 19.1   A Couple's Withdrawal-Plan Worksheet

Year	Withdrawal	Year-End Balance	Year	Withdrawal	Year-End Balance
1997	$60,000	$484,000	2002	$72,999	$328,914
1998	62,400	463,760	2003	75,919	278,295
1999	64,896	438,750	2004	78,956	219,273
2000	67,492	408,384	2005	82,114	150,874
2001	70,192	372,012	2006	85,399	72,023

redemption would occur immediately. When a portfolio's return exceeds the withdrawal percentage by a sufficient amount, you could continue to take out money for an indefinite period. Asterisks in the table denote these happy instances.

Finding the Best Withdrawal Rate

Figure 19.2 also can help you determine an appropriate withdrawal rate, based on how long your nest egg must last. First, decide how many years you think that you will require income. Suppose you will need to tap the account for at least 20 years, during which you expect 4-percent inflation and anticipate investment returns of 9 percent a year, in nominal terms. This translates into a real, or inflation-adjusted, return of 5 percent.

So how much can you safely withdraw? Find 5 percent in the "annual return" column. Now look to the right for the figure that comes closest to your 20-year holding period. As you can see, 23 years is in the 7 percent column, so you could withdraw up to 7 percent of your initial capital in constant dollars, in which case your principal should hold out for 23 years. It would be safer to withdraw a bit less than 7 percent to provide some margin for error. If you want the cash to last longer, reduce your withdrawals.

FIGURE 19.2   How Many Years Your Capital Can Last

Annual Return	Annual Withdrawal Rate*							
	5%	6%	7%	8%	9%	10%	11%	12%
1%	22	18	15	13	11	10	9	8
2	25	19	16	14	12	11	9	9
3	29	22	18	15	13	11	10	9
4	37	26	20	16	14	12	10	9
5	62	32	23	18	15	13	11	10
6	**	49	28	21	17	14	12	10
7	**	**	40	25	19	15	13	11
8	**	**	**	33	22	17	14	12
9	**	**	**	**	28	20	16	13
10	**	**	**	**	**	25	18	14

*Assumes withdrawals are made annually at the start of the year.
**Capital will last indefinitely in these scenarios.

Conversely, you could take out an increasing percentage of your account balance each year to liquidate it over a fixed period. You may be required to use this approach when making withdrawals from an IRA or other tax-qualified retirement plan. Specifically, after age 70½ you must cash out a minimum dollar amount annually, based on your life expectancy, or face a penalty tax. Consult IRS tables to determine this minimum required distribution.

Reallocating Your Assets

It's important to rebalance your portfolio at least every few years when following a systematic withdrawal program. As you grow older you may want to gradually cut back on your stock holdings. Figure 19.3 shows how a retired couple might reallocate their portfolio every five years. The numbers in each column represent percentages of the investment pie. Each column totals 100 percent.

Steering Your Investments to Safe Harbors

Many retirees take very good care of their investments. They have the time, energy and enthusiasm to devote to financial matters that they may not have had in their younger years. Perhaps you already are an astute market watcher. If not, let the following tips guide your decisions:

- *Make sure you have adequate emergency reserves.* Keep this money separate from your long-term investment portfolio so

FIGURE 19.3   Age-Specific Portfolio Allocations

Portfolio Category	Age Group					
	60	**65**	**70**	**75**	**80**	**85**
International stock	10%	10%	5%	5%	0%	0%
Growth	20	10	5	0	0	0
Equity income	30	30	35	35	35	25
Intermediate-term bond	20	25	25	25	25	20
Short-term bond	10	15	15	20	20	25
Money market	10	10	15	15	20	30

you won't be forced to liquidate stock or bond funds when they might happen to be depressed. As a rough rule of thumb, retirees and everyone else should have cash assets amounting to at least three months' living expenses.

- *Make sure you have adequate inflation protection.* Many people live a lot longer than they expect, and some folks spend as much as a third of their lives in retirement. The younger the age at which you stop working, the more you need stock funds. An affluent retired couple in their 50s might earmark 75 percent of their allocation to stock funds.

- *Don't stop investing when you enter retirement.* You may still have two or three decades to work with—practically an eternity in the financial markets.

- *Pay attention to estate planning as soon as possible.* Decide on a will and perhaps even a living trust or more complex arrangement. Review wills and living trusts every two years or when major changes occur in estate-tax laws, your personal situation or that of your beneficiaries. Don't forget gifts as an estate-planning tool. Giving money to children, grandchildren and others during your retirement years can be a wonderful experience and can help reduce the value of your taxable estate.

- *Let your tax-sheltered retirement nest egg compound as long as possible, drawing on amounts in taxable accounts first.* This means you might not want to touch your IRA or other tax-deferred plans before you must at age 70½. Variable annuities allow you to delay withdrawals until age 85, if not longer.

- *When you cash out of a retirement account or annuity, consider systematic withdrawals rather than a lump sum.* That way, you get a lot more tax deferral. Review the different options for withdrawing money and carefully determine what's best for you. You may want to consult a tax adviser or financial planner about this, especially when taking money out of an employer-sponsored plan.

- *Simplify your portfolio.* This will make it easier to withdraw cash and help you minimize paperwork and tax recordkeeping. For example, if you hold a half dozen IRAs, you may want to reduce the number to one or two. Of course, always keep your deductible and nondeductible IRAs separate.

- *Tap mutual fund companies for helpful pamphlets regarding retirement.* T. Rowe Price, Vanguard, Fidelity and Scudder's AARP program are among the fund groups with useful guides.

Street Smarts

Retirement can be a great time to travel or invest. Many retirees have enough assets to build nicely diversified portfolios. Most also can plan on living many more years, so they don't have to stick with fixed-income investments. In fact, you can tap a portfolio of conservative stock funds for a decade or two through a systematic withdrawal plan. If there's one common mistake retirees make, it's playing too safely.

CHAPTER 20

Getting on the Right Road to College

Most people traveling to Europe for the first time concentrate on the major destinations. They visit London and Paris, for example, while leaving Wales and Brittany for a return trip. There's only so much time in anyone's travel plans, after all, and you have to hit the highlights first.

So too with finances. Most people rank retirement planning as their top investment goal, for fear of becoming penniless in their old age. But preparing for a child's college education is another popular investment destination for people who can afford to do both. And just like saving for retirement, the earlier you begin the better. You can start contributing to a college kitty shortly after a child's birth, thereby allowing the powerful force of compounding to work harder for you.

Over the past decade, college tuition and fees have grown at a pace well above the inflation rate. Unfortunately, federal financial aid for students has not kept up. Although it's impossible to predict future college costs with any degree of accuracy, parents should plan on continuing escalation, to be safe. To complicate the forecasting process, different components of education costs (tuition and fees, food, housing, transportation, books, supplies and computers) increase at different rates. Parents who want to plan ahead should assume that tuition and fees will increase at 7 to 8 percent a year—a faster clip than the most likely overall inflation rate.

Estimating Future Costs

The first step in planning for a child's college education is to identify how much the schooling may cost when the time finally arrives. This depends on which school your child will be attending—something you often can't predict. Nonetheless, you need some ballpark figures to work with. Big variations exist, of course, in tuition and fees for private institutions—from less than $5,000 a year to more than $20,000. The costs run considerably less for a public college, especially if your child can commute from home.

The factors in Figure 20.1 can help you estimate future college expenses, given your projected inflation rate and the number of years until your child enrolls. Suppose your daughter is now five and you hope to send her to a private college that currently charges tuition and fees of $10,000. You expect her to begin college in 13 years, when she is 18, and you project an 8 percent inflation rate for tuition and fees.

How much will each of her four years of college cost? Simply multiply the $10,000 present expense by each of the 8 percent factors in rows 13 through 16 of Figure 20.1.

Year	Tuition
1	$27,200
2	29,400
3	31,700
4	34,300
Subtotal	$122,600

The costs for the four years total $122,600. And that's just for tuition and fees! But when you project room and board, books and supplies and other expenses, you may get by with applying a more modest inflation factor.

Room and board outlays could be determined by contacting schools that your child may attend. Find out the costs of both apartments and dormitories. The colleges may also provide ballpark figures for the annual costs of books and supplies, which is a minor portion of the total. If your child may attend a distant school, figure in the costs of air transportation as well.

Returning to our example, you estimate $7,000 per year for room and board and other expenses currently. You project a more modest 4 percent inflation for this set of costs. Because your child will begin college in 13 years, you multiply the $7,000 by each of the 4 percent factors in rows 13 through 16 of Figure 20.1.

Year	Expenses Other Than Tuition
1	$11,690
2	12,110
3	12,600
4	13,090
Subtotal	$49,490
Plus Tuition	122,600
Total	$172,090

These other expenses for the four years total $49,490. Adding this sum to the $122,600 tuition-and-fees figure equals a grand total of $172,090 for your child's four years of college.

It's certainly difficult to know where a newborn might go to school 18 years down the road, but starting to save modest amounts when the child is very young can really boost the value of your college kitty over time. If you have more than one child, it's especially important to plan carefully.

FIGURE 20.1   The Inflation Factor

	Projected Annual Inflation Rate						
Years	4%	5%	6%	7%	8%	9%	10%
1	1.04	1.05	1.06	1.07	1.08	1.09	1.10
2	1.08	1.10	1.12	1.14	1.17	1.19	1.21
3	1.12	1.16	1.19	1.23	1.26	1.30	1.33
4	1.17	1.22	1.26	1.31	1.36	1.41	1.46
5	1.22	1.28	1.34	1.40	1.47	1.54	1.61
6	1.27	1.34	1.42	1.50	1.59	1.68	1.77
7	1.32	1.41	1.50	1.61	1.71	1.83	1.95
8	1.37	1.48	1.59	1.72	1.85	1.99	2.14
9	1.42	1.55	1.69	1.84	2.00	2.17	2.36
10	1.48	1.63	1.79	1.97	2.16	2.37	2.59
11	1.54	1.71	1.90	2.10	2.33	2.58	2.85
12	1.60	1.80	2.01	2.25	2.52	2.81	3.14
13	1.67	1.89	2.13	2.41	2.72	3.07	3.45
14	1.73	1.98	2.26	2.58	2.94	3.34	3.80
15	1.80	2.08	2.40	2.76	3.17	3.64	4.18
16	1.87	2.18	2.54	2.95	3.43	3.97	4.59
17	1.95	2.29	2.69	3.16	3.70	4.33	5.05
18	2.03	2.41	2.85	3.38	4.00	4.72	5.56
19	2.11	2.53	3.03	3.62	4.32	5.14	6.12
20	2.19	2.65	3.21	3.87	4.66	5.60	6.73
21	2.28	2.79	3.40	4.14	5.03	6.11	7.40
22	2.37	2.93	3.60	4.43	5.44	6.66	8.14

Getting Started

One way to begin merely involves saving money as part of your own portfolio. This approach allows you to retain complete control over the funds—and if your child ultimately decides to head for the Navy or a local trade school instead of Princeton, you still have the money. The disadvantage of investing in your own name is that the investment earnings will be taxed at your higher rate rather than at the minor's lower bracket.

Custodial Accounts

As an alternative, you can establish a mutual fund account in your child's or grandchild's name, with you or another adult named as custodian. The first step is to get a Social Security card for your youngster. Depending on your state's laws, you would set up either a Uniform Gifts to Minor Act (UGMA) or Uniform Transfers to Minor Act (UTMA) account. Keep in mind that you are making an irrevocable gift, so you can't legally get the money back. Under current law, you can give as much as $10,000 a year to as many people as you choose with no gift-tax consequences. You and your spouse can jointly transfer as much as $20,000 to each person.

Some fund companies allow you to start a custodial account for less than their typical minimum investments. For example, Fidelity will reduce its usual $2,500 minimum to $1,000 for custodial investors in the Asset Manager, Blue Chip Growth, Growth & Income and Puritan portfolios. In addition, Fidelity will waive the normal 3-percent loads on its Blue Chip Growth and Growth & Income funds (the other two are no-load anyway). Other families with lower custodial-account minimums include Founders, Janus, & Babson, Neuberger & Berman, Scudder, Strong, T. Rowe Price, Twentieth Century and Vanguard. Fund companies also may waive their minimums if you agree to sign up for an automatic investment plan, in which you deposit $25, $50, or $100 into the account each month.

Twentieth Century also offers a program for custodial accounts in which it will automatically begin to shuttle your money from its Select Investors stock portfolio into a money fund as your child gets closer to college age. The amount transferred depends on the number of years over which you want the reallocation to occur.

As custodian in any of the preceding programs, you would have responsibility for investing the money prudently. Because a gift is irrevocable, the child would gain control of the funds when he or she becomes 18 or 21 years old depending on your state's laws. That means you can't stop him or her from spending the money on cars, clothes and even travel rather than schooling.

The "Kiddie Tax"

Tax planning is important if you place the investments in a custodial account. In particular, you need to understand how the *kiddie tax* works. Under age 14, a child's *passive income*—that is, dividends, interest and gains—is treated as follows:

- The first $650 of annual income and gains is tax free.
- The next $650 is taxed at the child's rate, usually 15 percent.
- Income and gains above $1,300 are taxed at the parents' marginal rate, which could expose a large college kitty to heavy taxation.

The situation improves when the child turns 14, because all income and gains more than $650 are taxed at the child's own rate, usually 15 percent. These rules were in effect in 1995 and are subject to change.

Make sure that the portfolio earnings for a child younger than 14 aren't so big that your own higher rate kicks in. The government wants to discourage parents from passing along lots of investments to their kids, thereby sheltering the income from considerably higher taxes. However, for college accounts under $10,000 or so, you don't have to be too concerned about a higher tax rate being applied.

One way to deal with the tax problem for younger children is to invest in a tax-efficient index fund, such as some of the products available from Vanguard or Schwab. In addition, you might keep a portion of the portfolio in municipal-bond funds, although you would be forsaking the greater growth potential of stock-market products.

Planning a College Portfolio

The type of investment plan you devise for a child depends largely on when you begin saving. We generally can break a college investment program into three age-specific phases:

Newborn to Age 5. During your child's younger years, go for maximum capital appreciation. Suitable funds include small-company, mid-cap and large-cap growth. Some international exposure also is desirable in case foreign stocks fare better than domestic during your investment period. Tax-efficient index portfolios could be attractive. For one-stop diversification, you might use a product like Fidelity Asset Manager Growth, T. Rowe Price Spectrum Growth or Vanguard Star LifeStrategy Growth.

By starting early on a newborn's college account, you may be able to get away with investing as little as $25 or $50 a month. For example, if

---

POINTS OF INTEREST:
Twentieth Century Giftrust

Twentieth Century, one of the larger no-load fund complexes, offers a unique twist for individuals who wish to give money to a person or charity: Twentieth Century Giftrust Investors, an aggressive-growth portfolio. Lipper ranked it the number one mutual fund performer over the decade ended December 31, 1994.

You can open a Giftrust account with as little as $250 and make subsequent investments of at least $50 whenever you choose. Your gifts are irrevocable, however. Every account must stay in force at least 10 years or until the child reaches the age of majority, whichever is longer. When you establish the trust, you must specify its duration. A lengthy horizon generally is desirable for capital growth. Donors can specify even longer periods, perhaps earmarking Giftrust for the stage in life when the child is likely to purchase a home. You also can set up accounts for the benefit of other adults.

Taxes are paid directly from assets in the trust account each year, based on the applicable trust rate. The tax situation becomes considerably more complex if the trust remains in operation after the child reaches 21 years. Once the trust terminates, the beneficiary may have to pay some additional taxes on the account's earnings.

you commit $25 at the beginning of each month to a stock fund that returns 10 percent annually, your college kitty would amount to nearly $9,200 after 14 years, which could be more than adequate if you plan to send your son or daughter to a public school near home.

Age 6 to 12. Make gradual changes during this intermediate phase. Long-term growth should still be your goal, with most of the portfolio in small-cap, mid-cap and international funds. However, as your son or daughter gets closer to age 12, shift toward income and growth.

Age 13 to 18. With five years or less until your child graduates from high school, you wouldn't want to gamble with an excessively large stake in growth-oriented funds. The emphasis should shift to income and capital preservation. Low-duration bond funds and money market portfolios might be suitable for much of the portfolio. If you are in a high-tax bracket and want to retain control of how the money is spent, consider using an intermediate-term municipal bond fund in your own name.

When your child gets to within a year of college, transfer to a money fund all the cash you'll need to meet the first year's costs. Preservation of capital is paramount now. Cash required for the next three years could be held primarily in short-term bond portfolios to garner higher yields than you could realize from a money fund.

A Passport for Your Child's Golden Years

College normally ranks as the top priority when you establish a savings program for a child, but some forward-looking parents also may want to help their toddlers finance a happy and secure retirement.

If you're so inclined, consider establishing a variable annuity for the young child or grandchild in your life. Teenagers can start IRAs under special arrangements with certain fund companies, but they must have sufficient earned income to make an IRA worthwhile. A variable annuity does not need to be funded with earned income, and unlike the $2,000 annual cap on IRAs, you face no contribution limits.

Because we're now working with an expansive time horizon, compound interest can easily make your child a millionaire when his or her golden years roll around. Let's assume you sock away $5,000 in a growth-fund subaccount for a 3½-year-old. If the money compounds tax-deferred at 9 percent annually during the next 62 years, your child would have more than $1 million by the time he or she turns 65. Of course, the money is subject to a 10-percent tax penalty if taken out before age 59½, but that penalty should encourage a long-term commitment.

You can choose among different ways to set up a variable annuity intended for a child. It can be established as a custodial account with the parent or another adult such as a grandparent named custodian. Some parents may want to open the account in their own names or that of a grandparent. This alternative allows you to retain total control of the money, even if you ultimately plan to give it to your children. Consider low-cost variable annuities for your youngster. For a list, see Chapter 18.

Street Smarts

When the destination is college, parents who plan wisely can make sure their children arrive on time and in good shape. A lot of cash can be stashed away in the years before a youngster graduates from high school, and the lengthy investment horizon makes appreciation-oriented products suitable. Depending on the child's age and portfolio balance, money invested in a custodial account or trust can compound at preferential tax rates. Parents should realize, however, that they will surrender control over the assets in accounts set up in this manner.

CHAPTER 21

Your Broker Is Your Travel Agent

Some people like to make all of their own travel arrangements—checking airline schedules, booking hotels and more. Others would rather call a travel agent, describe their dream vacation and pick up the tickets a few days later. Just as the travel business offers different degrees of service, so too mutual funds offer different degrees of service. Discount brokerages provide the convenience of "one-stop shopping," which appeals to a growing number of individuals who make their own financial decisions. Although we wrote *Building Your Mutual Fund Portfolio* with the do-it-yourself investor in mind, "full-service" brokerages and banks might prove helpful for those seeking personalized advice with their portfolios.

"One-Stop Shopping"

You can conveniently buy and sell hundreds of mutual funds through discount brokerages. Charles Schwab (800-266-5623) and Fidelity Investments (800-544-9697) are the biggest players and provide the most sophisticated programs, including 24-hour service in what has become a rapidly expanding field. Other discounters offering mutual fund trading—although not necessarily on the same terms—include Muriel Siebert & Co. (800-872-0666), Quick & Reilly (800-672-7220), Waterhouse Securities (800-934-4443) and Jack White (800-323-3263).

Discounter Benefits

In brief, these are the main advantages of buying mutual funds through a discount brokerage:

- You can consolidate all of your fund holdings on one account statement, along with other investments such as stocks, bonds and closed-end funds.
- You can move money from one family to another quickly and easily.
- You will find the information you need for tax purposes consolidated on a single statement.
- You can buy and sell a large number of funds at no charge.
- You can take advantage of services such as face-to-face dealings at local branches and margin accounts.
- You can reduce the amount of promotional materials received in the mail.
- You can place all trades through a single phone number.
- You can cut down on the opportunity costs that would otherwise result from the movement of money between families. Some funds require signature guarantees for redemptions, adding to the burden.

No-Transaction-Fee (NTF) Portfolios

Several hundred funds now can be bought and sold free of transaction costs through discount brokerages. Because the lists of NTF funds offered by various brokerages change, be sure to obtain the most recent updates. Fund companies absorb the cost of this service because they view it as a good marketing and asset-gathering strategy. Typically, they pay the brokerage 25 to 35 *basis points* each year on the amount people have invested in this manner, which works out to 25 to 35 cents for each $100 purchase. This cost shows up in a portfolio's expense ratio, which all investors shoulder, whether they use a discounter or deal directly with the fund family. As an offsetting factor, fund companies often can cut their advertising and shareholder-servicing costs by participating in a discount broker's program.

Discounters play a role that is somewhat analogous to that of a travel agent—they bring you and the fund together, and the fund family pays for this service just as an airline would pay a travel agent. Schwab and Fidelity each offer several hundred NTF funds.

What's in It for the Funds?

Discounters can help smaller fund groups attract shareholders. These lesser-known families can plug into the marketing clout of Fidelity or Schwab and reach potential new customers. However, many fund companies are cautious about such marriages, and some worry about the impact a severe bear market could have on their business. If investors flee stock funds, their cash would be switched into a Schwab or Fidelity money market product rather than their own in-house portfolio. This would cause the family to lose assets. The discounters' programs probably have weakened shareholder loyalties to certain fund families.

Transaction-Fee Funds

Some prominent no-load groups such as Vanguard, T. Rowe Price and Scudder have been reluctant to join the NTF programs. They don't want to pay the discounter 25 to 35 basis points, nor do they want to lose direct contact with shareholders. However, portfolios from these families are available through discounters. You pay a fee for trading these funds, but it's fairly reasonable if you're dealing with a relatively large dollar amount, such as $10,000 or more.

Beware of multiple fees. If you buy a transaction-fee fund that ordinarily imposes a low load, you might have to pay that charge in addition to the transaction fee. Plus, the transaction fee usually applies on both purchase and sale. At this writing, Jack White & Co., a smaller discounter based in San Diego, offered the lowest rates for trading transaction-fee funds and the largest selection of funds.

If you want exposure to a wider range of products and to different fee structures, you might use two discounters instead of one. This also can have advantages if you do a fair amount of buying and selling, because most discounters restrict how often you can trade NTF portfolios. Many investors use both Schwab and Fidelity, for example. A major advantage of dealing with Fidelity is that you gain access to the large stable of attractive Fidelity products.

Just because a discounter offers access to a particular family doesn't mean all members of that group will be in the program. For instance, a family may be reluctant to include a small, new portfolio through the brokerage because this could result in a huge influx of money within a short time. The fund may prefer more gradual growth, rather than being swamped with a large amount of cash.

Ten Questions To Keep in Mind

Buying no-load funds through a discounter has advantages and disadvantages. Here are ten questions to ponder if you're interested in opening an account.

1. *Which no-transaction-fee funds are offered?* As noted, the lists vary at each discount firm, and they change over time.
2. *What restrictions apply when trading NTF funds?* You face some limitations because the discounter incurs costs each time you buy or sell, yet does not receive a commission in return. Conversely, there are no restrictions when you trade transaction-fee funds because you pay for this service.
3. *What are the penalties for excessive trading in NTF funds?* If you trade too much, you may be charged for future orders, or even could be expelled from the discounter's program.
4. *Should you use more than one discounter?* Schwab and Fidelity make a good combination if you want to broaden your NTF holdings. But going with more than two discounters probably defeats the original purpose, if it's to simplify your investment life.
5. *What are the costs for trading transaction-fee funds?* Determine the commission you would pay based on the typical size of your trades. Fees become less onerous as you invest larger dollar amounts. You may receive a discount when you place a simultaneous order to sell one transaction-fee fund and use the proceeds to buy another.
6. *What are the cut-off times for same-day trades?* Generally, you must buy or sell by 2 pm Eastern Standard Time for funds other than the discounter's own proprietary products. If you're dealing with Schwab or Fidelity funds, your cut-off time for a same-day trade is 4 pm Eastern Standard Time. If you place an order before the applicable cut-off time, you get that day's price or NAV.
7. *Are you interested in using margin?* When you invest with a discount brokerage, you can borrow money either to speculate or to meet temporary cash needs, paying interest to the broker on your loan. Suppose you sell a closed-end fund and want to use the proceeds to simultaneously purchase an open-end fund. The trade on the closed-end portfolio settles in three business days whereas the mutual fund trade settles the next day. To

make this simultaneous transaction work, you could margin or borrow the money needed for your open-end purchase for the remaining two days.

8. *What kinds of supporting materials does the discounter offer?* Some brokerages publish mutual fund performance reports and retirement-planning software, for example.

9. *Do you like to visit your broker's office in person?* If so, you may want to pick a discounter that has a branch in your area.

10. *What do you intend to do with funds you now own?* To consolidate your holdings, you can transfer portfolios you already own into your new brokerage account without having to sell them and face possible taxable gains. Most discounters provide this service free of charge on funds they handle.

Should You Go?

A discounter makes a lot of sense for larger investors who hold perhaps ten or more funds from a half dozen or so families. To achieve an optimal mix of products, you need to pick the best of what each of several groups has to offer. This way you are sure to diversify by management and style. Smaller investors also can benefit when dealing with discounters by using their no-transaction-fee programs to avoid commissions.

Of course, you can select from an even broader array of choices when investing on your own. You also can tap into some especially low-cost funds, such as those in the Vanguard group, when proceeding in this manner. If you're content sticking with just a couple of large families, such as Fidelity and Vanguard, you are probably better off buying direct.

Dealing with a Full-Service Brokerage or Bank

Full-service brokers and bank representatives also can play an important role for many investors who simply don't have the time, interest or background to build and manage their own portfolios in today's increasingly complex financial world. If you decide to turn to a professional, however, you still should have at least a rudimentary knowledge of investing. You need a general understanding of what your adviser should be doing if you hope to evaluate his or her counsel and performance.

Good, trustworthy investment advice and assistance is well worth the cost. Choosing the wrong products or managing them inappropriately can be expensive, certainly more costly than the sales charges you pay for help. Nevertheless, paying a commission doesn't guarantee that your salesperson will provide good advice and service. Nor, of course, does it ensure profitable investing.

Load versus No-Load Funds

Academic studies have shown no basic difference in the performances of load and no-load funds before considering the impact of sales charges (which obviously tilt the argument in favor of the latter). You find top and bottom performers among both groups. Merrill Lynch Capital A, Templeton Foreign, United Income, Guardian Park Avenue, FPA Paramount and SoGen International are just some of the many examples of standout performers in the load arena.

Know Your Share Classes

But in an effort to make their products more palatable in view of the no-load competition, load groups have come out with a complex way to levy sales charges. Thus, the first thing to be aware of when you use a financial adviser is the different ways in which some funds impose commissions, and the reasonableness of those charges. These arrangements can be divided into three general methods of assessing fees, which correspond to three basic share classes:

- *Class A* shares are sold with a front-end load generally between 4 and 6 percent, possibly accompanied by a modest ongoing 12b-1 fee.
- *Class B* shares couple 12b-1 fees with a *back-end load* or *contingent deferred sales charge (CDSC)*. The back-end charge might begin at 5 percent or so in the first year, decline by one percentage point annually and disappear after five or six years.
- *Class C* shares apply no front-end loads, but impose a relatively high ongoing *level load* in the form of a 12b-1 fee. They also might feature a small back-end charge of 1 percent or so.

Class A shares generally make the best choice if you stay with a fund or family for a long period. You're paying the load up front and getting it out of the way. Class B shares may be a good choice if you plan to hold on for five or six years, which is about the time the CDSC disappears. B shares might convert automatically to A shares, with no front-end load required after several years. Use class C shares if you have a short time horizon, because you would pay nothing additional to invest in or redeem. But C shares make a poor long-term investment because the level load acts as a significant drain on performance over the years.

Brokers, Bank Representatives and Financial Planners

If you want help putting together and monitoring a mix of mutual funds, you may wish to use a full-service brokerage or bank. If you're looking to build a comprehensive financial blueprint covering your assets, income tax, estate planning and other areas, consider a financial planning firm. But middlemen in all three channels must be licensed by the National Association of Securities Dealers to sell mutual funds. That goes for insurance agents, too. So from a practical viewpoint, it doesn't really matter where you buy. In fact, the lines between the various camps have been blurring.

TRAVELER'S ADVISORY:
Be Aware of "Break Points"

If you're making a large investment—generally $50,000 to $1 million or more—ask your broker or bank representative about the so-called *break points* that front-end load funds usually offer. These are commission discounts for big purchases, spelled out in each fund's prospectus. For example, a fund that normally imposes a 5-percent front-end load on its class A shares might charge only 2.5 percent if you invest $250,000, 1.5 percent for a $500,000 purchase, or nothing if you invest $1 million or more.

Stockbrokers used to be compensated primarily through the commissions they earned on the products they sell, such as load funds. Today, it is much more common for them to generate fee income, although commissions still dominate. Financial planners, insurance agents and brokers working at banks also can earn a living from commissions, fees or some combination of the two. That's why it pays to ask!

Some investment professionals, especially in the financial-planner camp, charge fees only, either as an hourly rate or by the job. These planners often recommend no-load funds and may purchase them through a discount brokerage such as Schwab. The financial-planning business, like the brokerage industry, once was dominated by small firms that sold commission products. But these days you can find many fee-only planners, including those employed at major accounting or law firms.

To find a full-service broker, bank representative or financial planner, begin by asking friends and associates for referrals. In addition, the Institute of Certified Financial Planners (800-282-7526) will provide the names of three certified financial planners (or CFPs) in your area. For referrals on fee-only planners, contact the National Association of Personal Financial Advisors (800-366-2732).

Checking Candidates

Develop a list of adviser candidates and ask about their qualifications. Some states, such as Arizona, operate hotlines that you can call to inquire about a broker or planner's disciplinary history. Interview at least three candidates, asking about the products they like to use, their philosophy toward investing and the manner in which they earn compensation. Here are some questions to ask:

1. What kinds of clients do you focus on, in terms of their average net worth and investment sophistication?
2. In what kinds of investments, if any, do you specialize?
3. Do you recommend products from a variety of load-fund families or just one or two that are important to your firm?
4. What are your educational and professional credentials? (For instance, ask a financial planner if he or she has the CFP designation.)
5. How much investment experience do you have, and where have you worked?

6. How do you research investments? (You might ask if the person follows the suggestions of his or her firm or outside advisory services.)

7. What is your overall investment philosophy, and what are your favorite kinds of products?

8. What are your three favorite fund families, and why do you like them?

9. Do you believe in market timing, or do you recommend a buy-and hold strategy? (Avoid aggressive market timers because they generally do not fare well.)

10. Does your firm offer a mutual fund asset-allocation program?

11. In broad terms, how would you advise me to allocate my assets?

12. How frequently do you typically talk with customers? Do you have face-to-face meetings or take care of most business by phone?

13. Will you provide performance reports on my portfolio and explain them to me?

14. Can you provide illustrations of how some of your clients have done, especially those who have situations similar to mine?

15. Will you be providing me with educational literature and helping me understand it?

16. How do you manage your own portfolio?

Watch for Red Flags

During the interview, be sure to ask for an explanation of anything you don't understand, including commissions and fees. If the adviser isn't specific or fails to provide clear answers, regard this as a warning. You want someone who will listen attentively and respond fully to questions and requests. You also want a person who will clearly explain the potential risks of every investment he or she recommends. Steer clear of those who make outlandish claims like promising a 20-percent return on your dollars. And remember, there's no such thing as a risk-free investment. If you're seriously considering hiring an adviser, ask for references and check them.

If you decide to work with an adviser, you normally will be given a questionnaire to help determine your objectives, time horizon, risk tolerance, income needs and so on. Your adviser is responsible for becoming acquainted with your financial profile and developing a suitable mix of funds.

Now that you know what to expect from a full-service broker, bank representative or financial planner, deal cautiously with your adviser at first—treat it as a probationary period. If you suspect that you're getting a bum deal, you're probably right. Don't hesitate to make a change. It's *your* money!

Investigating Wrap Programs

Brokerage firms, banks and fund companies pair relatively affluent clients with suitable money managers through *wrap* (or *wrap-fee*) programs. The name "wrap" signifies that the money-management fees, service costs and transactions expenses are bundled together into a single asset-based charge. For example, if the fee is 1.5 percent a year and the client has a $100,000 account, the annual cost would be $1,500. Wrap programs represent a way to bring top managerial talent to a wider market, using brokers as intermediaries.

The original concept offered personalized service for a client's portfolio of individual stocks and bonds. Newer wrap programs using mutual funds have been growing in popularity and had attracted more than $12 billion in assets by year-end 1994, according to Cerulli & Associates, a Boston research firm. Brokerages have been the leaders in this field, but banks and fund companies also have stepped in. The minimum investment threshold varies but generally ranges from $25,000 to $200,000 or more. The percentage fee you pay declines with larger purchases—so if you're investing $500,000 or $1 million, you should expect a discount.

Many individuals are not comfortable making their own investment decisions, or they simply don't want to take the time. The typical wrap-account client might be a recent retiree who is rolling several hundred thousand dollars from a 401(k) plan into an IRA. Paying an annual fee of, say, 1.25 percent might seem reasonable to some investors.

With a mutual fund wrap program, you provide basic information about yourself to get the process started. You complete a questionnaire that deals with factors such as your age, time horizon, risk tolerance, income needs and size of your portfolio.

Then the firm feeds the information into a computer and comes up with a recommended stock-bond-cash allocation built around eight to ten mutual funds. In addition to picking funds and making the appropriate allocations, the company provides you with periodic performance reports, access to an account executive and 1099 forms at tax time. Investment-related tax advice also may be available. Your account rep monitors your portfolio regularly and rebalances positions based on changes in the stock and bond markets as well as in your personal circumstances.

Smith Barney has the oldest and largest of the mutual fund wrap programs. The New York-based brokerage has established a stable of 13 no-load TRAK portfolios, separate from its in-house load funds. The Smith Barney program charges clients an annual fee of 1.5 percent and requires a $10,000 minimum, a relatively low threshold by industry standards. Merrill Lynch, Prudential Securities and Linsco Private Ledger are among the other full-service brokerages offering these programs.

No-load fund groups with wrap programs include Fidelity, SteinRoe and Strong. More low-cost groups are expected to enter the business in the near future. The largest such program, Fidelity Portfolio Advisory Service, requires a $200,000 investment and imposes a 1-percent annual fee. A typical portfolio consists of eight to ten funds chosen from Fidelity's stable of over 200 products. Any applicable loads on those funds are waived. On average, portfolio revisions are made four to six times a year.

The main criticism of wrap programs is their cost, which can be as high as about 1.75 percent a year, on top of the individual expenses charged by the underlying funds. On funds with expense ratios of 1.5 percent or more, your total outlays could easily exceed 3 percent. But fees are negotiable, especially if you are investing several hundred thousand dollars.

You want to make sure that a wrap program offers a sufficiently wide selection of good-performing funds and that the fees on the funds themselves are reasonable. In addition, make sure that you won't be paying any loads on purchases. Some firms impose a relatively low annual wrap-account fee but then tack on load charges. However, most brokerages waive the loads in these programs.

Wrap-account fees likely will come down in the future because the competition has heated up. At this writing, Vanguard, the low-cost leader, was expected to introduce a wrap program with rock-bottom fees. Needless to say, high expenses can exert a big drag on performance.

Here are some general guidelines if you're shopping for a wrap program:

1. *Evaluate some of the funds in a program.* You don't want to pay a wrap fee only to end up with mediocre performers.
2. *Look for a sufficiently wide range of attractive portfolio choices.* You might not want to be restricted to a particular family of funds.
3. *Check out the costs and benefits.* Make sure you understand what you are paying and what you are getting in return.
4. *Do your homework.* Compare at least three different programs before making your final choice.
5. *Compare a wrap program to working with a financial planner.* The service you get in a mutual fund wrap program is similar to what you might expect from a fee-only financial planner. But you may get more in-depth counseling on tax and other matters from the latter. You can receive both, if you sign up for a wrap program through a financial planner.
6. *Consider one or more asset-allocation funds instead.* Investors with smaller portfolios may find all-in-one funds the better choice.

Street Smarts

- Discount brokerage programs may be attractive if you invest in funds from several families and want the advantages of one-stop shopping. These programs appeal to do-it-yourself investors.
- If you need advice, find out what local full-service brokerages, banks and financial-planning firms have to offer. Interview at least three investment professionals, making sure the chemistry is right between you and the adviser.
- Learn what you can about financial products. Even if you pay a professional to manage your money, you still need a basic knowledge of investing to evaluate the wisdom of your adviser's decisions.

CHAPTER 22

Knowing When To Head for the Exits

You're in Florida, Hawaii or the Virgin Islands and it has been raining for several days in a row with no signs of letting up. Do you cut your vacation short and head home, or do you stick it out for a bit longer? This is the sort of dilemma investors face when it comes time to consider selling. Your fund's performance, tax considerations and changes in your personal circumstances all can play a role. Although you might hang on to a mutual fund longer than a stock, it's not a good idea to fall in love with your holdings.

When to Sell

There can be many good reasons for packing up and going home.

Altering Your Allocation

Sometimes, it's wise to sell even when your funds have been performing well. For example, if you're following an asset-allocation plan, you may want to make a change when your asset class weights no longer fall within their target ranges, as explained in Chapter 3. Suppose you normally allocate between 60 and 70 percent of your portfolio to stocks, but your share has grown to 75 or 80 percent. It could be time to trim and prune, especially if you feel the market has become expensive or if you are nearing retirement. Which stock funds should you sell? Good candidates are those that are not living up to your expectations or those that no longer mesh with your goals.

Weeding Out Laggards

Poor performance is the number one reason people become dissatisfied with an investment, but you don't want to dump a good fund just because it had a bad quarter or two. Moving frequently among funds on the basis of quarterly results gets expensive and normally doesn't make sense. However, if a mainstream stock portfolio has significantly lagged behind its peers for perhaps eighteen months, it's probably time to move on. You should give a faltering aggressive-growth fund even less time to prove itself, before a volatile laggard does some really bad damage.

A good way to keep up-to-date with the performance of a volatile fund in relation to its closest competitors is to check the total-return numbers reported daily in *The Wall Street Journal* or *Investor's Business Daily.* For most other types of funds, quarterly performance results, as reported by newspapers such as *The Arizona Republic* and the *Los Angeles Times,* are probably sufficient. When making such comparisons, analyze similar types of portfolios. For example, compare a large-stock value fund with other large-stock value funds.

You also may want to sell a fund because you feel it won't fare well in the future, even if its past performance has been adequate. Maybe the manager holds too much or too little cash to suit your preferences. Some stock funds keep 50 percent or more of their assets in cash because their managers worry about an approaching bear market. If you are bullish but your fund manager isn't, it's time to move on.

Sticking with Styles

Even if the investment style or approach pursued by your fund is out of favor, that's not necessarily a good reason to dump it. It's wise to remain diversified across different styles because you can't predict when a particular approach will come back into the limelight. Don't think so badly of your large-stock growth fund if similar types of portfolios also have been in the doghouse.

Check to see how your portfolio has fared relative to an appropriate index. You can, for example, compare a growth-and-income fund against the S&P 500, a small-stock portfolio with the Russell 2000, an international fund with the EAFE, and a junk-bond product with the Salomon high-yield corporate bond index. For a sharper gauge on large stocks, use S&P's/BARRA Growth and S&P's BARRA/Value indexes.

A New Tour Director

A change in management also might justify selling your fund. The change could raise a big red flag if the portfolio is a solo fund or part of a small group, because it may not be feasible to replace the talented individual. However, if your fund is a member of a large, respected family, you can be confident that the complex will do its best to replace the star with a competent successor, as Fidelity did when Peter Lynch retired from Magellan in 1990. In addition, the big fund outfits usually have large research departments and many analysts to assist managers.

A change might be inconsequential if a committee runs the fund, as at American Funds, Dodge & Cox and Twentieth Century. It's worth noting that management transitions are generally more important with stock funds than with fixed-income portfolios because stock fund managers have considerably more opportunity to add value or lose ground.

Rising Expenses

This represents another possible reason to sell, so it's wise to keep tabs on your fund's expense ratio. Costs are especially important with bond funds because they generate lower returns than stock funds and every bit of economizing counts. Maybe you already own some bond

---

TRAVELER'S ADVISORY:
Has Your Small Stock Fund Grown Too Big?

If you own a small-company fund, it pays to keep up to date with its size. An overgrown portfolio (with upwards of, say, 1 billion million in assets) might be a sell candidate if it has underperformed its peers recently. Rising assets make these types of funds less nimble.

portfolios with above-average expenses. This could be a good opportunity to make some changes. Or perhaps you bought a fund when its
costs were capped at a modest level, but now the cap has been lifted so
the expense ratio is much higher. Money market funds are notorious
for temporarily waiving fees.

Perhaps your fund has instituted a 12b-1 fee since you acquired
shares, so the annual cost burden has grown significantly. Some people
hold investments with high 12b-1 fees and don't realize the longer-
term impact of this drain on performance. A bond or money market
fund with a 12b-1 fee is a candidate for selling. A stock fund with a
12b-1 fee higher than 0.25 percent falls into the same category if it has
not performed well.

If you decide to sell a fund with a 12b-1 fee, don't let any contingent
deferred sales charges take a big bite out of your investment. These
declining exit charges are associated with broker-sold funds and might
start out at 5 percent or so in the first year and then drop by one percentage point annually until the charge eventually disappears. You can pay
heavily if you sell such a fund too soon. If you must get out, consider
switching to another portfolio in the same family to avoid the charge.

Changing Personal Circumstances

On the personal level, many factors could justify a sale. You might
decide to make some switches after learning more about investing in
mutual funds or because you are nearing retirement or have length-
ened or shortened your time horizon. Perhaps you have a decreased (or
increased) tolerance for risk, have changed jobs recently or have
moved to another state. For tax reasons, you might want to unload a
fund that has lost money if you can use the loss to offset gains on other
positions. All are common examples of factors that could lead you to
alter your objectives.

Boosting Your Emergency Reserves

Keep cash that you might need to meet emergencies in a money
market or short-term bond fund, separate from your long-term investments. If you require more cash than you anticipated, add to your
safety net by pruning out laggard funds among your long-term holdings and transferring the proceeds to your emergency account. You

also could trim overpriced investments such as a small-stock fund that sports an excessive PE ratio.

When To Hang in There

There are many good reasons to sell, but you also must know when to stay put. Here are five suggestions for holding the line:

1. *Don't jump around frequently.* It's easy to switch in and out of mutual funds via toll-free numbers, usually with no transaction fee. Investors have become accustomed to making instant changes in their portfolios. Wider fund choices and better investment information tempt us to revamp our holdings. But you won't earn the advertised returns on a portfolio unless you hang on through at least a full market cycle. Don't sell without a real reason.

2. *Don't drop a top performer too soon.* What goes up doesn't always come down. Just because a fund has delivered above-average returns for many years does not necessarily mean that it's due for a fall. There are always a select number of funds, such as some of those on the *Forbes* honor roll, that outperform the market for remarkably long spans. Besides, selling shares in a long-term winner can give rise to a premature tax liability.

3. *Don't bail out because you fear a market crash.* As we've said, market timing usually doesn't work. Stocks can remain over-valued for surprisingly long stretches of time. The best strategy is to follow a long-term buy-and-hold policy because the market has a distinctly bullish bias. But you may want to cut back on your aggressive holdings if you're losing sleep over them. Pare them back to your "sleeping point."

4. *Don't panic and sell just after a plunge.* It's human nature to overreact to unfavorable developments or bad news. The market usually recovers at least a portion of its loss after it has taken a spill.

5. *Don't sell on the basis of a tip.* Even if you trust the tipster and feel the advice has merit, do your own analysis before you sell out. Only you know how the fund fits into your overall portfolio given your time horizon, risk tolerance and other factors.

CHAPTER 23

Charting Your Course for the 21st Century

The next millennium is just around the corner, and many people are wondering what their financial future holds. Clearly, mutual funds will play an increasingly greater role in people's lives. Even sophisticated investors realize the considerable difficulty of putting together a globally diversified portfolio consisting only of individual stocks and bonds. At a minimum, many people will look to mutual funds for their all-important international holdings and for exposure to other specialized areas such as high-yield bonds and real-estate stocks.

What investment strategies make most sense for the long haul? In general, the common-sense approaches that have served well in the past should prove equally desirable for the future. Put as much money to work as you can in a portfolio consisting of various asset classes. Your mix should be diverse enough that you can beat inflation, but not be so volatile or complicated that you can't live with it.

The Next Millennium—Where the Road to Wealth Is Headed

What can you expect of the financial markets as we get ready to turn our calendars to the 21st century? Though we don't have a crystal ball, we can make some statements with a high degree of confidence. Most reflect trends already in force and not easily reversed.

Inflation Won't Go Away.   Increases in the Consumer Price Index likely will average at least 4 percent or so on an annual basis early in the 21st century. The costs of certain items such as a college education may continue to grow at an even faster clip. In any event, you don't want to have too much stashed away in money market portfolios unless your time horizon is fairly short or you're wealthy enough that you don't mind earning lower returns.

Life Expectancies Will Be Longer.   More individuals will live into their 80s, 90s and 100s, making the need for a substantial nest egg greater than ever. A major danger people face is outliving their savings, and many Americans worry about it. Longer life spans coupled with inflation make the role of stocks more vital than ever, even for retirees.

A Continued Shift to Employee-Directed Pensions.   More people will take responsibility for managing their own retirement nest eggs simply because employers will force them to do so. These days, companies are less likely to adopt traditional *defined-benefit* pension plans in which employers put aside money for their workers and manage it for them. Instead, they are offering *defined-contribution* programs such as 401(k) and 403(b) plans, where employees must take an active role in selecting and managing investments themselves. This is a major reason why widespread investment education will be of paramount importance.

Markets Will Fluctuate.   Stock and bond prices will rise and fall, just as they always have. For long-term gains, you've got to accept some short-term risk. Dollar cost averaging should continue to rank as a popular strategy for easing into volatile investments. If you're willing to spend more time tinkering with your portfolio, look at value averaging, which we covered in Chapter 6. The only safe prediction we can make about the stock market over any time frame is that it will fluctuate.

Expect Bear Markets.   There probably will be a down market within the next decade, if not before the end of the century. Many people will panic and lock in losses. Yet a major bear market can represent the chance of a lifetime to go bargain hunting. Bear markets tend to be shorter than bull phases, so it would be rare to see a severe downturn lasting more than two years. History tells us that about seven out of every ten years are up periods for stock investors. There is no reason to expect this pattern to change.

Asset Allocation Will Grow in Importance.   Asset allocation will play a bigger role than before, especially as global investing gains in importance. The advantage of an eclectic approach is that one type of fund may be holding its ground while another is suffering, leading to an overall smoother ride and lower volatility. A well-diversified portfolio contains a broad mix of securities, possibly including large and small stocks, foreign shares, real-estate securities, high-grade bonds, high-yield bonds, foreign bonds and municipals. The recent proliferation of asset-allocation and life-strategy funds offered by major families such as Fidelity, T. Rowe Price and Vanguard makes it possible for even the smallest investors to get started.

International Investing Will Expand.   As the world continues to shrink, more people will be comfortable owning foreign stocks, especially through mutual funds. Global stock markets may gradually become more highly correlated with one another over the next couple of decades as capital moves more quickly and freely. This will mean reduced diversification benefits. But foreign markets still will offer the potential for higher growth.

Emerging Markets Will Grow Richer.   Markets in developing nations should be top performers over the next several decades. About 85 percent of the world's population resides in emerging economies. A higher rate of literacy coupled with advances in medicine and technology promise longer, better lives for these people. The demise of communism and the dramatic increase in the number of privatized companies have opened the door to unparalleled opportunities for international investors. Developing markets represent less than 10 percent of the world's total stock market capitalization, but offer high long-run potential.

Capital will continue to flow freely from mature economies, such as the United States, Japan, Germany and Britain, to exciting growth areas in the Middle East, Southeast Asia and Latin America. Stock markets in huge countries such as China and India will gradually become more liquid and efficient and of higher investment quality. Continuing strong expansion in foreign economies should cause their currencies to appreciate against the dollar, giving Americans who invest abroad a boost from currency profits.

Stocks Will Beat Bonds Long Term.   We don't know what kinds of returns you can expect from stocks. Just because equities have averaged around 10 percent a year over the past 70 years or so doesn't mean that they will fare the same during the 21st century. However, over periods of a decade or more, equities should outperform bonds, cash and the inflation rate. By increasing your percentage allocation to stocks, your overall return will be higher.

Index Funds Will Continue To Grow in Popularity.   With lower returns in store for the next decade or so, it's particularly important to pare your costs. Index funds represent an excellent way to do this, and they will surely beat the majority of actively managed alternatives. They're appropriate candidates for taxable accounts because they feature minuscule portfolio turnovers and thus rate as highly tax efficient. We expect to see more investor dollars flowing into this arena as knowledge of the advantages of indexing spreads.

Interest Rates Will Continue to Confound Bond Investors. Interest-rate forecasters have a poor batting average, and that won't change in the next millennium. But this doesn't mean you should give up on bond funds. Just be prepared for interest rates to rise on occasion, resulting in lower bond prices. As a compromise, diversify your bond or bond-fund holdings and avoid committing too much to long maturities. Also, add a modest international stake. To further reduce volatility, consider dollar cost averaging into a fixed-income portfolio.

Gold Won't Sparkle for Long.   Gold will continue to be a poor performer generally over the next century. The metal will enjoy a sprinkling of brilliant years as in 1993, but it's impossible to predict when these will happen. If you're uncertain about whether to include gold in your asset mix, here's a word of advice: don't. As an alternative asset class, we recommend real estate, which we expect to far outperform gold in the 21st century.

Real-Estate Funds Will Gain in Importance.   Worldwide inflation could heat up a bit in the decades ahead, making hard assets like real estate a good long-term hedge. Most individuals don't have adequate exposure to real estate even though they might own a home and perhaps a rental property or two. What they lack is diversification by property type and geographic region. Real-estate funds provide wide exposure to many different segments in the industry, including shopping malls, hotels, office buildings, recreation facilities and health-care complexes. Real-estate funds shift your money around to different areas as economic conditions change. They invest mainly in publicly traded real-estate investment trusts or REITs (see Chapter 15), which have become the preferred vehicle for raising capital for real estate.

Mutual Funds Won't Collapse.   The mutual fund industry will remain a sound destination for your long-term investment money, provided you're holding a good mix of assets. The industry is strong, healthy and highly regulated. The risks of investing in funds result from the inevitable fluctuations in stock and bond prices, not bankruptcy of fund families. By the turn of the century, perhaps 40 percent or more of all American households will entrust money to mutual fund companies, an increase from about 33 percent today.

Mutual Fund Mergers Will Continue.   Look for continued consolidation within the industry, as economic forces pressure smaller players to sell out. Fund companies make their money from management fees, which are assessed as a percentage of assets. So the more assets a group has, the higher its take. Larger companies also benefit from economies of scale, which lead to lower costs. The big families will become bigger through internal growth as well as acquisitions. Growing fund complexes benefit investors who like one-stop shopping by providing access to a broader menu of portfolios. Also, they can afford to hire top analysts and portfolio managers, which obviously benefits investors. Finally, they can afford to offer top-quality services for shareholders.

Discount Brokerage Programs Will Expand.   More people will deal with discount brokerages to build their mutual fund portfolios. Expect a continuing increase in the number of funds offered by the discounters, including those in the no-transaction-fee programs. These programs make it easy to assemble a diversified portfolio that contains the best of what each of several fund complexes has to offer. The danger is that people will buy and sell too frequently because it's so simple.

Banks Will Play a Greater Role in the Mutual Fund Business. It will be increasingly common for people to shop for mutual funds at their local bank branch. Banks now represent an important entry point for many first time mutual fund investors. This is a logical extension of the banking function, which involves managing customer money. The distinctions between banks and brokerage firms gradually have been fading and the antiquated Glass-Steagall Act (a 1933 federal act separating the activities of banks and brokerages) likely will be repealed within the next five years. With the barriers to competition eroding, more people will consolidate all financial activities in one house. An individual who goes to Bank of America for CDs and to Merrill Lynch for stocks may decide to go to either institution for both. The enhanced competition benefits investors.

Closed-End Funds Will Grow in Popularity.   Closed-end funds will appeal to more mainstream investors as vehicles to achieve broader diversification. Most likely, closed-end funds will continue to target specialized areas, such as sectors and emerging stock markets. Investors will have opportunities to pick up these portfolios at attractive discounts when pessimism prevails during downturns.

Derivatives Are Here To Stay.   *Derivatives* are financial vehicles whose returns are linked to those of some underlying instrument or security such as the S&P 500 index, the Japanese yen, the T-bill rate or the price of General Motors stock. Derivatives made headlines in 1994 when several mutual funds, corporations and municipalities sustained staggering losses through their misuse. Despite the outcry, this heterogeneous assortment of esoteric financial vehicles is here to stay, and

---

POINTS OF INTEREST:
Mutual Funds Are Derivatives

Mutual funds themselves fit the technical definition of a derivative, although they're never labeled as such. A fund's NAV fluctuates in sync with the aggregate ups and downs of the stocks or bonds held, which are the primary securities. As a form of derivative, mutual funds perform vital functions, including risk reduction through diversification.

that's probably all right. It's fine that fund managers use derivatives provided they're appropriate, sensibly employed, used in moderation and properly disclosed. Certainly, the increased attention given to derivatives will benefit investors in the decades ahead.

Street Smarts

Common-sense investment approaches will continue to prove profitable in the years ahead. Unfortunately, many people will probably make the same common mistakes in the next millennium as they have in the past. The first step in building a winning 21st century portfolio is to steer clear of the hazards. The Epilogue provides a comprehensive, 101-tip checklist to help you sidestep the potholes that line the investment superhighway.

EPILOGUE

101 Tips for a Safe and Profitable Journey

Remember to pack the following investment gems in your luggage as you set forth on your financial journey. These guideposts reinforce and expand the key points covered throughout *Building Your Mutual Fund Portfolio*.

1. *Diversify for investment success.* Steer clear of all-or-nothing bets by thoughtfully allocating your assets. Develop a solid plan based on your age, time horizon, liquidity needs, income and risk tolerance. Stick with it until your circumstances change.

2. *Periodically rebalance your holdings to your original asset-allocation benchmarks.* By doing this, you will wind up selling shares in expensive funds and reinvesting in cheaper ones.

3. *Invest as much as you can in stock funds.* As a rough rule, try to hold a percentage at least equal to "100 minus your age" in stocks. Senior citizens might consider 110 minus their ages to avoid growing too conservative.

4. *Don't hop from fund to fund.* Traders often lag the long-range returns of the stock and bond markets.

5. *Set your sights on building wealth slowly.* Get-rich-quick schemes often backfire. People who amass fortunes through speculation frequently also learn how it feels to get poor quickly.

6. *Keep it simple.* Basic investment plans often work best on the quest for wealth.

7. *Avoid gimmicks.* Don't invest in anything you don't understand. Plain-vanilla funds survive the test of time better than faddish peers that make use of derivatives and other arcane strategies.

8. *Do your homework before starting out.* Never buy or sell mutual funds solely on the basis of tips. If a suggestion seems to have merit, do your own analysis.

9. *Focus on risk, return and cost when evaluating funds.* Keep in mind that a fund's risk and expenses are easier to predict than its return.

10. *Judge past performance with a grain of salt.* Historic returns don't always predict future results, especially if a fund's management or investment style has changed recently.

11. *Don't neglect the prospectus.* You'll find the guts of this document in the "financial-highlights" table. Look for past expense ratios, portfolio turnovers, total annual returns and year-to-year changes in assets.

12. *Scan fund expenses in the prospectus "fee table."* Watch out for 12b-1 fees, which nibble incessantly at your wealth. Think doubly hard about a bond fund with 12b-1 charges.

13. *Consider hiring a stockbroker or financial planner if you need help with your portfolio.* Just make sure the individual is competent and will look out for your needs. The more you understand about investment risks, returns and costs, the better you can evaluate the kind of job your adviser is doing.

14. *Don't overlook estate planning in your investment game plan.* A living trust has important advantages over a will.

15. *Make sure your mutual fund accounts are titled correctly.* Individual, joint, custodial and trust accounts are four common alternatives. The manner of titling takes precedence over any instructions in your will when it comes to transferring assets to heirs. Make sure your heirs know about your accounts.

16. *Take advantage of fund-company services.* Telephone reps often can furnish answers to your questions, but they won't give specific advice.

17. *Let time work for you.* At 10 percent annually—the long-run average return on stocks—your money doubles every 7.3 years, quadruples every 14.6 years and expands tenfold every 24.2 years.

18. *Emphasize time over market timing.* Buy good stock funds and stay with them for the long haul. Even professionals have trouble predicting the market's next move.

19. *Invest regularly.* It's been demonstrated that you can do well over the long haul even if you invest money each year at or near the market's annual peak.

20. *Recognize that the risk of being in stocks decreases as your holding period lengthens.* Known as *time diversification,* it works because the good years far outweigh the bad over lengthy periods. On average, seven out of every ten years are winners in the stock market.

21. *Start investing as soon as possible, even if you must work with small sums.* Just $25 a month in a stock fund that returns 10 percent yearly would compound to $132,778 after four decades.

22. *Save as much of your paycheck as you can.* The older you get and the higher your income, the larger the percentage you should strive to set aside.

23. *Take advantage of individual retirement accounts for their tax-deferral benefits.* IRAs represent ideal long-term savings vehicles for younger people. They also can benefit older people, given today's lengthier life expectancies.

24. *Consider painless and efficient automatic investment plans,* as offered by many fund companies. Your monthly investments go straight into your chosen fund from either a bank account or your paycheck.

25. *Don't waste time searching for elusive risk-free investments.* Even T-bills will succumb to inflationary dangers.

26. *Be cognizant of bond-market perils.* Simply put, bond prices go down when interest rates go up. But they appreciate when rates drop.

27. *Be familiar with duration,* the best measure of a bond fund's interest-rate risk, and know how to apply it. Duration readings of eight or more reflect high vulnerability.

28. *Don't expect as much from star bond managers compared with top stock managers.* Fixed-income portfolios display smaller variances in performance than their stock counterparts. Bond managers simply have less opportunity to add value, except in special areas such as junk bonds where pockets of inefficiency may exist.

29. *Never invest in a bond or money market fund unless you know its expense ratio.* Avoid money funds with expense ratios higher than 0.5 percent and bond products with costs exceeding 0.75 percent. The best bond deals feature rock-bottom expenses.

30. *Remember that a bond fund's monthly dividends are not fixed like a bond's interest.* Payments could rise or fall with changing interest rates, and as investors move into and out of the portfolio.

31. *Consider municipal-bond funds for a portion of your portfolio if you're in a higher tax bracket.* But realize that most muni funds are long-term in nature, which means they can be volatile.

32. *Buy a single-state muni fund instead of a national portfolio if you live in a populous state with reasonably high tax rates.* Your interest earnings will be double tax-exempt—that is, exempt at both the state and federal levels.

33. *Don't allocate too large a slice of your investment pie to money market funds,* because inflation can be devastating. Don't earmark more than 10 to 15 percent of your nest egg to this category unless your time horizon is fairly short.

34. *Conversely, don't use stock funds for cash that you will need in three to five years or less.* Keep near-term savings separate from long-term investments.

35. *Don't try to time the market by moving heavily into cash.* There's a large risk to being on the sidelines, provided you're working with a long time horizon and hold sufficient liquid assets to meet short-term needs. You never know when stock prices might go through the roof. The really big surges don't last long. Be there for the party!

36. *But consider changing your stock-fund mix if you're concerned with downside risk in a pricey market.* Move a portion of your more aggressive holdings into less volatile stock choices such as equity-income funds.

37. *Pay attention to what T-bills yield relative to stocks,* by dividing the yield on the former by the yield on the latter. When 91-day T-bills yield more than twice the S&P 500's dividend yield, it could signal that stocks have become overpriced.

38. *Conversely, recognize the excellent value offered by stocks anytime the T-bill/stock yield ratio is considerably below 2.0.* At the extreme, stock-market conditions could be highly favorable when both numbers are about equal.

39. *Don't expect good or bad times to last forever.* Stocks can stay overvalued or undervalued for surprisingly long stretches, but bull markets always come to an end, and so do bear markets.

40. *Use standard deviation instead of beta to evaluate a mutual fund's risk.* The former is a pure, unbiased measure of volatility, which is not tied to a particular stock-price index as is beta. Standard deviation measures the extent to which returns bob up and down around their average. Mutual fund rating services such as Morningstar and Value Line publish this number.

41. *Examine your fund's composite PE ratio—the average price-earnings ratio for all the stocks it holds.* If a fund's PE is well above that of the S&P 500, it faces greater possible losses in a correction or bear market.

42. *Remember that volatile funds might not be so bad when held in appropriate proportions within a broad portfolio.* Combining funds that rise and fall at different times could result in an overall smoother ride.

43. *Combine funds that follow the growth and value stockpicking styles,* as one style normally is out of favor when the other is in. Your portfolio's fluctuations will be less erratic if you include investments from both camps.

44. *Don't forsake stock funds, even if you're retired.* A 65-year-old retiree can expect to live another 20 years or so. If you need income, take your dividends in cash. If that's insufficient, make systematic withdrawals from a diversified portfolio.

45. *But don't set up a systematic-withdrawal plan without first calculating how long your capital will last,* given your expected return and withdrawal rate. Considering the impact of taxes and inflation, you risk depleting your nest egg if your annual withdrawal rate exceeds about 6 percent.

46. *Stay away from funds that are not members of reputable families,* unless you know the manager has an excellent record. In particular, avoid tiny funds—those with assets less than $10 million—unless they are promising members of an established group.

47. *Don't assume that laggard funds will bounce back.* Long-term losers have perennially poor performance records, along with outsized expenses, a small and declining asset base, high portfolio turnover and, sometimes, legal problems.

48. *Don't look to your nest egg for thrills and excitement.* Sometimes, relatively dull investments, such as index funds, are best.
49. *Keep in mind that about 70 percent of actively managed funds underperform the market* because operating expenses, transaction costs and cash holdings lower returns. This represents the main argument in favor of index funds.
50. *Favor index funds for a meaningful "core" portion of your stock allocation*—say, 25 to 50 percent or so. With these portfolios you need not worry that a star manager might jump ship. With a passive approach, it doesn't matter so much who's at the helm.
51. *Beware of gimmicks when shopping for an index fund.* Avoid "enhanced" index portfolios that claim they can outperform the S&P 500 or other benchmarks. Plain-vanilla products with rock-bottom costs are best.
52. *Include small-cap and international funds in your portfolio for better risk-adjusted performance.* Younger investors with long time horizons should take a significant stake in these categories.
53. *Look beyond a fund's name to its actual investment policies and portfolio holdings.* ABC Emerging Growth might have substantial positions in large rather than small stocks. XYZ Growth might focus on value stocks rather than growth.
54. *Don't invest in a small-stock fund without knowing the average size of its holdings.* Check its median market cap as published by Morningstar or Value Line. A true small-stock portfolio invests in companies with capitalizations less than $600 million. A fund that focuses on "micro caps" should own corporations worth about $200 million or less.
55. *Avoid small-stock portfolios with assets greater than $500 million or so* unless you're convinced the management is exceptionally talented.
56. *Keep in mind that small stocks move in cycles of five to seven years,* during which they either outperform or underperform the large blue chips.
57. *Don't invest heavily in small companies when they're pricey.* As a rule, they're expensive when the PE ratio of the T. Rowe Price New Horizons Fund approaches two times that of the S&P 500. Analysts track New Horizons for this purpose because it's the oldest small-company fund around.

58. *Conversely, do take bigger positions in small stocks when they're cheap.* Small companies represent excellent value when the PE of New Horizons approximates that of the S&P 500.

59. *Don't hesitate to venture abroad.* International investing is a great way to round out a portfolio, since about two-thirds of world stock-market values exist outside the United States.

60. *Lean to international rather than global funds for your overseas exposure.* The former invest exclusively in foreign markets, whereas the latter have stakes in stateside stocks as well. With international funds, you can fine-tune your overseas exposure more precisely.

61. *Check the foreign weightings of your domestic stock funds,* which could hold up to 15 percent or more of their assets in non–U.S. issues to try to improve performance. You may already have more international exposure than you think.

62. *Maintain modest stake in emerging stock markets as well* if you have a lengthy investment horizon. Developing nations offer exciting long-term growth potential.

63. *Don't expect international diversification to reduce your portfolio's volatility all the time.* Normally, it works reasonably well, but during a global panic, all the world's major stock exchanges could tumble together.

64. *Turn negatives into positives by bargain hunting abroad.* Global stock-market crashes are great times to search for values. Even in normal times, there's almost always some place where stocks are cheap.

65. *Don't write off individual retirement accounts (IRAs),* even if you're not eligible to make deductible contributions. Tax-deferred compounding by itself can be a powerful force over time.

66. *Consider growth-stock funds paying little or no dividends for taxable accounts.* They usually offer more tax efficiency than income-oriented stock portfolios, which might work better inside retirement accounts.

67. *Check on upcoming capital-gains distributions before you invest in a stock fund toward year end.* Buy in after the ex-distribution date so you don't get saddled with a current tax bill. This tip wouldn't apply if you're investing inside a tax-sheltered retirement account.

68. *Use variable annuities only after you already have contributed all you can to tax-deferred retirement plans such as IRAs and 401(k)s.*

69. *Favor no-load variable annuities* offered by firms such as Janus, T. Rowe Price, Schwab, Scudder, USAA and Vanguard.

70. *Plan to hold on to any variable annuity at least ten years* and preferably for more than 20. This way, the benefits of tax-deferred growth can overcome the drag of higher costs associated with annuities.

71. *Place the most aggressive part of your portfolio inside a variable annuity to offset the higher costs with greater long-run gains.* Emphasize categories such as growth, small-company and international-stock funds.

72. *Consider index funds as another way to minimize your tax bite.* An index fund with turnover of less than 10 percent will distribute little in the way of taxable gains to shareholders. This strategy could serve you better than a variable annuity, because you don't have to deal with higher ongoing costs and premature-withdrawal penalties.

73. *Follow a dollar cost averaging strategy if you want to ease into risky positions gradually.* This involves investing a fixed sum of cash every month or quarter.

74. *Conversely, consider putting a large sum of cash to work all at once,* if you can stand the fluctuations. Dollar cost averaging helps smooth out your returns, but you could miss a big upward move in the initial weeks or months.

75. *Be aware that a dollar cost averaging approach will succeed only if you have the courage to stick with it,* which means you need to keep socking away cash even when the outlook appears bleak.

76. *If you follow a dollar cost averaging program, consider doubling your monthly investments during corrections and, especially, full-fledged bear markets.* Emotionally, this isn't easy to do, but your performance will improve once your funds bounce back.

77. *Recognize that mutual funds invariably recover after they've taken a plunge.* Individual stocks might not come back because a weak company could go bankrupt. It's often wise to average down with mutual funds by acquiring more shares at depressed prices, thereby reducing your average cost per share. However, this practice is dangerous with stocks.

78. *Stay away from closed-end funds unless you're willing to put in more time and effort.* These investments demand more sophistication and patience than regular open-end funds.

79. *Never buy a closed-end stock fund on the initial public offering.* It's highly likely to slip to a discount several months later. Be patient.

80. *Don't overlook the opportunities in closed-end domestic equity funds,* some of which have been around since the late 1920s. Unlike many other closed-end products, these investments are fairly conservative.

81. *Bargain hunt for closed-end funds during tax-selling season in December,* especially after a flat to down year. That's when double-digit discounts often develop.

82. *Use limit orders whenever you invest in a closed-end fund.* With these orders, you're instructing your broker to buy or sell shares at your specified price or better. Getting a bargain often takes a little patience.

83. *Be wary of single-country closed-end funds, especially when they're trading at high premiums.* They can fall fast and far when investor sentiment sours.

84. *Be careful of volatile sector funds such as technology and health-care portfolios.* Don't allocate more than 5 or 10 percent of your total assets to these funds.

85. *Don't earmark more than 10 percent of your portfolio to gold funds.* Gold has been a poor long-term performer, even though it sometimes rises in contrast to stock and bond prices during troubled times. If you want a modest stake in a gold fund, consider doing so gradually through dollar cost averaging.

86. *If you want sector holdings, go for stable industries or those that can offer diversification benefits.* Utility, real-estate and natural-resource funds are three sensible choices for long-term investors.

87. *Don't own more funds than you can effectively monitor.* It's probably time to trim and prune if you have more than a dozen positions.

88. *Consider consolidating your holdings by opening an account with a large discount brokerage.* No-transaction-fee funds are the best deals discounters offer.

89. *Resist the temptation to jump in and out of funds if you deal with a discounter,* even though it's easy to do so.

90. *Be careful about mutual funds that own other funds,* as you could pay two layers of fees. Worthy exceptions include T. Rowe Price Spectrum Growth, T. Rowe Price Spectrum Income and the Vanguard Star LifeStrategy portfolios, because these don't double dip.

91. *Beware of flashes in the pan.* Don't buy funds that finish number one in a year or quarter. Even long-term losers can be super performers over short periods. Funds that finish top-ranked usually have to take big risks to get there.

92. *Avoid new funds, as you can usually find proven performers of the same type.* The exceptions here are new stock portfolios run by established managers. Large fund groups often nurture offspring with their best investment ideas.

93. *Don't panic and sell a fund on a day when the market takes a big drop.* Corrections often last just a few days at a time.

94. *Sell a conservative stock fund if it significantly underperforms its peers for six or more consecutive quarters.* Be less patient with volatile funds that have been lagging.

95. *But don't sell a good fund too soon.* Just because a portfolio has had a lengthy climb does not mean it's due for a fall. Some managers outperform the market for remarkably long periods.

96. *If you want to realize a tax loss, wait more than 30 days after selling a fund if you desire to repurchase the same one.* Otherwise, you could run afoul of the "wash sale" rule. You also can bypass this rule if you reinvest the proceeds in a different fund, even if it's in the same investment category.

97. *Keep an eye on tax simplification when selling shares.* If you liquidate a position in many pieces over the years, you may create a tax nightmare when it comes time to calculate your cost basis. The situation would be worse if you have purchased shares at different times and reinvested distributions along the way.

98. *Keep in mind that prices will "regress to the mean" over time.* The long-run average return on large stocks has been a little over 10 percent a year. If funds have done much better than that lately, they might be due for a breather.

99. *Don't expect your manager to shine in all seasons.* Funds that excel in bull markets often take big hits during bearish phases. And portfolios that weather down markets best tend to look sickly when the bull charges ahead.

100. *Lean toward stock funds that stay fully invested rather than those that retreat heavily into cash.* It's very difficult to be consistently successful at market timing.

101. *Don't worry so much about individual fund losses. Rather, assess the damage in terms of your overall portfolio.* If you have allocated assets properly, you should have some winners to offset the losers. Good weather eventually comes after a storm. You've got to ride out the squalls to bask in the sunshine.

Glossary

adviser   The management company employed by a mutual fund that's responsible for making investment decisions.

aggressive-growth fund   A portfolio managed with the objective of realizing maximum capital gains, often by investing in small- and medium-size firms or by using speculative strategies.

annuity   A series of payments, either for a fixed number of years or continuing until the death of an individual. *See* fixed annuity and variable annuity.

asked price (or offering price)   The per-share price you pay to buy an investment. For a mutual fund, it is the current net asset value plus any applicable front-end load or sales charge. For a closed-end fund or stock, the asked is always higher than the bid price. For example, a closed-end fund might be quoted at 10 bid, 10⅛ asked. The resulting price spread does not include applicable brokerage commissions. *See* bid price.

asset allocation   The process to determine the relative proportions of stocks, bonds and cash to be held by an investor. *See also* strategic asset allocation and tactical asset allocation.

asset-allocation fund   A portfolio that shuttles its money between stocks, bonds and cash, normally remaining within target ranges for each category. Many asset-allocation funds follow a global orientation, moving money among U.S. and foreign markets.

asset-class risk   A danger you face if you have a disproportionately large amount of wealth in one asset category, such as foreign stocks. The idea behind asset allocation is to spread your wealth among different classes to lessen this risk.

automatic investment plan A program set up with your bank or employer to transfer a specific amount of money directly into a mutual fund at regular intervals such as monthly.

balanced fund A portfolio consisting of both stocks and bonds, typically favoring the former by a 60-40 ratio.

beta coefficient A measure of market risk. A fund with the same volatility as the Standard & Poor's 500 is defined to have a beta of 1.0. Higher-risk portfolios have betas greater than 1.0, and lower-risk funds have betas below 1.0.

bid price The per-share price at which you can sell an investment. For a mutual fund, this is usually the net asset value. For a closed-end fund or stock, the bid price is always below the asked. For example, a closed-end fund might be quoted at 10 bid, 10⅛ asked. This spread does not include applicable brokerage commissions. *See* asked price.

breakpoints Investment thresholds at which quantity discounts are offered to people making large investments in a fund that charges a front-end load. Greater discounts would be available with larger investments.

capital-gains distribution A payment to shareholders generated by profits in a fund's portfolio. Mutual funds are required by law to distribute to shareholders virtually all of their realized net capital gains. Most funds pay such distributions once a year, in December.

closed-end fund An investment company that trades like a stock, usually on the New York Stock Exchange. Like mutual funds, these portfolios are diversified and professionally managed. Closed-end funds normally sell at either a discount from NAV or are priced at a premium.

contingent-deferred sales charge (CDSC) A back-end load commonly attached to broker-sold funds that have a 12b-1 fee but no front-end load. The CDSC declines yearly, typically phasing out after five or six years.

correlation A statistical measure of the degree to which returns from two different investments or asset classes move together. The more closely different assets move in tandem, the higher the correlation.

country fund *See* single-country fund.

credit risk The danger that a bond issuer will not meet its obligation to pay interest and principal to its creditors. Junk bonds have high credit risk whereas Treasury securities are considered to have none. Credit risk is measured by a bond's rating.

currency risk The danger of adverse currency fluctuations faced by international investors. Generally, this poses problems for Americans investing in foreign markets if the dollar strengthens.

derivative (or derivative security) A financial contract generating a return that is linked to the performance of some underlying asset such as a bond, stock, foreign currency or an index. These securities can be standardized—such as a plain-vanilla option or futures contract—or customized to suit the needs of large investors or speculators.

discount With respect to closed-end portfolios, a markdown from a fund's net asset value. For example, a closed-end fund trading at $8 with an NAV of $10 would be selling at a 20-percent discount.

discount brokerage A brokerage that generally charges lower commissions because it normally provides no investment advice.

dollar cost averaging The process or strategy of investing equal dollar amounts at predetermined intervals, such as $100 monthly.

duration The most sophisticated measure of interest-rate risk for a bond or bond portfolio. Duration numbers range from near zero (for money market funds) to 10 or more (for long-term bond funds). The higher the number, the more a portfolio will fluctuate in response to a change in interest rates.

efficient market The concept, demonstrated by academic research, that stocks generally sell for what they're worth.

equity-income fund A portfolio that emphasizes stocks with above-average dividend yields. Similar to a growth-and-income fund, an equity-income portfolio normally places more emphasis on yield and less on appreciation.

expense ratio The ongoing expenses of a fund divided by its average net assets. Expenses include management fees, shareholder-servicing costs and 12b-1 fees.

fixed annuity An annuity contract that guarantees a fixed rate of interest for a specific period such as three years, after which the guaranteed rate is reset.

401(k) plan An employer-sponsored retirement plan that allows workers to defer taxes on the portion of their salary that they contribute or invest each year.

403(b) plan An employer-sponsored retirement plan that allows employees of nonprofit organizations such as public schools and colleges to defer taxes on the portion of their salary that they contribute each year. A 403(b) plan operates similarly to a 401(k) plan.

Ginnie Mae (or GNMA) fund   A type of fixed-income portfolio popular with retirees that produces high monthly dividends by holding mortgage securities backed by the Government National Mortgage Association (or Ginnie Mae). Each monthly payment on a Ginnie Mae consists of a return of principal as well as income.

global fund   A fund that invests worldwide. A global stock fund holds both U.S. and non–U.S. equities, with a heavier weighting on the latter. Global bond funds mix foreign and domestic debt securities.

growth-and-income fund   A portfolio that seeks a combination of capital appreciation and dividends, commonly by investing in the stocks of larger companies. The relative emphasis on appreciation or income is usually about equal, but varies somewhat among funds.

growth fund   A stock portfolio that has capital appreciation rather than income as its primary objective. These funds typically invest in medium and large companies.

growth investing   An investment strategy designed to realize high capital appreciation by focusing on companies and industries with above-average prospects for increases in revenues and earnings. These stocks typically trade at above-average PEs.

high-yield bond fund (or junk-bond fund)   A portfolio that emphasizes speculative bonds rated below triple-B by major rating agencies. These are known as *non-investment-grade* bonds.

income distribution   Payment of a fund's net investment income to shareholders each year. This consists of interest and dividends earned on the portfolio, minus expenses. Bond and money market funds typically make income distributions monthly, whereas stock funds may make them just once a year along with their capital gains distribution, usually in December.

income fund   A portfolio that seeks dividend and interest income as opposed to capital appreciation by holding a mixture of bonds as well as stocks paying generous dividends. Compared with balanced funds, these portfolios typically place a lower emphasis on stocks.

income ratio   A mutual fund's net investment income—dividends plus interest minus expenses—divided by its average net assets.

index fund   A low-cost, passive portfolio designed to track a market benchmark, such as the S&P 500 or the Wilshire 5000. True index funds have very low portfolio turnovers, often less than 10 percent.

individual retirement account (IRA)   A tax-sheltered account that can be established by investors to save a portion of their earned income for retirement.

inflation risk   The danger that an investment's return will not be sufficient to protect against declining purchasing power over long periods.

international fund   A portfolio that invests in foreign stocks. Unlike global funds, which may have some U.S. holdings, international funds normally invest exclusively outside the United States.

interest-rate risk   The danger that rising interest rates will lead to falling bond prices.

investment company   A general term that refers to open- and closed-end funds. Both are professionally managed portfolios of investments regulated by the Securities and Exchange Commission.

junk-bond fund   *See* high-yield bond fund.

leverage   The use of borrowed money to try to amplify gains. Investors who buy stocks or funds on margin through a broker are using leverage. A double-edged sword, leverage can magnify losses as well as gains.

limit order   An order entered through a stockbroker to buy or sell a stock or closed-end fund at a specific price or better. Limit orders can be entered either for the day or on a good-till-canceled basis.

living trust (or inter vivos trust)   A trust created during a person's lifetime to provide for the orderly transfer of wealth to designated beneficiaries. Such an arrangement is usually revocable, meaning that its terms can be changed by the grantor. Property within a living trust is held in the name of the trust so that those assets will pass to the intended survivors without regard to any will, thereby avoiding probate.

load fund   A fund that charges a sales commission. When buying a fund with a front-end load, investors pay the charge when they initially purchase shares. However, some load portfolios do not charge anything up front. Rather, they assess an annual 12b-1 fee coupled with a contingent deferred sales charge. In addition, some funds with neither a front-end load nor contingent deferred sales charge may impose a level load, in the form of a relatively high 12b-1 fee. *See also* contingent deferred sales charge and 12b-1 fee.

low-load fund   A portfolio that imposes modest sales charges, typically a front-end load ranging from 1 to 3 percent.

management fee   The fee paid by shareholders to a fund's adviser. The management fee, which is specified in the prospectus, is included as part of the expense ratio. *See also* adviser.

market risk   The danger that a substantial decline in stock prices generally will reduce the value of your portfolio.

nominal return   The stated return on an investment, unadjusted for inflation. *See* real return.

nondiversified fund   A mutual fund that takes large positions in a relatively small number of stocks and sectors, making it more volatile than its broadly diversified relatives because of this higher degree of concentration. Some aggressive-growth and sector portfolios are nondiversified, but most funds are not classified as such.

national municipal-bond fund   A portfolio that invests in bonds issued by a variety of states and municipalities. The income produced by these funds normally avoids federal taxation. In addition, the proportion of income derived from securities issued within your state also would be tax-exempt at the state level.

net asset value (or NAV)   The price or per-share value of a mutual fund. It equals the total market value of all securities held in the portfolio, less the liabilities. Fund companies calculate the NAV once a day, after the market's close.

no-load fund   A mutual fund that doesn't impose any front-end load or contingent deferred sales charge. If such a fund has a 12b-1 fee, it must be 0.25 percent or less annually for the fund to be considered no-load. *See* contingent deferred sales charge and 12b-1 fee.

offering price   *See* asked price.

portfolio turnover rate   An indication of trading activity for a mutual fund. Turnover is defined as the dollar value of securities either sold or purchased during the year, whichever is less, divided by average monthly assets. A turnover of 100 percent would indicate that each security was held for one year on average. Higher turnovers are associated with greater trading activity and higher transaction costs.

premium   With respect to closed-end funds, the amount by which a fund's market price exceeds its NAV. If a fund has a share price of $12 and an NAV of $10, it would be trading at a 20-percent premium. Buying a closed-end fund at a premium is often risky. *See* discount.

prospectus   A mutual-fund disclosure document required by the SEC. The prospectus contains most of the facts about a fund that prospective investors need to know, such as the portfolio's objectives, risks, costs, past performance, shareholder services, investment minimums and other data.

purchasing-power risk   *See* inflation risk.

real return   The inflation-adjusted return on an investment, equaling the nominal return minus the inflation rate. *See* nominal return.

regional fund   A fund that invests in the stocks of companies located in broad areas such as Europe, Latin America or Asia.

rights offering   A technique used by closed-end funds to raise additional money from existing shareholders by giving them the opportunity to buy new shares at a discount to the market price. Shareholders receive one right for each share held.

sector fund   A portfolio that specializes in the companies of a particular industry, such as gold, health care, real estate or technology.

Securities and Exchange Commission (SEC)   A federal government agency that regulates both open- and closed-end funds as well as other securities. The SEC also oversees the U.S. stock and bond markets, registered investment advisers and brokerages.

SEP-IRA (simplified employee pension)   A retirement plan for small businesses or self-employed individuals.

short sale   The sale of a security that the seller hopes to purchase at a lower price in the future, thereby closing the position at a profit. Short sellers normally sell borrowed securities, which they feel are ripe for a fall. If the price rises, the short seller loses.

single-country fund   A portfolio investing in the stock market of a specific nation. Most are closed-end, although some open-end portfolios target the Canadian, Japanese and other stock markets.

single-state municipal bond fund   A portfolio consisting of the bonds of a specific state. These funds generate income that is exempt from state as well as federal income taxes for residents of their states. They therefore appeal to investors who reside in states with high tax rates.

specialty fund   A portfolio that invests in a specific industry or has some other unusual feature, such as pursuing a course of socially responsible investing. *See* sector fund.

standard deviation   A statistical measure of the volatility of a portfolio's past returns. In contrast with beta, which gauges market risk, standard deviation measures total risk and is therefore a superior tool. The higher the number, the more volatile an investment.

strategic asset allocation   A process to determine long-term benchmark norms and target ranges for holdings of stocks, bonds and cash. A person's allocation weightings should reflect individual characteristics such as age, time horizon and risk tolerance. *See* tactical asset allocation.

systematic withdrawal plan   A program established with a mutual fund company whereby an investor automatically receives fixed dollar payments at periodic intervals from his or her fund account.

tactical asset allocation   A process to establish specific short-term holdings in stocks, bonds and cash within a predetermined range. Suppose your strategic allocation calls for you to hold between 60 and 75 percent of your total assets in stocks. With a tactical asset allocation approach, you would fine-tune your current stock holdings to a percentage within that range based on your near-term outlook. *See* strategic asset allocation.

tax efficiency   The extent to which a fund exposes shareholders to tax liabilities. Funds that pass little in the way of taxable gains to investors are relatively efficient.

total return   The percentage return of an investment that includes both its income and capital appreciation (or depreciation). Mutual fund results are typically measured in terms of total return. Fund returns reflect the subtraction of expenses (including 12b-1 fees), but normally do not reflect the payment of any front- or back-end loads.

turnover   *See* portfolio turnover rate.

12b-1 fee   An ongoing fee charged by some funds to pay for marketing and distribution costs, often including compensation to brokers for selling the fund. The prospectus will specify if a fund charges any 12b-1 fees, named for a 1980 ruling by the Securities and Exchange Commission.

value investing   A style of investing that aims to find bargain stocks based on common benchmarks such as low PE or price-to-book ratios or a high dividend yield. Value investors are sometimes called bottom fishers.

variable annuity   An investment product that features a stable of mutual funds inside an insurance wrapper that offers tax-deferred earnings, a minimal death benefit and various annuitization options.

wash sale   The sale and repurchase of substantially identical securities with the apparent intent of realizing a tax loss. The IRS disallows losses realized in wash-sale transactions. If you wait at least 31 days after the sale to repurchase the securities, the transaction is not considered a wash sale. (The securities can't be purchased within the 30-day window prior to the date of sale, either.)

withdrawal plan   *See* systematic withdrawal plan.

yield   The income generated by an investment, expressed as a percentage of its price.

yield curve   The relationship between the yields on Treasury securities and their time to maturity. An upward sloping yield curve, which is typical, would indicate that Treasury bonds have higher yields than Treasury notes, which in turn yield more than Treasury bills.

APPENDIX 1

Toll-Free Phone Numbers of Selected Fund Families

Fund Family	Phone	Fund Family	Phone
AARP	800-253-2277	Gabelli	800-422-3554
Acorn	800-922-6769	Gateway	800-354-6339
AIM	800-347-1919	G. T. Global	800-824-1580
Alliance	800-227-4618	Heartland	800-432-7856
American	800-421-0180	Hotchkis & Wiley	800-346-7301
American Heritage	800-828-5050	IAI	800-945-3863
Babson	800-422-2766	INVESCO	800-525-8085
Benham	800-321-8321	Janus	800-525-3713
Berger	800-333-1001	Kaufmann	800-237-0132
Brandywine	800-656-3017	Lexington	800-526-0056
CGM	800-345-4048	Lindner/Ryback	314-727-5305
Clipper	800-776-5033	Longleaf	800-445-9469
Cohen & Steers	800-437-9912	Meridian	800-446-6662
Columbia	800-547-1707	Merriman	800-423-4893
Crabbe Huson	800-541-9732	Montgomery	800-572-3863
Dodge & Cox	800-621-3979	Mutual Series	800-448-3863
Dreyfus	800-645-6561	Neuberger & Berman	800-877-9700
Evergreen	800-235-0064	Nicholas	800-227-5987
Fidelity	800-544-8888	Oakmark	800-476-9625
Founders	800-525-2440	One Group	800-338-4345
FPA	800-982-4372	L. Roy Papp	800-421-4004
Franklin/Templeton	800-632-2180	PBHG	800-809-8008
Fremont	800-548-4539	Phoenix	800-243-4361

Fund Family	Phone	Fund Family	Phone
T. Rowe Price	800-638-5660	Strong	800-368-3863
Putnam	800-225-2465	Tweedy Browne	800-432-4789
Royce	800-221-4268	Twentieth Century	800-345-2021
Rushmore	800-622-1386	United Services	800-873-8637
Salomon Brothers	800-725-6666	USAA	800-531-8181
Schwab	800-526-8600	Vanguard	800-662-7447
Scudder	800-225-2470	Wasatch	800-551-1700
Stagecoach	800-222-8222	Warburg Pincus	800-257-5614
SteinRoe	800-338-2550	Yacktman	800-525-8258
Stratton	800-634-5726		

*You can find phone numbers of families not listed above by calling 800-555-1212.

APPENDIX 2

Sources of Investment Information

Mutual Fund Guides

The Individual Investor's Guide to Low-Load Mutual Funds and *Quarterly Low-Load Mutual Fund Update.* Published annually and quarterly, respectively, by the American Association of Individual Investors. Covers about 900 funds.
Phone 312-280-0170.

Morningstar Mutual Funds. Published biweekly, covers 1,500 funds.
Phone 800-876-5005.

Morningstar Mutual Funds on Floppy. Updated monthly, covers 5,700 funds on a computer diskette.
Phone 800-876-5005.

Morningstar Mutual Fund 500. Published annually, covers 500 leading funds.
Phone 800-876-5005.

The Mutual Fund Encyclopedia, by Gerald Perritt. Covers more than 3,400 funds. Published annually by Dearborn Financial Publishing, Inc.
Phone 800-829-7934.

Mutual Fund Profiles. Published quarterly by Standard & Poor's. Covers about 1,200 funds using data provided by Lipper Analytical Services.
Phone 800-221-5277.

The Value Line Mutual Fund Survey. Published biweekly, covers 2,200 funds.
Phone 800-634-3583.

Closed-End Fund Guides

Morningstar Closed-End Funds. Published biweekly, covers more than 350 funds.
Phone 800-876-5005.

Morningstar Closed-End Funds on Floppy. Updated monthly, covers more than 500 funds on a computer diskette.
Phone 800-876-5005.

Morningstar Closed-End Fund 250. Published annually, contains 250 leading funds.
Phone 800-876-5005.

Standard & Poor's Stock Reports. Updated quarterly. Reports on virtually all closed-end funds in customary S&P format.
Phone 800-221-5277.

The Value Line Investment Survey. Updated quarterly, covers the leading closed-end funds in customary Value Line format.
Phone 800-634-3583.

Variable Annuity Guide

Morningstar Variable Annuities/Life. Published biweekly, covers 60 variable annuities.
Phone 800-876-5005.

INDEX